"At last, a book which restores the proper genius of Perls and of the Californian style of Gestalt therapy, giving the right place to the right brain! Year after year, I was worried by more and more dogmatic publications, trying to seduce the academic intelligentsia, but taking the risk of losing the real spirit of Gestalt, imprisioning clients within an over-rigid theory.

I loved the clarity of the concepts allied with such a lively presence of the author, personally involved in his memories, witnesses, sharing of thoughts, and clinical illustrations...

I am delighted by the appearance of this book by my 'American cousin' (whom I finally met in Sienna), who considers—like me—that Gestalt Therapy is more an Art than a Science and underlines that Life, like art, contains more than theory spells out (p. 215)."

—Serge Ginger
author of La Gestalt, une thérapie du contact *and founder of the*
Ecole Parisienne de Gestalt

"The book is a work of Magic. Its scope and its depth make it an extraordinary achievement. What merits the rarer epithet 'Magic,' is the fact that it succeeds in performing a paradoxical task. So far the East Coast people, who see Gestalt Therapy as more theory-bound, less Zen-like, based more on Gestalt Psychology and less on intuition, have had the edge over their West Coast colleagues in the area of published articles and books. Now at last West Coast Gestalt therapists, who see the late work of Fritz as his greatest, will have found a marvellous 'spokesman for the nonverbal.' "

—Gideon Schwarz
professor, Hebrew Union University, and Gestalt Teacher

"This translation of the soul of Gestalt (rather than its skeleton) comes to fill a hole; it constitutes a reflection on an intuitionism that acknowledges itself as such."

—Paco Peñarrubia
former President, Gestalt Therapy Association of Spain

Books by Claudio Naranjo

Ennea-type Structures

Gestalt Therapy:
The Attitude and Practice
of an Atheoretical Experientialism

How to Be

La Vieja y Novíssima Gestalt

Techniques of Gestalt Therapy

The Healing Journey

The One Quest

The Psychology of Meditation

"To Fritz Perls...

... and Jim Simkin, of course."

GESTALT THERAPY

THE ATTITUDE AND PRACTICE OF AN ATHEORETICAL EXPERIENTIALISM

Claudio Naranjo, M.D.

Gateways/IDHHB Publishing
Nevada City, California

ISBN: 0-89556-090-9

© 1993 by Claudio Naranjo, M.D.
All Rights Reserved. Printed in the U.S.A.

Published by GATEWAYS / IDHHB, INC.
PO Box 370
Nevada City, CA 95959
(800) 869-0658; (916) 477-1116

"Protoanalysis" is a registered service mark
of the Arica Institute, Inc.

Library of Congress Cataloging in Publication Data

Naranjo, Claudio.
    Gestalt therapy : the attitude and practice of an
atheoretical experientialism / Claudio Naranjo.
        p.   cm.
    Includes bibliographical references and index.
    ISBN 0-89556-090-9 : $29.95
    1. Gestalt therapy.   I.   Title.
RC489.G4N37   1992
616.89'143—dc20   92-19329
                                                CIP

TABLE OF CONTENTS

Book Two:
Gestalt Therapy Revisited

FOREWORD

Reading Naranjo's work on Gestalt therapy is an education, an inspiration, a fulfillment. But perhaps above all—a pleasure. How gratifying to be able to use the words so often employed by book reviewers in referring to works of fiction: "A good read." And an excellent read it is; no small accomplishment for a serious work on the theory and specific practices of a most significant development in the field of psychotherapy—Gestalt therapy.

That his book is a pleasure and exciting to read is integral to the spirit and flavor of his ambitious undertaking.

To begin with, the author is blessed with a clarity of style which itself seems an outgrowth of his dedication to understanding and to his passion for teaching. It is safe to say that Claudio is incapable of writing an incomprehensible sentence. How to explain such a felicitous predicament? I believe it to stem from a powerful intellectual digestive system with an instinctive talent for clarifying, re-structuring and assimilating.

How fitting. Fritz Perls emphasized again and again the parallels between good eating and the requirements for emotional growth and conflict resolution. Emotional experiences—like food—were to be carefully tasted, chewed, liquefied, swallowed, digested and assimilated. Then they were truly part of you and not a bolus of indigestible stuff in your belly leading to indigestion and insomnia.

There is evidence that Claudio Naranjo has a sensitive intellectual stomach, easily upset by food which does not make a good "fit." So he works and chews on it (not that this aspect of his preparation is in the least visible) and when he is ready to share it, it is tasty, satisfying, nourishing.

Take, for instance, such a relatively esoteric phrase as Gurdjieff's "conscious suffering." Naranjo deftly relates it to the Gestaltian "non-evasion of suffering" (obviously related to the careful eating referred to above). So what was in Gurdjieff's opaque style rather puzzling is now seen simply as the idea of confrontation rather than avoidance of pain or frustration. This sort of masterly noting of parallels and overlaps among diverse fields is richly scattered throughout the book.

Considerable care has evidently gone into the selection of the title. Most books would have used the standard title "Theory and practice of...." Naranjo makes it clear that his choice of "attitude" rather than "theory" is of the essence of his theme. I am reminded of two personal incidents between myself and Fritz. Early in my training with him I kept hounding him with questions about "technique." Finally he could no longer contain his exasperation. "Abe, you're driving me crazy with all these 'technique' questions. The point is not technique; the point is *perspective*." His point hit home although it took years to really assimilate. On another occasion we were speaking about his startling therapeutic skills. He said, "I'm good at this because I have eyes and ears and I am unafraid."

So here we have a delightful commentary on the matter of practice. Naranjo points out that Gestalt therapy is unique in that it is a system built on intuitive understanding rather than on theory. Throughout the various chapters on expression, integration, dream interpretation, etc., the book is replete with illustrations of how this intuition is enacted with a variety of clients.

Chapter 2 on present-centeredness is one of the gems of the book. It is a chapter which was originally included in Fagan and Shepherd's early compendium *Gestalt Therapy Now*.[1] In this chapter particularly we are treated to a rich cultural feast in which quotations from British and Latin poetry are gracefully employed to enhance the points being made. I find it deeply satisfying to observe the workings of a lively, well-stocked mind which naturally sees things in broad context and perspective. The results are far from "intellectualized" but on the the contrary are engagingly intelligent and carry the reader on a journey in which every spot observed is experienced as an interesting element both for itself and for its place in the larger order. Again, how fitting for a writer on Gestalt.

A further remark on the matter of titles: let us remember the sub-title of Perls' main work, *Gestalt Therapy*. Curiously the subtitle is never referred to and I would venture to guess that few Gestalt therapists would remember it. The subtitle is "Excitement and Growth in the Human Personality."

There is much excitement in the present book; a solid sort of excitement which derives from casting rays of light and understanding on so many corners of life and living.

[1] *Gestalt Therapy Now*, Joan Fagan and Irma Lee Shepherd, editors. Palo Alto, 1970: Science and Behavior Books.

On page 42 we find "If we can discover our freedom within our slavery, we can also discover our joy under the cover of victimization." On page 52 we come across the thought, "Once we accept nothingness everything is added unto us." It would be difficult to find a better explication of the not-so-easily-understood notion of the fertile void.

Claudio had a good deal of opportunity for close association with Fritz Perls and developed a deep appreciation of his unique gifts and his creative genius. The depth of Claudio's appreciation can be felt in his statement, [it is] "particularly true of Gestalt therapy where the therapist is more challenged than in others to be both a naked human being and an artist." Admiration need not aspire to greater heights than is represented in such a statement.

At the same time, this appreciation of Perls' achievements does not blind Naranjo to some of the shortcomings of Fritz as a person and some of the limitations of Gestalt as a way of growth. Using Fritz's own idea of "holes," i.e., blind spots or undeveloped areas in an individual, Naranjo correctly identifies some important "holes" in Gestalt itself. The disdain for the interpretive, the overstrict avoidance of intellectual understanding, the inclination towards the "tough" attitudes towards clients rather than the supportive, tender or friendly, these are indeed limitations in the Gestalt approach. No damage whatsoever to the essential spirit of Gestalt is done by correcting these limitations. What would, in fact, be a serious betrayal of Gestalt would be *not* to maintain our constant interest in deepening and broadening our understanding and our ways of doing.

In conclusion, a final word of appreciation. There are many sound, solid, competent works in our field of psychotherapy. But there are not many feasts. And this work is a feast, a flow of observations, analyses, integrations almost bewildering in their richness. I believe the book can serve as an overview—both for the neophyte *and* for the experienced therapist—of some of the problems of psychotherapy and their relation to the explosive growth of interest in the transpersonal and spiritual realms of understanding. One senses, in his writing, in his ways of thinking, nothing less than a reverential fascination with the perennial human efforts at self-knowing, self-transcendence, self-creation.

It is all too apparent how pleased I am to have the opportunity to write this introduction. It gives me pleasure to celebrate Claudio Naranjo's contributions to our knowledge and to acknowledge my appreciation of our friendship.

Abraham Levitsky
Berkeley, California
April, 1991

PREFACE TO THE ENGLISH EDITION

In consequence of the initiative of publishers abroad the present book, which was the first I have written in the English language, has appeared already in Spanish and Italian. While the title under which it appeared in the Spanish edition, *La Vieja y Novísima Gestalt*, was intended to convey something roughly equivalent to "that old and ever new Gestalt," it was interpreted by many as rather something more like "Old Gestalt vs. New Gestalt," and I have been proclaimed an original innovator. Nothing has been further from my intent in this book. While it is true that I have contributed novel reflections on the transpersonal aspect of Gestalt therapy and on its place among traditional "ways of growth," and while it is true as well that I have created a variety of Gestalt exercises and included in the book a chapter on a "fourth way" characterology that has enhanced my personal practice and that of my students, it is also true that the book mostly constitutes an echo of what Gestalt therapy I learned from Fritz Perls, just as my own practice is an echo of his style.

Indeed, I could just as well have called it "California Gestalt" in view of the distinction introduced after Fritz Perls' death by his earlier New York collaborators. The expression has often been used with an implicit deprecatory implication—as in "that is only *California* Gestalt," where California carries combined associations of New Age and spiritual supermarket. Yet it is also possible to say "California Gestalt" with dignity, for many of us believe that Fritz's California years were his ripest, and it is not trivial that California has been the Mecca of both a world-wide cultural wave and the starting point of the Humanistic-Transpersonal revolution in psychology.

In the Introduction to this book, written five years ago, I have explained why I originally used "Attitude and Practice" instead of "Theory and Practice."[1] I do not think that there can be any doubt concerning Fritz Perls' anti-intellectual style in his California years, when the expressions "mind-fucking," "verbiage" and "bullshit" were so present in his vocabulary. Certainly he was wise enough to appreciate the great ideas of his time: the organismic and holistic conceptions and an appreciation for the process of Gestalt formation in particular. Yet I think that his theoretical best was that of his late years when he claimed that he no longer needed a conceptual apparatus to therapize or live, and had come to be supported in nothing outside himself—i.e., his consciousness in the present. It was at this time that we may say that he wrote with blood—when he stood on his own two feet and when he was most nakedly himself.

---

[1] As in the way *The Gestalt Journal* announces its yearly conferences, for instance, or the Polsters' "Gestalt Therapy Integrated: Contours of *Theory* and Practice."

Though I can claim to have been a theorist of spiritual disciplines and psychotherapy alike, and have authored a book on personality that is scheduled to appear after this present volume, when I practice Gestalt Therapy I am at least as atheoretical as Fritz was, and feel not only deeply sympathetic to his position, but also interested in celebrating it at a time when most gestaltists feel embarrassed vis-a-vis the academicians who disdain them for not having enough of a theoretical edifice (i.e., one comparable in sophistication to that provided by the psychoanalysts and the behaviorists, as is deemed a necessary support for permissible practice). Like Fritz, who in his autobiography shared with us that dream of his of launching an education of physician-philosophers, I have never underestimated the intellectual component in the education of either therapists or human beings in general, and I believe that I am less ambivalent than Fritz concerning the issue for I think that he was not at peace in regard to the matter: there was an anti-intellectual side to him and also, as I see it, an intellectual insecurity that often made him bombastic and may have stimulated his dream of launching and educating physician-philosophers. (I am convinced that his vehemence against "bullshit" was the reflection of his earlier excesses). His atheoretical stance was purest and most tenable, I think, in reference to the view that therapeutic activity can be intensified through the inhibition of conceptualization and can be guided through intuition better than through discursive "computing." It certainly did not involve the belief that therapists should be ignorant.

I have explained most of my book's new title thus far, and it only remains for me to point out that the Gestalt way is not only an experientialism in that—from the therapist's point of view—it is a working *out of* experience, but in that for the individual undergoing it, it is a way *through* experience—a way in which moving along is propelled, as it were, by the very act of experiencing: the deepening of awareness and the clarification of experiential understanding (including the experience and understanding of his or her attitude-in-face-of-experience).

I hope that, just as Fritz's legacy to contemporary psychotherapy has been much vaster than what stimulus it gave in the specialized field of Gestalt Therapy, this book may be of service (as Abe Levitsky anticipates in his generous foreword) to those who are interested in therapy in general, including those who are not specialists or even professionals. Particularly, I hope that it may provide stimulation and inspiration to those involved in the growing network of psychologically sophisticated support and co-therapy groups.

Claudio Naranjo
Berkeley, California
1992

Author's Introduction

Sometime in 1966 I was approached by Michael Murphy on the lawn in front of the Esalen Big House with a request for an article on Gestalt Therapy that he wished to publish (and eventually did publish) as an Esalen monograph. He had recently approached Fritz Perls, who suggested that he ask me to do it instead. I had at the time taken part in several workshops with Fritz and he had become very fond of me—to the point of granting me a permanent scholarship to his Esalen activities. I accepted with pleasure, and the result was my first piece of writing in English—which in retrospect I understand as a blessing, for through it I discovered that I could express myself more easily than I had thought.

Nothing had been published on Gestalt therapy at the time, except for Perls' two early books, some articles of his and a short statement from Van Dusen claiming that Gestalt therapy is the most consistent therapeutic application of phenomenology. Two additional papers circulated in mimeographed form in those days (while I attended Perls' and Simkin's first professional training workshop at Esalen) — one by Simkin and another by John Enright. (Both have since appeared in proper chronological sequence, along with mine, in Stephenson's *Gestalt Therapy Primer*[1]).

---

[1] *Gestalt Therapy Primer: Introductory Readings in Gestalt Therapy* , F. Douglas Stephenson , ed. (Springfield, Ill.: Charles C. Thomas, 1975).

I carried out the assigned task with much satisfaction, since I had been keenly aware of how difficult it was to imagine Gestalt therapy in action from the reading of Perls' two early books. Through a caprice of destiny I had been among the first readers of *Gestalt Therapy . . .*, when the book was published by Julian Press in the fifties, for it had been sent by the publisher to my uncle Ben Cohen, co-founder of the U.N. who lived, of course, in New York. My uncle, being Under-Secretary for Press and Information, was constantly receiving many books from many sources, and occasionally forwarded to me those which he thought would especially interest me. It turned out that this particular one had considerable influence on my professional activity—though not as a therapist, but as a researcher and teacher; yet I must say that I imagined Perls through that writing (in spite of the exercises at the beginning of the volume) as a young intellectual rather than an old experientialist, and I was equally far from imagining the practice of Gestalt therapy. It now seems to me that Fritz had a genius for therapeutic interaction, but that he was neither gifted nor properly trained as a theorist, and that in his early years he relied heavily on theoretically inclined peers for the promotion of his therapeutic approach in an academic world dominated by psychoanalysis. Yet I think that Gestalt therapy always transcended the theoretical formulations about it, and that it came into its own when Fritz, later in his life, broke free from "elephant shit" and the need to validate his praxis through academic rationalizations.

Fritz, I believe, saw his work better reflected in my piece than in his early writings, for I never saw him so happy throughout the years of our friendship as on the day when he told me how much he liked it—not even when he felt that he had triumphed over Maslow at the memorable Esalen meeting at which he bit Abe's leg.

When Fritz was approaching his seventieth birthday and Jim Simkin invited contributions for a Festschrift in his honor, I wrote for it the paper called "Present Centeredness—Technique, Prescription and Ideal."[2] After reading it Fritz suggested that I put my two papers (and perhaps some further contributions, along with articles from other contributors) together as a book. In spite of my enthusiasm for Arnold Beisser's "Theory of Paradoxical Intention" and Bob Resnick's "Chicken Soup is Poison" I was slow in carrying out the project. When I saw Fritz again, after a year or so in Chile, he told me he had in the meantime suggested to the "Miami girls" (Fagan and Shepherd) to bring out such a collection, and stimulated me to write a Gestalt therapy book of my own.

I don't think I would have undertaken the task of this book without such stimulus; writing about somebody else's creation would have competed for what time I had for writing about what seemed more personal work; also, I think I felt that anything I could say beyond what I had already written might seem too obvious. In the course of the years, however (after reading what has been published since Fagan and Shepherd's *Gestalt Therapy Now*) I have the impression that what seemed obvious to me was not so obvious to others.

Except for its first two chapters, *Gestalt Therapy: The Attitude and Practice of an Atheoretical Experientialism* was written in the weeks that followed Fritz's death in 1970. Since I was at Fritz's memorial service in San Francisco when my only son died in a car accident in the Big Sur Hills, this writing was done at a time of deep mourning, and the fact that I chose to undertake it conveys how significant it was for me at the time to complete this piece of "unfinished business." In the first place, this was a time when I was

[2]Included in Fagan and Shepherd's *Gestalt Therapy Now*.

getting ready for a journey which, as I have explained in the introduction to *The Healing Journey*, I thought would be without return. I had decided to join a spiritual teacher in an attitude of total availability and it seemed to me that I should pay my debts to my past so as to embark in a new stage of life without plans or obligations. The Gestalt Therapy book was one of my pending projects, and one which at Fritz's death seemed the appropriate one to tackle.

Even though the 1970 trip to the Chilean desert was in an inner sense indeed without return, I did come back to Berkeley in 1971 and offered the Gestalt Therapy book to Stuart Miller — then in charge of the Viking Esalen series, that had already published my earlier books *The One Quest* and *On the Psychology of Meditation* (currently titled, *How to Be*[3]). The manuscript would have been printed long ago if it had not been lost at a xeroxing place. Such has been the density of my life, both inwardly and outwardly, ever since, that it would have been preposterous to dig in old filing cabinets for the originals from which the book could be reconstituted. Only a portion of it was published as *Techniques of Gestalt Therapy*, first for the benefit of my Berkeley students, then as part of Hechter and Himelstein's *Handbook of Gestalt Therapy*[4], and finally by *The Gestalt Journal*.

Yet at last I find myself at a time when the completion of the long-interrupted and postponed task becomes figure again upon the background of other projects. It is a time of harvesting again, as in 1969-1970, and one in which I am not only occupied with writing new books but with finishing the old ones.

[3] *How To Be*, Claudio Naranjo (Los Angeles: Jeremy Tarcher, 1991).

[4] *The Handbook of Gestalt Therapy*, edited by Chris Hatcher and Philip Himelstein (New Jersey: Jason Aronson, Inc., 1990).

Along with chapters belonging to the earlier *The Attitude and Practice of Gestalt Therapy*, I am introducing under the title "Gestalt Therapy Revisited" a number of statements belonging to a time of return to psychotherapy after my not very long and yet deeply life-changing South American pilgrimage. While in the 1970 book I essentially spelled out my experience of Gestalt therapy with Perls and Simkin, the later batch of essays, though not of much volume, contains a more personal contribution: the underscoring of the transpersonal aspect of Gestalt, a critique of the "holes" in the approach, some illustration of later clinical work, a statement of my attitude in regard to therapeutic and training exercises along with some sharing from my "bag of tricks" and considerations on the affinity between Gestalt and some spiritual traditions. The first three of these pieces have already appeared in *The Gestalt Journal* (the second being an edited transcript of the opening address at the Baltimore Conference in 1981); two of the others originated as presentations at the 2nd International Gestalt Conference, in Madrid in 1987; while the chapter on Gestalt Exercises, a subject which I might consider one of my specialties, has been written expressly for this book. Shortly before going into print, I decided to include still another chapter—"Gestalt After Fritz"—that addresses itself to the history of the movement. It constitutes the edited transcript of a talk given at the Fourth International Gestalt Conference (in Siena, 1991) and is self-explanatory.

One thing has seemed incomplete in the present book even after the additions: my failure to have included, in my discussion of the implicit life philosophy of Gestalt, the issue of trust in organismic self-regulation. I have said that Gestalt is (on the patient's side) fifty percent attention and fifty percent spontaneity. I would also say that in "Techniques of

Integration" (Book One, Chapter 6) I have emphasized awareness over spontaneity.

Fritz's trust in individual self-regulation stands in contemporary psychotherapy as a contribution comparable to that of Rogers' trust in the self-regulation of groups: both have influenced psycho-therapeutic practice through a contagion of attitude transcending intellectual influence.

I have conducted a computer search for the appearance of the expression "organismic self-regulation" in the titles and abstracts of two hundred psychological and medical journals since 1966, and I think readers may be interested in knowing that the phrase does not appear a single time. It was certainly Fritz Perls who popularized the expression, and he used it in such manner that he seemed to be making reference to a well known concept. I think I have not been the only one of his listeners to assume that he was quoting Sherrington or Goldstein. The concept was certainly a familiar one to his listeners, and yet the implicit attribution of "organismic self-regulation" to the authority of the scientific establishment may have involved a shamanistic sleight of hand. Trust in organismic self-regulation is embodied in Gestalt therapy as a trust in spontaneity—which goes hand in hand with what I have called "humanistic hedonism" and is not a different issue but a biological translation of the existential one of "being oneself." In either case, what is meant is a living-from-within rather than a living-from-without—i.e., out of obedience to obligation or concern for self-image. The ideals of spontaneity and authenticity imply a faith similar to that of the indwelling perfection of Mahayana Buddhism and other spiritual traditions.

It seems appropriate that Fritz came into his own and was appreciated for what he truly was—in the nude, so to say—at Esalen Institute, a center created in part through the inspiration and support of Alan Watts and where one of the earliest community members was Gia-Fu-Feng, who then covered many walls with his beautiful calligraphy and taught Tai-Chi and later gave us one of the modern translations of Lao-Tzu. These outer circumstances echoed an affinity of Fritz with Taoism which was reflected in his life and work. When Fritz said "organismic self-regulation" he also meant "Tao" at least in the sense of "the Tao of man," which the Taoists distinguish from the supraindividual "Tao of Heaven"; a course of appropriate action dictated by deep intuition rather than reason (and involving a Dionysian yielding to preferences rather than a Sartrean striving for choices).

In his allegiance to organismic self-regulation Perls was not only an inheritor of Freud, who first pointed out to us the vicissitudes of repression, but a continuator of Wilhelm Reich (his analyst), who was the first to believe in instinct more than in present civilization. By default of a chapter on organismic self-regulation in this book I have wanted to highlight the issue in this introduction, and feel pleased that in so doing I have touched upon the subject before and not after the subject of awareness—as befits the unique manner in which it is emphasized in the Gestalt approach as well as the predominantly Dionysian quality of the Gestalt ethos.

While I have grouped together as a "theory" my statements on the primacy of attitude over technique (Chapter 1) and my discussion of present-centeredness (Chapter 2), I have deliberately refrained from calling my early book *The Theory and Practice of Gestalt Therapy*. The choice, rather, of *Gestalt Therapy: Attitude and Practice* implicitly reflects my view that Gestalt therapy has not arisen as the application of a body of theory (that might be called its foundation) but is, rather, a matter of being in the world in a certain way.

Of course we can spell out Fritz Perls' psychological outlook (it is primarily in *his* outlook that I am interested) and in so doing we may find a certain view of the ego as a factor of internal interference—in *Ego, Hunger and Aggression*[5]—and as an "identification function"; we find certain ideas about the self and contact — in addition to the open systems view of an organism in the environment and the holistic Gestalt approach. Even though we can find all this and more, I conceive of Fritz's psychological ideas as a context of his work rather than as a foundation, an explication rather than a skeleton. Because of this, when I defined Gestalt Therapy on the occasion of presenting Esalen and Herbert Otto with my "I and Thou Here and Now" in the mid-60s, I avoided a conceptual definition (as was noted by a reviewer in *Etc.: The Journal of General Semantics*) by simply pointing to it as "the approach that originated in the work of Fritz Perls."[6]

When in the late 60s I was searching for a better understanding of the "theoretical foundations" of Gestalt, I appealed to Gene Sagan (about whom Fritz was greatly excited in the early 60s and who constituted the link to Esalen Institute). He refreshingly told me that he thought that Gestalt therapy had more in common with the Stanislawsky method of acting than with Gestalt psychology. I continue to agree with him. I also shared at the Baltimore conference my view that Fritz sought intellectual support in Gestalt psychology at a time when he was in need of intellectual support against the academic world.

Far from being adverse to theory, I have professed criticism in face of Fritz's anti-intellectual orientation, inherited by many. Yet I think that the theory that Gestalt therapy might need (if any) will

---

[5] *Ego, Hunger and Aggression*, F. S. Perls (New York: Random House, 1969).

[6] "Contributions of Gestalt Therapy." In *Ways of Growth: Approaches to Expanding Awareness*, edited by Herbert Otto and John Mann (New York: Grossman, 1968)

not be the collection of Fritz's personal beliefs, such as "anxiety is excitement minus breathing" or "to die and to be reborn is not easy"—however insightful many of these may be. What the psychotherapist could draw most benefit from is a conceptual frame of reference to the understanding of the psyche and the growth process not so provincial as a specific Gestalt theory. At least, personally, I am more interested in a theory of health and sickness (that is to say, more ambitiously: a theory of enlightenment and endarkenment) that would bring together not only the inspiration of Gestalt psychology but what we know of conditioning, psychodynamics and, beyond that, the contribution of the Eastern spiritual traditions.

Less ambitious than such a comprehensive undertaking and still more relevant than Paul Goodman's attempt in the mid-50s (the "Gestalt theory" embraced by today's emerging Gestalt orthodoxy) would be a *"theory of Gestalt therapy"*—an enterprise comparable to the theory of psychoanalytic therapy that has recently emerged as an alternative endeavor to the psychoanalytic theory of the mind. Of this I have spoken in this book without making it its foreground, and my view can be summarized in the formula:

Gestalt therapy = (Awareness/Naturalness + Support/Confrontation) Relationship

or in other words: the therapeutic process rests, on the patient's side, on the two transpersonal factors of awareness and spontaneity; while the therapist contributes to it (as I discuss under Gestalt Techniques) the stimulation and support of genuine expression and negative reinforcement ("ego reduction") of the pathological. To the extent that psychotherapy may be learned, this activity of eliciting genuine expression and confronting the dysfunctional constitutes strategy; to the extent that therapy derives from the degree of development of the therapist's being, both of these will be the spontaneous outcome of uncontrived relationship and individual creativity.

GESTALT THERAPY

THE ATTITUDE AND PRACTICE
OF AN ATHEORETICAL
EXPERIENTIALISM

BOOK ONE

THE ATTITUDE AND PRACTICE OF GESTALT THERAPY

I. THEORY

Chapter One

The Primacy
of Attitude

The different schools of psychoanalysis and, even more so, behavior therapy, are based on the application of certain ideas and theories: that is, of assumptions as to the nature of lawfulness of psychological phenomena. Such assumptions, when brought to bear on the therapeutic situation, give rise to the characteristic procedures or techniques of the different approaches. The techniques represent the practical expression of the ideas that characterize a given system and may be regarded as a behavioral definition of that school of psychotherapy.

But is it the *techniques* of a given tradition that account for the success claimed by the practitioners that employ them? If the effectiveness of psychotherapy were completely dependent upon the totality of its techniques, we would be entitled to expect that computers will some day take over the functions of the professional, and that do-it-yourself approaches laying out the procedural detail of the approach will be as effective as the interpersonal situation.

This is a view that most psychiatrists today would reject out of a conviction that it is the *personal relationship* between doctor and patient that is critical in the healing process. What the nature of such a relationship is, though, is a subject on which much remains to be said, for the opinions of psychotherapists tend to differ on this matter just as they do in their theoretical conceptions.

The now-classic studies of Fiedler on the nature of
the therapeutic relationship have been important in
showing that experts of different schools resemble each
other more than they resemble the less skilled professionals in their own school, both in their conception of
the ideal therapeutic relationship and in their behavior
during sessions with their patients. When it comes to
the issue of defining the nature of such successful behavior, or of defining the ideal held by the more experienced therapists, we may feel dissatisfied with
Fiedler's information, however, for the only clear-cut
trait demonstrated by him in such behavior is that of
"understanding" the patient. Whereas professionals of
different schools differed from each other with regard
to supportiveness or punitiveness, participation or non-
participation (non-directive), the assumed superior
status or an equalitarian collaborative role of the
therapist, all the more successful representatives of
these approaches were seen as listening to and understanding their patients rather than interrupting their
thoughts or being unable to understand by reason of
the therapist's personal needs.

The experimental finding of a convergence of
psychotherapeutic systems at the higher levels of
understanding confirms, I think, the belief held by
many of us on the basis of experience, and constitutes
an echo of the growing recognition in our day of a
similar convergence "at the top" among the ways of
different religions. If the crux of such convergence
and the "personal element" under discussion is *not*
to be found in the intellectual formulations or in the
explicit techniques defining the various approaches,
we may ask whether it can be found among a list of
"behavioral traits" at all, but rather, in an *attitude,* a
state, a characteristic "state of mind" which is to such
traits as a *Gestalt* is to the component elements.

In her well-known book, *You Are Not the Target,*
Laura Huxley stresses a point quite relevant to this
discussion. Again and again throughout its pages, in

connection with certain procedures, she insists: "*It works if you work.*" The same could be said of many spiritual disciplines, and yet it is perhaps the greatest limitation of any solitary practice. Even in the learning of a language or a musical instrument, few have the persistence to carry out on their own the discipline required to master even the less subtle and outward aspects of the skill involved. When it comes to the question of inner change, though, the difficulty increases, for *who wants to change?* and *who is really able to "work"?*

In behavioristic terms psychopathology consists in addictions and avoidances which can only be changed through punishment and rewards in a chosen direction. In psychoanalytic terms, psychopathology is the outcome of "defenses" which inevitably will become manifest in psychotherapy as "resistances." In the light of such formulations the role of the psychotherapist is not merely that of somebody who applies certain techniques, but one who can make the patient work with them — in spite of himself.

The individual's means of defeating his own therapeutic intent, however, are more subtle than mere omission. He may *think* that he is free-associating or expressing his present feelings or being himself, for instance, and in fact he may be doing something quite different; or, more subtly yet, he may respond to indications or follow the steps of a given technique in a mechanical, feelingless fashion. If so, he is only apparently "doing" something, and there is little to wonder if he accomplishes nothing.

The skilled professional in psychotherapy is, above all else, he who can elicit real doing, beyond the superficial actions which, when not backed by the appropriate attitude, are no more than an empty ritual. He is able to detect the proper attitude, reinforce it, require it, teach it, because he knows it in himself. Any book can describe a technique, but an attitude needs to be conveyed by a person.

The central role of the proper attitude is not only to be seen in the field of psychotherapy but in every psychological exercise or spiritual discipline. If we seek the heart of a technique we invariably arrive at instructions that transcend behavioral description, which are difficult to communicate, even through personal supervision, and are frequently referred to as ultimately inexpressible. It may be necessary, for instance, that the person engaging in a certain form of practice should be in an attitude of "openness", that he "let go", that he place himself in an attitude of receptiveness, or surrender, or equanimity, or trust, or faith, or longing, and so forth. Even in the case of a practice of non-doing such as Zen meditation, the meditation instructor is imminently concerned with conveying *how* the technique must be put into practice to be effective. Even though the external aspects of no-action may be clear, "Just to sit," as Shrunyu Suzuki said, "embraces all the koans."

In order to be not only a demonstrator of techniques but one who can see that they serve their function, the therapist, like the spiritual guide of different traditions, must be an expert in the *howness* of the techniques. He might be likened to the watch repair man who, according to a well-known joke, charged a large sum for blowing hard at the mechanism of a watch. "All that money just for blowing!" was the natural reaction of the customer, though he could not help admitting that the watch was now functioning. "Only ten cents for blowing, the rest for knowing where," was the answer. Much of the extant writing on psychotherapeutic systems deals with techniques, and yet, like the blowing in the foregoing story, techniques are not the point. Techniques, it could be said, are the *occasions* for the expression—by patient and therapist alike—of the attitudes that constitute the real work. They are a series of actions to be engaged in *in a certain spirit*, and the therapist is one who has some mastery of that spirit. His knowledge of what to do or how to act does not derive principally from molecular formulas, but from a global understanding of "where it is at"— an understanding that he is not necessarily able to formulate explicitly. Moreover, his implicit under- standing — which he has developed through his life and training—is not necessarily related to his theoretical outlook.

Gestalt therapy is unique among the major schools of psychotherapy because of *the extent to which this is a system built upon intuitive understanding rather than theory.* This does not mean that intuition was not important in the creative process of Freud, Jung or others. Perhaps each effective system stems from a personal realization. Nor does it mean that intuition is not part of psychotherapeutic practice in general. The uniqueness of Gestalt therapy, rather, lies in the fact that a direct grounding of practice upon intuition or living understanding never was replaced by a foundation upon theoretical assump- tions. Ideas are certainly part of the system, yet ideas are its flowers and never its roots. Moreover, the nature of these ideas is generally an explication of attitudes rather than of theoretical constructs. They are ideas rooted in experience rather than in specula- tive activity, and do not lend support to the therapeutic activity but constitute, like it, an alterna- tive avenue of expression.

Perls believed that to be a psychotherapist was to be himself, and vice versa. He employed and generated techniques (just as he used pens to write or silverware to eat) but warned us about *props* — procedures employed with the belief that *they* will do something while we sit back. There was no division in his mind between being what he was and doing his job, and what he "taught" when "training" psychotherapists was a bringing them to be them- selves. He trusted *being* to be infectious and *intrinsic learning* of psychotherapy to be sufficient. To *be*, meant, to him, to be here and now, to be aware and to be responsible—that is, to stand behind one's own actions and feelings.

These three—an appreciation of *actuality*, of *awareness*, and of *responsibility*—constitute the core attitude of Gestalt therapy. Though three different attitudes in appearance, they are but aspects or facets of a single mode of being in the world. To be responsible (response-able) entails being present, being here. And being truly present is being aware. Awareness, in turn, is presence—reality—and a condition incompatible with the illusion of irresponsibility by means of which we avoid living our lives (or knowing that we do live them, whatever we may think).

The Implicit Philosophy of Gestalt Therapy

The basic attitude of appreciation of actuality, awareness and responsibility becomes manifest in a number of more specific attitudes that Gestalt therapists learn in their training and communicate without preaching in their work. These more specific attitudes may be regarded as corollaries of actuality, awareness, responsibility. I believe that these, together with their threefold marrow, constitute the real tradition of Gestalt therapy, while techniques are only a convenient means for the expression and transmission of their understanding. To give some examples:

1. There is in Gestalt therapy an attitude of respect for the person's illness rather than an attempt to effect change. It is paradoxical to say that a psychotherapeutic activity, which we naturally understand as one oriented toward change, is in this case based upon the stance of accepting a person as he *is*. On the other hand, we know from every form of psychotherapy that in fact, if not in theory, acceptance (in the form of self-acceptance sometimes facilitated by genuine external support) leads to growth rather than stagnation. Life is process, and

living it is all that is required to maintain its flow. In the view of Gestalt therapy, one way of *not* living is to stand aside from life telling ourselves what we *should* be doing. By *shouldism* we do not increase our being but lose sight of what we are. Gestalt therapy in this respect stands out more by what it refrains from doing than by what it does. It claims that awareness is enough; that for change to take place nothing else is needed but presence, awareness, responsibility. This is what Dr. Arnold Beisser has called "the paradoxical theory of change." I would argue with the term "theory" because of the experiential foundation of this attitude. At its best it is not the intellectual stance of "I know that he will change once he stops trying. I will trust this theory and trick him out of his vicious circle," but a genuine interest in having the patient be what he is (or lack of interest in changing him). If a therapist wants "change" at all, he wants more of the same. He wants the patient to be more present, more responsible for what he is and more aware. The patient wanting to "change" *wants as little as possible of himself,* and thus avoids, lies, pretends, et cetera. And yet he will eventually learn, through the simple *experience of being,* that he need not seek to be what he is not.

2. Another expression of what I am calling the basic attitude of Gestalt therapy is that particular stance which Dr. Resnick has discussed in his paper "Chicken Soup is Poison." If our being (presence, awareness, responsibility) is all that we need, this is not all we *want.* In the view of Gestalt therapy, many of our wants are not grounded in needs, but are a craving for environmental substitutes of what we are disowning in our being. Perls understood maturation as the transition from environmental support to self-support, and Gestalt therapists since him are well aware of the double repercussion that support may have in the therapeutic setting: a basis for growth, or a substitute for it. The Gestalt therapist sees the therapeutic role of a "helper" with reservations since he believes that "helping" can be the main obstacle to his real helpfulness. Accordingly, he detaches himself from compulsive lovingness and

seeks either that balance of support and frustration which is most conducive to growth, or the spontaneous expression of himself.

3. Still another corollary of the basic stance of Gestalt psychotherapy is the attitude with which the therapist contemplates the seemingly undesirable aspects of his patient's personality. The Gestalt therapist is, at his best, equally appreciative of his patient's impulsive nature and of his defense mechanisms. In both he sees energies which operate destructively in the dark but will find constructive expression in awareness. To say that it is enough for the therapist to increase his patient's awareness, his sense of actuality and his responsibility, or to say that these three are enough for us in order to become fully human entails a *basic trust in the rightness of our own nature.* Given this trust we need not manipulate ourselves or others to preserve our "goodness" and avoid the catastrophe of chaos or destructiveness. The Gestalt therapist believes such manipulation to be not only superfluous and wasteful of our energies, but destructive, in that it alienates us from what we are, creates unhappiness within and without, and thence leads to the need for further manipulation in order to avoid unhappiness or fill our emptiness.

To say that the Gestalt therapist trusts the rightness of human nature does not mean that he conceives of authenticity as a condition of no friction and no pain. As Fritz Perls has expressed it: "All I can do is, possibly, to help people to reorganize themselves to function better, to enjoy life more, to feel — and this is very important — to feel more real. What more do you want? Life is not violins and roses."

The Gestalt therapist does not say that aggression does not destroy or hurt, but that the measure of aggression is part of our organismic functioning and that, when unacknowledged, suppressed, disowned, distorted, this aggressive potential is likely to result in greatly increased destructiveness as well as personal unhappiness. Accordingly, the work of the Gestalt therapist is characterized to a high degree by the extent to which he invites explosive behavior, aggressive or otherwise. He does not fear the extremes of feeling or lack of control, but on the contrary, sees them as the occasion for the required awareness of impulses, and for the patient's taking responsibility for them, acknowledging them as part of his being.

What is true of impulse expression—including, particularly, expression of anger—is equally true of the expression of control. Gestalt therapy does not view resistance as something to be smashed, but as one more activity to become aware of and responsible for. Defenses are not something that *happen* to us and of which somebody can make us free, but something that *we do*, and may choose to continue doing or not, according to our evaluation of our needs and the situation. As in Judo or Tai Chi Chuan, the attitude of the Gestalt therapist is to guide the patient to *use* the energies of what he would rather resist as an opponent. To do that, he first must come in *contact* with his opponent: listen to him, see what he is about. Eventually he will realize that there is no "other."

4. Still another attitude expressed in the activity of the Gestalt therapist is a disregard for explanations, interpretations, justifications and conceptual activity in general. The derivation of this stance from that which I am calling the basic attitude is easy to see if we consider that in talking *about* things we are at once standing aside from our direct experience of them.

Justification usually stems from the person's lack of self-acceptance—at least at the moment of justifying—and reveals that he is choosing to avoid his experience of discomfort by seeking external approval. A Gestalt therapist would have him, first of all, own up to his experience rather than play a social game. Beyond that, he may help the patient to take responsibility for his self-accusation or, if that be a phantom, dissolve it in awareness and reconcile himself with his action. Explanations generally rest upon the same emotional ground as justifications. Behind most "whys" there is

the tacit echo of a parent's warning: "If you cannot
explain your reaction—or action—you have no right
to it." This type of explanation may be seen as a
justification in terms of causes rather than a justification in terms of purposes and intentions or extrinsic
standards. Justification, whether in terms of past or
future, causes or goals, is an attempt to base the *isness*
of an experience upon a reality other than that in the
present. To the Gestalt therapist there is no reality
other than *this* one, here and now. Acceptance of what
we are here and now is taking responsibility for being
what we are. Not doing so is hanging onto the illusion
of a god greater than reality.

Gestalt therapy, in contrast to psychoanalysis,
has little to add to the dynamic interpretation of
psychopathological phenomena. It is a "therapy"
more than a theory, an art more than a psychological
system. Yet, like psychoanalysis, Gestalt therapy involves a philosophical underpinning. The attitudes
listed above, such as their threefold premise, constitute a philosophical foundation of Gestalt therapy.
More than that: Gestalt therapy *rests* on an implicit
philosophical posture which is transmitted from
therapist to patient or trainee by means of its procedures without need of explication. And more yet: I
would like to suggest that the experiential assimilation of such implicit *Weltanschauung* is a hidden key
to the therapeutic process. This amounts to the claim
that a specific *philosophy* of life provides the background of Gestalt therapy just as a specific psychology provides that of psychoanalytic therapy.

The transmission of attitudes such as those listed
above through the use of the tools characteristic of
Gestalt therapy may be likened to the process
whereby a sculptor creates a form with the tools of
his art. In both instances the content transcends the
instruments, though the instruments have been conceived for its expression. Unfortunately, it is one of
our human weaknesses to trust that formulas and

techniques will do everything for us, as is shown by the history of every cult, the story of incessant petrifaction of truth in rigid forms.

In calling the philosophy of Gestalt "implicit," I am not saying that it is, as in psychoanalysis, covert. It is *simply* implicit, this implicitness being itself the outcome of its nature or content: the Gestalt therapist places more value in action than in words, in experience than in thoughts, in the living process of therapeutic interaction and the inner change resulting thereby than in influencing beliefs. Action engenders substance or touches substance. Ideas can easily float by, cover up, or even substitute for reality. So nothing could be more remote from the style of Gestalt therapy than preaching. Yet, it involves a kind of preaching without injunctions or statements of belief, just as an artist preaches his world-view and orientation to existence through his style.

Ideas are as dangerous as techniques as substitutes for real experience, since they tempt us with their clarity and clear-cutness. Thus we fall into the "magical" pitfall of equating knowledge and being, understanding and action, utterance and effectiveness. And yet, there is nothing else that we have but ideas and techniques, and we must accept that what serves us can also put us to sleep and take our place.

Morality beyond good and evil

"Good" and "evil" are suspicious to the Gestalt therapist, who is used to perceiving most of human advice as subtle manipulation, discussion on moral issues as self-justification and rationalization of needs, statements of worth or worthlessness as over-generalizations and as projections of personal experience onto the environment in people's attempt to avoid responsibility for their feelings and reactions.

As Fritz Perls has put it:

Good and bad are responses of the organism. We say, "You make me mad." "You make me feel happy," less frequently, "You make me feel good," "You make me feel bad." Among primitive people such phrases occur with extreme frequency. Again we use expressions like, "I feel good," "I feel lousy," without considering the stimulus. But what is happening is that an ardent pupil makes his teacher feel good, an obedient child makes his parents feel good. The victorious boxer makes his fan feel good, as does the efficient lover his mistress. A book or a picture does the same when it meets your aesthetic needs. And vice versa: if people or objects fail to meet needs and produce satisfaction, we feel bad about them.

The next step is that instead of owning up to our experiences as ours, we project them and throw the responsibility for our own responses onto the stimulus. (This might be because we are afraid of our excitement, feel that we are failing in excitement, want to shirk responsibility, etc., etc.) We say the pupil, the child, the boxer, the lover, the book, the picture "is" good or bad. At that moment, labeling the stimulus good or bad, we cut off good and bad from our own experience. They become abstractions, and the stimulus-objects are correspondingly pigeon-holed. This does not happen without consequences. Once we isolate thinking from feeling, judgment from intuition, morality from self-awareness, deliberateness from spontaneity, the verbal from the non-verbal, we lose the Self, the essence of existence, and we become either frigid human robots or confused neurotics.[1]

In spite of such views on the good and bad, Gestalt therapy abounds in injunctions as to the desirability of certain attitudes toward life and experience. These are *moral injunctions* in the sense that they refer to the pursuit of the good life. Even though the notion of morality in common parlance has come

[1] *Complex*, #9, 1955 (pp. 42-52) © 1955 by the 5 x 9 Press. Reprinted with permission of *The Gestalt Journal*.

to indicate a concern about living up to standards extrinsic to man, it is possible that all the great issues in morality have once originated in a humanistic ethic where good and evil were not divorced from man's condition. Thus the concept of *righteousness* in Judaism, that eminently law-giving religion, once indicated the condition of being in tune with God's law or will, which we may understand as similar to that alluded to by the non-theistic Chinese as living in the Tao—following one's proper *Way*. So it would seem that what, in a living vision of life is seen as right, just, adequate, or good, after being expressed in laws, turns against man and enslaves him by claiming some authority greater than himself.

If we want to list the implicit moral injunctions of Gestalt therapy, the list may be longer or shorter according to the level of generality or particularity of our analysis. Without claiming to be systematic or thorough, here are some that may give an impressionistic notion of the style of life entailed:

1) Live now: be concerned with the present, rather than the past or future.
2) Live here: deal with what is present rather than with what is absent.
3) Stop imagining: experience the real.
4) Stop unnecessary thinking; rather, taste and see.
5) Express rather than manipulate, explain, justify, and judge.
6) Give in to unpleasantness and pain just as to pleasure; do not restrict your awareness.
7) Accept no *should* or *ought* other than your own: adore no graven image.
8) Take full responsibility for your actions, feelings, and thoughts.
9) Surrender to being as you are.

The paradox that such injunctions may be part of a moral philosophy that precisely recommends giving up injunctions may be resolved if we look at them as statements of truth rather than duty. Responsibility, for instance, is not a *must*, but an unavoidable fact: we *are* the responsible doers of whatever we do. Our only alternative is to acknowledge such responsibility or deny it. All that Gestalt therapy is saying is that by accepting the truth (which amounts to a non-undoing rather than a doing) we are better off: awareness cures. Of course, it cures us of our lies.

I think that all these specific injunctions of Gestalt therapy may in turn be subsumed under the three more general principles that I have mentioned earlier in the text:

1)   Valuation of actuality (temporal present
      vs. past or future), spatial (present vs. absent),
      and substantial (act vs. symbol)
2)   Valuation of awareness and the acceptance
      of experience
3)   Valuation of wholeness, or responsibility.

To consider these *merely* as technical points of view or therapeutic devices would be to underestimate their role. Consider, for instance, interactions like the following, which I do not think are exceptional in Gestalt therapy sessions:

(On actuality)

P.:   I felt very depressed yesterday . . .
T.:   I see that you are beginning to tell me a story.
P.:   I see . . . It is true that I am not depressed
      now, but I thought that it would be good to
      understand what happened; otherwise,
      I worry that the next time . . .
T.:   You see how you worry?
P.:   Well, if I don't think about my future,
      what am I doing here, then?
T.:   Let us find out.

Or consider the following, on the matter of responsibility:

P.: I feel anxious because I feel that you expect me to come up with something . . .
T.: I do?
P.: Well, I imagine . . . or rather, I would like to please you, or impress you . . .
   though I should not feel that way.
T.: Who says so?
P.: I don't like to feel that way. It makes me feel weak.
T.: What is the "it"?
P.: I make myself feel weak. I shrink. I turn my power off.
T.: So that is how you make yourself anxious . . .
P.: Yes, I do it. I have the choice . . .

I think that these are instances where the therapist's interaction may be viewed as one of practical demonstration of the validity or merits of a life philosophy. More often than not, the scope of the issue will be narrow in its particularity, but the consistency in the point of view will gradually lead to the building up of a new pattern of convictions. A patient may experimentally find out, for instance, that by yielding to feelings that he had been avoiding, they undergo a transformation; that by accepting them they change, whereas in his ordinary policy of warding them off he had only perpetuated them. Or in the processes of intentional temporary "forgetting" of past and future worries, he may discover to his surprise that he does not need to hold on to them all the time; in fact he can, with this new attitude, cope better, not worse, with practicalities. This type of interaction in Gestalt therapy parallels that in Zen:

Sengtsan asked Huike, saying, "I am diseased: I implore you to cleanse me of my sin." Huike said, "Bring me your sin and I will cleanse you of it." Sengtsan thought a while; then said, "I cannot get at it." Huike replied, "Then I have cleansed you of it."

Beyond attitude: direct experience.

The basic attitude of valuing the present and presence, awareness and responsibility becomes—as white light broken into the rainbow colors—the more specific attitudes or ideals that inspire the behavior of the Gestalt therapist in his practice. Each one of these specific attitudes or implicit injunctions stems from that which we have posited as the threefold central one as a particular form of expression of a single law. Yet it would not be accurate to think of their derivation as a purely logical one, explicit as their inter-relatedness may be shown on logical terms.

In speaking of attitudes, indeed, I have not been stressing enough the *experiential* foundation of the behavior or beliefs implied in the foregoing descriptions. The term "attitude" is adequate in that it denotes a global response, it suggests the area of life philosophy and behavioral aspects. It may be well to clarify, however, that the learning of attitudes that I am pointing out as the central process in Gestalt therapy is not to be taken as a matter of changing beliefs nor imitation of behavior. The substance of the transmission that takes place in psychotherapy is not ideas or styles of behaving but an experience from which both ideas or behavior may derive—not a description but an *experience* of presence, awareness, responsibility, which carries with itself the guarantee of its all-rightness and the perception of its possibility for other beings. He who *is* not only can stand on his own and enjoy rather than suffer his circumstances, but he can see the *is-ness* that others are wasting energy in both denying and striving for. He does not have to *adopt* an attitude. He experiences himself as worthy of existence, and so does he experience the other. Just as the therapist is for himself he is *for* his patient; and not *against*, but *disinterested* in the games that obscure his being.

To say that the learning process taking place in Gestalt therapy is experiential rather than intellectual and merely behavioral is obvious. Yet I think it deserves to be stated that if this is true *the therapeutic process consists in the transmission of an experience.* Much has been written on psychotherapy as technique—that is, from the standpoint of the *effects* upon the patient of the therapist's actions or interpretations. In discussions of this sort, the patient's experiences are always seen as *elicited* by deliberate choices of behavior on the part of the therapist. What is left out, however, is the notion that *experience may be passed on,* and that, as life proceeds from life, a certain depth of experience may perhaps be only brought about by the *presence* of another being partaking in that depth, and not by manipulations. If attitude is a deeper issue than technique, and if techniques issue from attitudes, experience is still a deeper issue than attitudes and constitutes *their* source. Without the appropriate attitude techniques become empty forms. Without experience even attitude becomes second-hand dogmas. Just as a dead organism cannot reproduce itself, mere dead attitudes cannot engender any corresponding attitude in another being. Experience, on the other hand, is self-duplicating. It creates the external forms that convey its pulsating heart.

I believe the foregoing to be true of every successful psychotherapy, yet particularly true of Gestalt therapy where the therapist is more challenged than in others to be both a naked human being and an artist. In the same sense that Beethoven said of his music that it went from the heart to the heart, I see the actions of the Gestalt therapist as meaningful only to the extent to which they are, more than techniques, *expressions of a perspective,* embodiments of a living understanding, that may generate that understanding in another person. To the extent that they are grounded in this living or experiential understanding, they will generate the trust or faith required to make psychotherapy a communication in depth rather than a game with words.

Chapter Two

Present-Centeredness

To me, nothing exists except the now.
Now = experience = awareness = reality.
The past is no more and the future not yet.
Only the now exists.

Fritz Perls

I.   *All issues reflected in present-centeredness*

I have been positing in the previous chapter:

1)   that the techniques of Gestalt therapy are rooted in certain attitudes,

2)   that these attitudes are manifestations of a basic attitude that may be understood from a threefold point of view of awareness, responsibility and actuality, *and*

3)   that this basic attitude is not merely an ideological issue but is itself rooted upon an experience: the *evidence* of actuality (i.e. the apprehension of the *fact* that we are living here and now and we are one with our concrete actions); the evidence of responsibility (the fact that we do what we do and that we are no different from what we are), and the evidence of awareness (that we at some level know what we are doing and experiencing, no matter how much we lie to ourselves pretending that we do not).

In the following pages I will examine in some detail one aspect of the threefold attitude of Gestalt therapy, as an instance of a work of explication that could be done with each one of the three. More specifically, I will be explaining an *aspect* of actuality, in itself an aspect of the philosophy of Gestalt Therapy. Yet, as I expect to show, all issues are reflected in this one, or in any, for the questions of actuality, awareness, and responsibility are only superficially distinct. On close examination we may discover, for instance, that the question of actuality is not only related to the valuation of present tense and present locus, but to that of concrete reality, of sensing and feeling rather than thinking and imagining, to awareness and to self-determination. More specifically, I hope that the following pages may show that the willingness to live in the moment is inseparable from the question of openness to experience, trust in the workings of reality, discrimination between reality and fantasies, surrender of control and acceptance of potential frustration, a hedonistic outlook, awareness of potential death, and so on. All these issues are facets of a single experience of being-in-the-world, and looking at such an experience from the perspective of present-centeredness amounts to an arbitrary choice.

II. *Present-Centeredness as Technique*

Although the *hic et nunc* formula recurs in scholastic literature, the relationship of the here and now to contemporary psychotherapy has been the outcome of a gradual evolution.

Psychoanalysis began with a past-oriented approach. Freud's discovery of free association had its origin in his experience with hypnosis, and his first explorations into the method were in the nature of an attempt to do away with the trance state and yet elicit the same clues for the understanding of his patient's past. He would, in those days, pose a question to the patient and ask him to report the first thought that came to his mind at the moment of touching his forehead. With increasing experience, he found that he could omit the touch of the forehead and also the question, and regard instead every utterance as an association to the preceding one in the spontaneous flow of thoughts, memories, and fantasies. At the time, this was to him no more than the raw material for an interpretive endeavor, the most precious associations being those related to the patient's childhood. His assumption then was that only by understanding the past could the patient be free from it in the present.

The first step toward an interest in the present in psychoanalysis was Freud's observation of "transference." Insofar as the patient's feelings toward the analyst were understood as the replica of his earlier feelings toward parents or siblings, the understanding of the therapeutic relationship became at once significant to the understanding of the still basic issue of the patient's past.

At the beginning, the analysis of transference was still subservient to retrospective interpretation, but we may assume that it led more and more to an understanding of its value in its own right, for the next step was a gradual shift in stress from past to present, not only as the medium or material being examined but as the very goal of understanding. Thus, while at first the analysis of the present was a tool or a means for the interpretation of the past, many today regard the analysis of childhood events as a means toward the understanding of present dynamics.

The lines of development have been multiple. Melanie Klein, for instance, retains an interpretational language based on assumptions about early childhood experience, but the trend of her school in actual practice is to focus almost exclusively on the understanding of the "transference relationship." A similar focus upon the present was carried by Bion into the group situation.

Wilhelm Reich's shift toward the present was the outcome of his shift of interest from words to action. In his character analysis, the issue is that of understanding the patient's form of expression rather than the content of his speech. There can be no better way of doing so than by observing his conduct in the ongoing situation.

A third contribution to the valuation of the present in the therapeutic process is Karen Horney's, which touches the very foundation of the interpretation of neuroses. In her view, emotional disturbances that originated in the past are sustained now by a false identity. The neurotic once sold his soul to the devil in exchange for a shining self-image, but he is still choosing to respect the pact. If a person can understand how he is burying his true self in this very moment, he can be free.

The growing emphasis in present-orientation in contemporary psychotherapy can be traced to the impact of two other sources aside from psychoanalysis: encounter groups, and the Eastern spiritual disciplines. Information on the latter is now widespread in the West and practice in some of them is increasing. Zen, in particular, can be listed among the influences that have contributed to the shaping of Gestalt therapy into its present form.

The now in presentification and in "the continuum of awareness."

There are at least two ways in which present-centeredness is reflected in the technical repertoire of Gestalt therapy. One is the outspoken request to the patient to the effect that he attends to and expresses what enters his present field of awareness. This will most often be coupled with the instruction of suspending reasoning in favor of pure self-observation. The other is the *presentification* of the past or future (or fantasy in general). This may take the form of an inward attempt to identify with or re-live past events as in the *returning* of dianetics, or, most often, a reenacting the scenes with gestural and postural participation as well as voice, as in psychodrama.

Both these techniques have antecedents in spiritual disciplines older than psychotherapy, and it could not be otherwise, given their importance. Presentification is found in the history of drama, magic and ritual, and in the enacting of dreams among some primitive people. Dwelling in the present is the cornerstone of some forms of meditation. Yet both presentification and dwelling in the present find in Gestalt therapy a distinctive embodiment and form of utilization which deserve discussion at length. In the following pages I will concentrate on the approach called in Gestalt therapy the exercise of the continuum of awareness. Since it is very much like a meditation translated into words, and its role in Gestalt therapy is comparable to that of free-association in psychoanalysis, I will deal with it mostly in comparative terms.

Gestalt therapy and meditation

The practice of attention to present experience has had a place in several traditions of spiritual discipline. In Buddhism, it is a corollary of "right-mindfulness," one of the factors in the "Noble Eightfold Path." An aspect of "right- mindfulness" is the practice of "bare attention."

Bare Attention is concerned only with the *present*. It teaches what so many have forgotten: to live with full awareness in the Here and Now. It teaches us to *face* the present without trying to escape into thoughts about the past or future. Past and future are, for average consciousness, not objects of observation, but of reflection. In ordinary life, the past and the future are taken but rarely as objects of truly *wise* reflection, but are mostly just objects of day-dreaming and vain imaginings which are the main foes of Right Mindfulness, Right Understanding and Right Action as well. Bare Attention, keeping faithfully to its post of observation, watches calmly and without attachment the unceasing march of time: it waits quietly for the things of the future to appear before its eyes, thus to turn into present objects and to vanish again into the past. How much energy has been wasted by useless thoughts of the past: by longing idly for bygone days, by vain regrets and repentance, and by the senseless and garrulous repetition, in word or thought, of all the banalities of the past! Of equal futility is much of the thought given to the future: vain hopes, fantastic plans and empty dreams, ungrounded fears and useless worries. All this is again a cause of avoidable sorrow and disappointment which can be eliminated by Bare Attention.[1]

Past and future do not qualify as "bare objects" in that they are in the nature of imagining, but are also to be avoided because dwelling in them entails a loss of freedom: illusion ensnares us in its recurrence. As Nyaponika Thera puts it:

> Right Mindfulness recovers for man the lost pearl of his freedom, snatching it from the jaws of the dragon Time. Right Mindfulness cuts man loose from the fetters of the past which he foolishly tries ever to reinforce by looking back to it too frequently, with eyes of longing, resentment or regret. Right Mindfulness stops man from chaining himself even now, through the imaginations of his fears and hopes, to anticipated events of the future. Thus Right Mindfulness restores to man a freedom that is to be found only in the present.[2]

The most important practice related to the view in the quotation above is that form of meditation that the Chinese call *wu-hsin* (or idealessness), which

[1] Nyaponika Thera, *The Heart of Buddhist Meditation* (London: Rider, 1962) p. 41.

[2] Ibid.

consists, as Watts puts it, in "the ability to retain one's normal and everyday consciousness and at the same time let go of it."

That is to say, one begins to take an objective view of the stream of thoughts, impressions, feelings, and experiences which constantly flows through the mind. Instead of trying to control and interfere with it, one simply lets it flow as it pleases. But whereas consciousness normally lets itself be carried away by the flow, in this case the important thing is to *watch* the flow without being carried away.

This is a state in which. . .

> one simply accepts experiences as they come without interfering with them on the one hand or identifying oneself with them on the other. One does not judge them, form theories about them, try to control them, or attempt to change their nature in any way; one lets them be free to be just exactly what they are. "The perfect man," said Chuang-tzu, "employs his mind as a mirror; it grasps nothing, it refuses nothing, it receives but does not keep." This must be quite clearly distinguished from mere empty-mindedness on the one hand, and from ordinary undisciplined mind-wandering on the other.[3]

The practice of attention to the present in the context of Gestalt therapy is very much like verbalized meditation. Moreover, it is a meditation carried into the interpersonal situation as an act of self-disclosure. This permits a monitoring of the exercise by the therapist (which may be indispensable to the inexperienced) and may also add significance to the contents of awareness.

I would not doubt that the search for words and the act of reporting can interfere with certain states of mind; yet the act of expression also adds to the exercise in awareness, beyond its being merely a means of information for the therapist's intervention.

---

[3] Alan Watts, *The Supreme Identity* (New York: Farrar, 1957) p. 176.

At least the following advantages of communicated awareness over silent meditation may be listed:

1) The act of expression is a challenge to the sharpness of awareness. It is not quite true to say that we know something but cannot put it in words. Of course, words are mere words and we can never put *anything* in words; yet within limits clarity of perception goes together with the ability to express, an artist being a master in awareness rather than a skilled pattern-maker. And in art as in psychotherapy, the task of having to communicate something involves having to really look at it rather than dreaming about looking.

2) The presence of a witness usually entails an enhancement both of the attention and of the meaningfulness of that which is observed. I think, too, that the more aware an observer is, the more our own attention is sharpened by his mere presence, as if consciousness were contagious or a person could not as easily avoid seeing what is exposed to the gaze of another.

3) The contents of consciousness in an interpersonal setting will naturally tend to be that of the interpersonal relationship, whereas the solitary meditator focused on the "here and now" will systematically fail to find such contents in his field of awareness. Since it is mainly the pattern of relating and the self-image in the process of relating that are disturbed in psychopathological conditions, this factor looms large in making the here-and-now exercise a therapy when in the I-thou setting.

4) The interpersonal situation makes present-centeredness more difficult, for it elicits projection, avoidances and self-delusion in general. For instance, what for the meditator in solitude may be a series of observations of physical states, in the context of communication may become embedded in a feeling of anxiety about the therapist's eventual boredom, the assumption that such observations are trivial or show the patient's essential barrenness. The elicitation of such feelings and fantasies is important:

a) If present-centeredness is a desirable way of living which is usually marred by the vicissitudes of interpersonal relationships, the challenge of contact entails the ideal *training* situation. I would like to invite the thought that the practice of living-in-the-moment is truly an *exercise* and not merely an occasion for self-insight. Just as in behavior therapy, this is a process of desensitization in the course of which a person becomes free of the central conditioning of avoiding experience, and he learns that there is nothing to fear.

b) Related to the above is the fact that it is precisely the awareness of the difficulties in present-centeredness that can provide the first step toward overcoming them. Experiencing the compulsive quality of brooding or planning may be inseparable from an appreciation of the alternative to them, and of a true understanding of the distinction between the said states of mind and present-centeredness.

5) The therapeutic context allows for a monitoring of the process of self-observation, whereby the therapist brings the patient back to the present when he has been distracted from it (i.e., from himself). There are mainly two ways of doing this. The simplest (aside from merely reminding him of the task) is that of waking him up moment after moment to what he is doing unawares. This is accomplished by directing his attention to aspects of his behavior that seem to form part of his automatic patterns of response or clash with his intentional actions. Such simple action of being a mirror to him may serve to bring into focus his relationship to himself and his actions in general.

P.:   I don't know what to say now . . .
T.:   I notice that you are looking away from me.
P.:   (Giggle)
T.:   And now you cover up your face.
P.:   You make me feel so awful!
T.:   And now you cover up your face with
      both hands...
P.:   Stop! This is unbearable!
T.:   What do you feel now?
P.:   I feel so embarrassed! Don't look at me!
T.:   Please stay with that embarrassment.

    P.:   I have been living with it all my life!
          I am ashamed of everything I do!
          It is as if I don't even feel that
          I have the right to exist!

An alternative to this process of simply reflecting the patient's behavior is that of regarding the occasions of failure in present-centeredness as cues to the patient's difficulties (or rather, living samples thereof) just as in psychoanalysis the failure to free-associate is the target of interpretation. Instead of interpretation, though, we have in Gestalt therapy *explication:* the request that the patient himself becomes aware of and expresses the experience underlying his present-avoiding behavior. For one of the assumptions in Gestalt therapy is that *present-centeredness is natural:* at depth, living-in-the-moment is what we want most, and therefore deviations from the present are in the nature of an avoidance or a compulsive sacrifice rather than random alternatives. Even if this assumption were not true of human communication in general, it is made true in Gestalt therapy by the request to the patient of staying in the present. Under such a structure deviations may be understood as either failures, as a sabotaging of the intent, or as distrust in the whole approach and/or the psychotherapist.

In practice, therefore, the therapist will not only coach the patient into persistent attention to his ongoing experience, but he will especially encourage him to become aware and express his experience at the point of failing at the task. This amounts to stopping in order to fill in the gaps of awareness:

    P.:   My heart is pounding. My hands are sweating.
          I am scared. I remember the time when
          I worked with you last time and...
    T.:   What do you want to tell me by going back to
          last week?

P.: I was afraid of exposing myself, and then I felt relieved again, but I think that I didn't come out with the real thing . . .

T.: Why do you want to tell me that now?

P.: I would like to face this fear and bring out whatever it is that I am avoiding.

T.: O.K. That is what you want now. Please go on with your experiences in the moment.

P.: I would like to make a parenthesis to tell you that I have felt much better this week.

T.: Could you tell me anything of your experience while making this parenthesis?

P.: I feel grateful to you, and I want you to know it.

T.: I get the message. Now please compare these two statements: "I feel grateful," and the account of your well-being this week. Can you tell me what it is you feel that makes you prefer the story to the direct statement of your feeling?

P.: If I were to say, "I feel grateful to you," I would feel that I still have to explain... Oh! now I know. Speaking of my gratefulness strikes me as too direct. I feel more comfortable in letting you guess, or just making you feel good without letting you know my feeling.

In this particular instance we can see that the patient has: 1) avoided expressing and taking responsibility for his feeling (as it later became apparent, because of his ambivalence), and 2) acted out his feeling instead of disclosing it in an attempt to manipulate the therapist's state of mind into contentedness rather than becoming aware of his desire for him to be pleased.

Whenever the experience motivating activities other than the mere act of consciousness becomes explicit through such inquiries, it frequently happens that the patient can let go of the roundabout ways of expression involved in the deviation from the present. Direct expression, in turn, can lead to richer awareness.

T.: Now see what it feels like to tell me of your gratefulness as directly as possible.

P.: I want to thank you very much for what you have done for me. I feel that I would like to recompense you for your attention in some way... Wow! I feel so uncomfortable saying this. I feel that you may think that I am being a hypocrite and a boot licker. I guess that I feel that this was a hypocritical statement. I don't feel *that* grateful. I want *you* to believe that I feel grateful.

T.: Stay with that. How do you feel when you want me to believe that?

P.: I feel small, unprotected. I am afraid that you may attack me, so I want to have you on my side.

We can look at the foregoing illustration in terms of the patient's initially not wanting to take responsibility for his alleged gratefulness. As it soon became clear, this was so because of his ambivalence and his reluctance to tell an explicit lie (or, at least, a half-truth). Finally, when he did take responsibility for *wanting the therapist to perceive him as grateful*, he could acknowledge his fear at the root of the whole event. It is true that his first statement referred to the pounding of his heart and his fear, but now in speaking of the expectation that the doctor might attack him, he has gone more into the substance of his fear. Looking back at the excerpt, it seems reasonable to assume that he deviated from present-centeredness when he implicitly chose to manipulate rather than experience. Mere insistence on returning to the present could have possibly told more of the contents of his surface consciousness, but failed to reveal the out-of-awareness operation of his avoidance.

The continuum of awareness and free association

Reporting the experience-at-the-moment not only holds a place in Gestalt therapy comparable to that of free association in psychoanalysis, but the difference between the two in practice is not as clear-cut as it would seem from their definitions.

In principle, "free association *of thought*" emphasizes what Gestalt therapy avoids the most: memories, reasoning, explanations, fantasy. In actual practice, however, the psychoanalytic patient may be primarily experience-centered in his communication, while a Gestalt therapy patient may frequently deviate from the field of present sensing, feeling, and doing. Aside from the instructions given to the patient in Gestalt therapy to the effect that his communication be limited to actuality and the field of immediate experience, there is a difference brought about by the therapist's approach to the patient's communication in both instances.

Let us take the case of a patient reminiscing about a pleasant event. An analyst might, in the first place, lead the patient to become engaged with the significance of the event remembered. The Gestalt therapist, on the contrary, will most probably attend to the missing report on *what is happening with the patient now, while he chooses to remember rather than dwell in the present.* Rather than with the content of his memory, he is concerned with his present *action* of bringing the event to mind or reporting it.

The analyst, too, may choose to focus on the patient's present. In such a case, he will most probably *interpret* his reminiscing as either a compensation and defense in face of his feelings at the moment, or as a cue or indirect indication of his actual pleasurable feelings. The Gestalt therapist, on the other hand, will consider interpretations as messages to the patient's analytical mind, which must step out of reality in order to "think about" it. His efforts are precisely those of minimizing the current estrangement from experience involved in abstraction and interpretation. Therefore, he will instead recruit the patient's effort as a co- phenomenologist to the end of observing, rather than theorizing about or labelling this act or remembering a pleasant incident. The awareness of "I am remembering something pleasant" is already a step beyond the act of remembering in itself, and may open up an avenue to the understanding of the actual motive or intent in the process. For instance, it might lead to the realization that: "I want to make you feel that I have lots of good friends so you think that I am a great guy," or "I wish that I could feel as happy as I did in those days. Please help me," or "I am feeling very well-cared for right now — just as on that occasion," and so on.

In fact, if the patient knew what he was doing in his actions of remembering, anticipating, interpreting, there would be nothing "wrong" with him. The usual trouble is that such actions replace, cover up, and amount to an acting-out of an ongoing experience rather than its acknowledgement and acceptance. What is wrong is that they stem from the assumption that something is wrong, and that our consciousness tends to be entrapped in them to the point of self-forgetfulness. Watts has commented that after practicing for some time the exercise of living in the moment it will become apparent:

> . . . that in actual reality it is impossible to live outside this moment. Obviously our thoughts of past and future transpire in the present, and in this sense it is impossible to concentrate on anything except what is happening now. However, by *trying* to live simply in the present, by trying to cultivate the pure "momentary" awareness of the Self, we discover in experience as well as theory that the attempt is unnecessary. We learn that never for an instant has the time-thinking of the ego actually interfered with the eternal and momentary consciousness of the Self. Underlying memory, anticipation,

anxiety and greed there has always been this center of pure and unmoved awareness, which never at any time departed from present reality, and was therefore never actually bound by the chain of dreams.

As soon as this is realized, he notes:

> . . . it becomes possible once more to entertain memory and anticipation, and yet be free from their binding power. For as soon as one is able to look upon memory and anticipation as present, one has made them (and the ego which they constitute) objective. Formerly they were subjective, because they consisted in *identifying* oneself with past or future events, that is, with the temporal chain constituting the ego. But when one is able, for instance, to regard anticipation as present, one is no longer identifying oneself with the future, and is therefore taking the viewpoint of the Self as distinct from the ego. To put it in another way: as soon as the ego's act of identifying itself with the future can be seen as something present, one is seeing it from a standpoint superior to the ego, from the standpoint of the Self. It follows that when our center of consciousness has shifted to the strictly present and momentary outlook of the Self, memory and anticipation guide peripheral and objective actions of the mind, and our being is no more dominated by and identified with the egoistic mode of thought. We have all the serenity, all the keen awareness, all the freedom from temporality, of one who lives wholly in the present, and yet without the absurd limitation of not being able to remember the past or to provide for the future.[4]

The exercise of the awareness continuum and asceticism

In spite of the last statement, it may be a psychological truth that a person can hardly attain present-centeredness while remembering, before having known the taste of it in the easier situation of

[4] *Ibid.*

reminiscence-deprivation. The same may be paren-
thetically said on the matter of contacting one's
experience while thinking. Ordinarily, thinking dis-
pels the awareness of the Self-in-the-activity-as-
thinker and the feelings constituting the ground
of the thinking-motivation, just as the sun during the
daytime prevents our seeing the stars. The experience of thinking and not being lost-in-thought
(i.e., caught up in the exclusive awareness of the
figure in the totality of figure-ground) is a condition
that can be brought about most easily by contacting
such experience-ground in moments of thoughtless-
ness. In this the Gestalt therapy techniques of
suspending reminiscence, anticipation, and thinking
fall in with the implicit philosophy of asceticism in
general: certain deprivations are undergone in order
to contact what is currently hidden by the
psychological activity involved in the corresponding
situations. Thus, deprivation of sleep, talking, social
communication, comfort, food, or sex is supposed to
facilitate the access to unusual states of consciousness but is not an end or ideal in itself—except
through cultural deterioration.

Not only does the practice of attention to the
stream of life relate to asceticism in that it entails a
voluntary suspension of ego-gratification and a
deprivation, but in the more general trait of presenting the person with the difficulty of functioning in a
way that runs counter to habit. Since the only action
allowed by the exercise is that of communicating the
contents of awareness, this precludes the operation
of "character" (i.e., the organization of coping
mechanisms) and even *doing* as such. In this, the
practice of the now is one of ego- loss, as emphasized
by Buddhism and commented on by Watts in the
quotation in the previous section.

III. Present-Centeredness as Prescription

Every technique a prescription?

Not all that is of value as a psychological exercise need automatically be a good prescription for living. Free association may be a useful exercise, but not necessarily the best approach to conversation, just as the headstand in Hatha Yoga need not be the best posture to be in most of the time. To a greater or lesser extent, techniques have a potential for being carried into ordinary life, thus making all of life the occasion for the soul-growth endeavor. Yet it is not only the individual value of a certain approach that counts when it comes to its appropriateness as prescription, but its compatibility with other desirable purposes in life, the degree of clash that it will bring about with existing social structure, and, especially, its compatibility with a conception of the good society. Thus, the abreaction of hostility in a situation of no constraints can be of value in psychotherapy, but is this approach the one that would maximize sanity and well- being in a community?

I think that opinions on the matter would be divided. They would be divided even on the question of truth. Whereas aggression tends to be socially reproved and the commandment states, "Thou shalt not kill," truth is commonly regarded as virtue, and lying a sin. One might therefore expect that the technique of self-disclosure, valuable in the context of psychotherapy, would be immediately applicable to life. Given the ordinary condition of humanity, though, truth has been and may continue to be not only uncomfortable or inconvenient but dangerous. The example of Socrates, Jesus Christ, or the heretics at the time of the Inquisition points out that an unconditional embracing of truth may mean the acceptance of martyrdom, for which I am sure that the average human being is not ready. The desire to turn feelings into prescriptions in cases where society did not make such projects feasible has been one of the implicit and explicit rationales in the creation of special communities among those who share the goal of living for the inner quest. In such groups, sometimes veiled by secrecy, man has sought to live according to principles not compatible with other than a monastic, therapeutic, or other special setting.

Humanistic hedonism

Living-in-the-moment, in contrast to other techniques, seems a perfectly appropriate prescription for life. Moreover, it appears to be more in the nature of a technicalization of a life-formula than the prescribing of a technique. The idea of prescription may evoke images such as that of the bad-smelling tonic that children were frequently compelled to take "for their good" before the time of gelatin capsules and flavor chemistry. This is part of a dualistic frame of mind in which "the good things" seem different from the "things for our good," and the goal of self-perfecting something other than "merely living."

This is not what the classic injunctions of present-centeredness convey. Take for instance, King Solomon's, "A man hath no better thing under the sun, than to eat, and to drink and to be merry" (Ecclesiastes 15) or the later version of the same thought in St. Paul's First Epistle to the Corinthians: "Let us eat and drink, for tomorrow we die."

The character of these, like that of most statements that stress the value of actuality, is hedonistic. And it could not be otherwise, for if the value of the present is *not going* to be for a future it must be *intrinsic:* the present must contain its own reward.

In our times, the hedonistic outlook seems to be divorced from and to run counter to religious feeling (just as to "prescription orientation" in general). Insofar as "body" and "mind" are regarded as incompatible sources of value, idealism and spirituality tend to be associated with a grim asceticism, while the defense of pleasure is most often undertaken by the cynically practical, tough-minded and hard-nosed "realists." This does not seem to have always been so, and we know that there was a time when religious feasts were real festivals. So, when we read in the Bible, "Let us eat, drink and be merry, for tomorrow we die," we should not super-impose on that statement our present body-mind split, or the tough-mindedness with which it is often repeated. Behind it was an outlook according to which living life and living it now was a holy action, a way in accordance with God's will.

Rarely do we find this balance of transcendence and immanence in Western thought, with the exception of remarkable individuals that seem to be marginal to the spirit of the times—heretics to the religious or madmen to the common folk. William Blake, for instance, was such a man in claiming that "Eternity is in love with the productions of time."

Even in psychoanalysis, which in practice has done much for mankind's *id*, the "pleasure-principle" is looked upon as a childishness and a nuisance that the "mature" reality-oriented ego must hold in check.

Contrariwise, Gestalt therapy sees a much stronger link between pleasure and goodness, so that its philosophy may be called hedonistic in the same sense as the good old hedonisms before the Christian era. I would like to suggest the notion of humanistic hedonism which does not necessarily entail a theistic outlook and yet seems to distinguish this approach from the egoistic hedonism of Hobbes, the utilitarian hedonism of J. S. Mill, and that of the regular pleasure-seeker. (If at this point the reader wonders how Gestalt therapy can be called ascetic and hedonistic at the same time, let him remember that Epicurus' view of the most pleasurable life was that of one devoted to philosophical reflection while on a simple diet of bread, milk, and cheese.)

Carpe diem

The hedonistic vein is inseparable from an intense appreciation of the present, not only in Gestalt therapy, but in the thinking of the many (mostly poets and mystics) who have voiced a similar prescription. Perhaps the most insistent on this subject was Horace, whose *carpe diem* ("seize the day") has become a technical label to designate a motif that runs throughout the history of literature. Here it is in its original context:

> *Dom loquimur fugerit invide aetas:*
> *carpe diem, quam minimum credula postero.*

> *In the moment of our talking,*
> *envious time has ebbed away,*
> *Seize the present, trust tomorrow*
> *e'en as little as you may.*

Horace's present-centeredness runs parallel to his awareness of the running away of "envious time": the irreparable loss of life that is the alternative to living in the moment. In the Biblical injunction to eat, drink and be merry, too, death is both the argument and the teacher. The same is true of many other statements, viz, the saying, "Gather ye rosebuds while ye may," or Ovid's, in the *Art of Love:*

> *Corpite florem*
> *Qui nisi corptas erit turpiter ipse cadet*

> *Seize the flower,*
> *for if you pluck it not 'twill fade and fall.*

> *Gather therefore the rose whilest yet is prime,*
> *For soon comes the age that will her pride deflowre;*

Gather the rose of love whilest yet is time,
Whilest loving thou mayst love be with equal crime.
(Spenser: *The Faerie Queene*)

Make use of time, let not advantage slip;
Beauty within itself should not be wasted:
Fair flowers that are not gathered in their prime,
Rot and consume themselves in little time.
(Shakespeare: *Venus and Adonis*)

If you let slip time, like a neglected rose
It withers on the stock with languished head.
(Milton: *Comus*)

As mentioned above, the focus of Gestalt therapy on the present is inseparable from its valuation of consciousness itself, expressed in its pursuit of relinquishing the avoidances with which our life is plagued. Most directly, not to avoid the present is not to avoid living in it, as we all too often do as a way of avoiding the consequence of our actions. Inasmuch as confronting the present is a commitment to living, it is freedom: the freedom to be ourselves, to choose according to our being's preference: to choose our way. Exposure to Gestalt therapy can demonstrate experientially that when the present is met in the spirit of non-avoidance—that is, with pleasure—it becomes what Dryden saw in it:

This hour's the very crisis of your fate,
Your good and ill, your infamy or fame,
And the whole colour of your life depends
On this important now.
(*The Spanish Friar*)

The issue is now, but we do not acknowledge it in our half-hearted way of living, thereby turning life into a deadly substitution of itself. We "kill" time or incur that "loss of time" at which "the wisest are most annoyed," according to Dante. Another way in which this particular aspect of living fully turns up in Gestalt therapy is in the concept of closure. Just as in Gestalt psychology closure is applied to perception, it is applied in Gestalt therapy to action: we are always seeking to finish the unfinished, to complete the incomplete Gestalt, and yet always avoiding doing so. By failing to act in the present, we increase "unfinishedness" and our servitude to the load of the past. Moreover, as Horace puts it in one of his Epistles, "he who postpones the hour of living as he aught is like the rustic who waits for the river to pass along before he crosses; but it glides on and will glide on forever."

Perhaps we would not suspend life in the present if it were not for the dream of future action or satisfaction. In this connection, the present-centeredness of Gestalt therapy bespeaks its realism in the sense of an orientation toward tangible existence and actual experience ahead of conceptual, symbolical, or imagined existence. Not only the future, but also the past, can only be alive in the present as thought forms: memories or fantasies, and Gestalt therapy aims at the subordination of these to life. Its attitude is the same as in Longfellow:

> *Trust no future, howe'er pleasant,*
> *Let the dead Past bury its dead!*
> *Act, act in the living Present!*
> *Heart within and God o'erhead.*

Or in the Persian proverb versified by Trench:

> *Oh, seize the instant time; you never will*
> *With waters once passed by impel the mill.*

or another, according to which:

> *He that hath time and looketh for a better time,*
> *loseth time.*

All these statements are inspired by the apprehension of a contrast between the *livingness* of the present in contrast to the non-experiential (therefore relatively unreal) nature of past and future:

Nothing is there to come, and nothing past,
But an eternal now does always last.
(Abraham Cawley)

More often than not, our life is impoverished by the process of substitution of substance by symbol, experience by mental construct, reality by the reflection of reality in the mirror of the intellect. Relinquishing past and future to come to the enduring present is an aspect of the prescription of "losing your mind and coming to your senses."

IV Present-Centeredness as Ideal

Der den Augenblick ergreift
Das ist der rechte Mann[5]
(Goethe)

The word "ideal" needs clarification. Ideals are frequently understood with a connotation of duty and/or intrinsic goodness that is foreign to the philosophy of Gestalt therapy.

If we deprive an ideal of its quality of should or ought, it remains as either a statement of the desirable way to an end, that is, a prescription, or else a "rightness." By this I mean an *expression* of goodness, rather than a means or an injunction: a sign or symptom of an optimal condition of life. This is the sense in which we may speak of ideals in Taoism, for instance, in spite of its being a philosophy of non-seeking. In spite of its non-injunctional style, the *Tao Te Ching* is always elaborating on the traits of the sage: "For this reason the sage is concerned with the belly and not the eyes" or "The sage is free from the disease because he recognizes the disease to be disease" or "The sage knows without going about," "accomplishes without any action," and so on. In the same sense, present-centeredness is regarded as an ideal in statements like: "Now is the watchword of the wise."

[5] He who seizes the moment is the right man.

Although some recipes for better living are means to an end that differ from such an end in quality, this is not true of present-centeredness. In the latter case (as in that of Gestalt therapy in general) *the means to an end is that of shifting to the end state right away:* the way to happiness is that of starting to be happy right away, the way to wisdom that of relinquishing foolishness at this very moment—just as the way to swim is the practice of swimming. The prescription of living in the now, therefore, is the consequence of the fact that we *are* only living in the now, and this is something that the sane person *knows*, but the neurotic does not realize while enmeshed in a dreamlike pseudo-existence.

In Buddhism, the now is not merely a spiritual exercise, but the condition of the wise. In a passage of the Pali Canon, Buddha first utters the prescription:

> *Do not hark back to things that passed,*
> *And for the future cherish no fond hopes:*
> *The past was left behind by thee*
> *The future state has not yet come*

and then the ideal:

> *But who with vision clear can see*
> *The present which is here and now*
> *Such wise one should aspire to win*
> *What never can be lost nor shaken*

Whereas the Buddhist version of the now-injunction stresses the illusoriness of the alternatives, the Christian view stresses the trust and surrender entailed by present-centeredness. When Jesus says, "Take therefore no thought of the morrow, for the morrow shall take thought for the things of itself," and he draws upon the example of the lilies of the fields (Matthew 6), he is not only saying, "Don't act upon catastrophic expectations," but more positively, "Trust!" While the Christian version is framed in a theistic map of the universe, and trust means trust in the heavenly Father, the attitude is the same as that regarded as the ideal in Gestalt therapy, which may be rendered as trust in one's own capacities for coping with the now as it comes. In this, therefore, we see that the idea of present-centeredness becomes one with that of experiencing rather than manipulating and that of being open to and accepting experience rather than dwelling in and being defensive in face of possibility. Such attitudes bespeak two basic assumptions in the *Weltanschauung* of Gestalt therapy:

1) Things at this moment are the only way that they can be
2) And behold, the world is very good!

If the present cannot be other than what it is, what the wise will do is surrender to it. Furthermore, if the world is good, why not, as Seneca puts it, "gladly take the gifts of the present hour and leave vexing thoughts." To say of anything that *it* is good is, of course, a statement alien to Gestalt therapy, according to the point of view of which, things can only be good to *us*. And the latter, in turn, depends on us and what we do with our circumstances. Our current perception of existence is full of pain, helplessness, and victimization. Moreover, as Edmund Burke remarked over two centuries ago: "To complain of the age we live in, to murmur of the present possessors of power, to lament the past, to conceive of extravagant hopes of the future are the common disposition of the greatest part of mankind."

In the view of Gestalt therapy, however, such complaints and lamentations are no more than a bad game we play with ourselves—one more aspect of rejecting the potential bliss of now. At depth we are where we want to be, we are doing what we want to do, even when it amounts to apparent tragedy. If we can discover our freedom within our slavery, we can also discover our essential joy under the cover of victimization.

The whole process of estrangement from reality as reality is given in the Eternal Now may be conceived as one of *not trusting* the goodness of the outcome, of *imagining* a catastrophic experience or at best an emptiness, for which we compensate by creating a paradise of ideals, future expectations, or past glories. From such "idols" we keep looking down upon present reality, which never quite matches our constructs, and therefore never looks perfect enough. This is how the question of present-centeredness ties in with that of acceptance of experience vs. judgmentalness. As Emerson has put it:

> These roses under my window make no reference to former roses or to better ones; they are for what they are; they exist with God today. There is no time to them. There is simply the rose; it is perfect in every moment of its existence . . . but man postpones and remembers; . . . He cannot be happy and strong until he, too, lives with nature in the present, above time.[6]

Searching for the ideal rose, we don't see that each rose is the utmost perfection of itself. For fear of not finding the rose we seek, we hang on to the concept of "rose" and never learn that "a rose is a rose is a rose." It is our greed and impatience that does not permit us to let go of the substitute through which we enjoy the reflection of reality in the form of promise or possibility, and by which we are at the same time cut off from its present enjoyment. The intuition of Paradise Lost and the Promised Land is better than total anaesthesia, but short of the realization that they are right here. Khayaam knew well:

> *They say that Eden is bejewelled with houris;*
> *I answer that grape-nectar has no price—*
> *So laugh at long-term credit, stick to coin,*
> *Though distant drums beguile your greedy ear.*

[6] Quoted by Watts.

And:

Never anticipate tomorrow's sorrow.
Live always in this paradisal Now—
Fated however soon to house, instead,
With others gone these seven thousand years:

My tavern comrades vanish one by one,
Innocent victims of Death's furtive stroke.
All had been honest drinkers, but all failed,
Two rounds before the last, to drain their bowls.

Rise up, why mourn this transient world of men?
Pass your whole life in gratitude and joy.
Had humankind been freed from womb and tomb,
When would your turn have come to live and love?

Allow no shadow of regret to cloud you,
No absurd grief to overcast your days.
Never renounce love-songs, or lawns, or kisses
Until your clay lies mixed with elder clay.[7]

---

[7] *The Original Rubaiyyat of Omar Khayaam,* a new translation with critical commentaries by Robert Graves and Omar Ali-Shah (New York: Doubleday, 1968).

Part II

TECHNIQUE

Chapter Three

Introduction to the Techniques of Gestalt Therapy

The techniques of Gestalt therapy are many and cover a wide spectrum of behaviors—verbal and non-verbal, structured and unstructured, introspective and interpersonal, inner- and outer- directed, symbolic and non-symbolic. Some of these techniques are not unique to Gestalt therapy, and perhaps every one of them may be regarded as a variation (intentional or not) upon a technique to be found in an alternative form of psychotherapy or in some system of spiritual guidance. Yet a session of Gestalt therapy could not be confused with any other, for the approach, we might say, constitutes a new and unique *Gestalt*.

The uniqueness of Gestalt therapy does not lie at the molecular level of elemental technical components nor at the molecular level of attitude, but at the intermediate level where an attitude gives form to the technical material and generates a new synthesis out of the available possibilities.

Gestalt therapy is, at the technical level, a synthesis above all else. What is typical to it is the particular "twist" given to old forms, the place and meaning that each one of these has taken in the context of the others, the organic sense with which the therapist moves from one to another keeping his attention upon an issue rather than upon a formula.

If practical gestalt therapy is a synthetic corpus of techniques, this is precisely because it is not technique-oriented. A synthesis exists only to the extent that many parts can crystallize around a unifying center. The center, in the present case, which brings together a surprising variety of resources, is that issue beyond techniques that we have referred to in earlier writings as one of actuality-awareness-responsibility.

During his lifetime Perls increased his repertoire with anything that served his aim of making his patients more aware and responsible. He adapted, borrowed, combined and never ceased to invent techniques, not deliberately, but with the spontaneous assimilation-creation of life itself.

From free association he retained the idea of sustained awareness, though switching in interest from content to form; from Reich he took his understanding of defense as a motor event and his recognition of the importance of expression; from Karen Horney's "tyranny of shoulds" he probably derived, in the course of time, the personification of "topdog"; from psychodrama the enacting of conflicts; from dianetics the re-enacting of traumatic episodes, and the techniques of sentence-repetition; from Zen Buddhism the rule of minimizing intellectualization, and so forth.

In no way, however, do we feel inclined to regard Gestalt therapy as a composite of approaches or as a merely eclectic approach. Just as we do not think of Bach's music as a composite of previous Italian, German and French styles (which in a way it is), but are more struck by the uniqueness of an emerging synthesis than by the recognition of its components, so the new *building* of Gestalt therapy impresses us more than the old bricks.

I will demonstrate in Chapter Four how a specific attitude — present-centeredness — has brought together some bricks into one part of the Gestalt therapy building: the "continuum of awareness" exercise. The experience of "being present" was here the seed, and Perls found this seed not in any form of psychotherapy, but in his own awareness (particularly in personal experiences, to which he has referred as *satori*.) This seed, which in the historical past has originated forms of meditation, Perls brought into contact with a soil familiar to him: free association—and he found that to enlightened eyes this was a free *dissociation* which was missing the point. The point, in this case, was *the obvious*.

I have examined present-centeredness as an *ideal* (an aspect of the good life) which the therapist offers the patient as a broad *prescription*, and in which he trains him through a specific *technique*. The same may be said of each aspect of the three-fold ideal of Gestalt therapy: actuality-awareness-responsibility.

Practically every technique in Gestalt therapy might be seen as a particularized embodiment of the broad prescription: "be aware." This prescription, in turn, is an expression of the therapist's belief and experience that only with awareness can there be true living, and that the light of awareness is all that we need to come out of our confusion, to realize the foolishness of the ones creating our conflicts, to dispel the fantasies that are causing our anxiety.

Likewise, we can look upon practically every technique in Gestalt therapy as the particular crystallization of the one prescription: "Take responsibility, experience yourself as the doer of your actions, experience *you*." This prescription, in turn, is an expression of the therapist's belief—based upon experience—that only when we *are* what we are, can we say that we are living: that if we only start to be ourselves—or acknowledge that we already are— we will find a fulfillment greater than that brought about by the satisfaction of any particular want.

To say that Gestalt therapy aims at the awakening of awareness, of the sense of actuality and of responsibility, is equivalent to saying that its aim is the ability to *experience*.

In a sense we are "experiencing" something all the time. Yet we are in meager contact with our experiences, only half awake to reality. In that sense, we may say that we are not truly experiencing.

To the Gestaltist, true experience is therapeutic or corrective by itself. A wakeful moment—a moment of contact with reality—is one where our daydream phantoms may be seen for what they are. Also, it is a moment of training in experiencing: one in which we can learn, for instance, that there is nothing to fear or that the reward of being alive surpasses the pains or losses that we might like to avoid in our slumber.

A thirst for experience is part of all life. Often though, this takes the form of a wanting to move on and on to *other* experiences than those at hand. A craving for *more* replaces the need for *depth* that could be our natural mode of contacting the world, had we not become desensitized to it. Intuitively seeking that depth or fullness of awareness that is our birthright, and not finding it, we seek the substitute of environmental stimulation: spicy foods, rock climbing, high-speed sportscars, competitive games, tragedies on the movie screen.

The approach of Gestalt therapy is the converse. Experiencing is sought, not by stimulation but by sensitization. The gestaltist sees arousal-from-without as a form of environmental support not necessary to him who has developed arousal-from-within, thus coming to his senses.

In two ways the techniques of Gestalt therapy can serve to bring the patient into contact with his experience. One way of experiencing is *to stop avoiding*, ceasing to cover up experience. The other is bringing our energies to bear upon the content of awareness in the form of intensified attention or deliberate exaggeration. Even though these two are interdependent, so that suppressive and expressive techniques may be regarded as the right and the left hands of the psychotherapist, I will deal with them under separate headings.

Chapter Four

Suppressive Techniques

Have you ever been in what passes for group therapy?
Everybody throws his opinion on a victim and everybody in-
terprets everybody. Argumentations, verbal ping pong games,
at best, an attack: "You are projecting, my dear," or a "poor
me" crybaby performance. What kind of growth can you
expect in these "self improvement clubs?"

Fritz Perls

The first prerequisite for experiencing what we can potentially experience is to stop doing something else. A number of activities, other than those of attending and expressing, keep us so busy that we hardly have any attention left for the moment in which we are living. If we can only stop playing some of our customary games, we will find that experiencing is not any more something we have to seek, but something we cannot avoid. Indeed, as said before, we *are* experiencing something all the time at a level we are only intermittently in touch with, and with which we do not identify. Our eyes see, "we" do not. Our dreams can remember what we are not aware of seeing and tell us things "they" know, not "us."

To experience, we must be present, we must be *here* and *now*. We cannot "experience" (only recreate in imagination) what is past or absent. Reality is always now. Even while remembering, our reality is our present action of remembering, our wanting to remember, our reactions, here and now, to our memories.

There is little place for the now in ordinary conversation. Much of what we say is a telling of anecdotes, sharing plans, communicating beliefs or opinions. Not even our private mental activity is centered primarily on the present. Much of it consists of anticipations, memories, fantasies and "fitting games." We Gestalt therapists look at such activities with suspicion. Each one of them constitutes a legitimate and functional ability of ours; and yet, most of the time, we use these abilities, not for a functional, constructive purpose, or even pleasure, but as a mechanical diversion equivalent to a tapping of our fingers, or doodling. More specifically, the Gestaltist's view is that all these activities, other than noticing the present, constitute an act of *avoidance of the present.*

By means of the simple technique of *ceasing to do anything other than experiencing,* therapist and patient alike may be able to test the validity of this assumption.

The experience of doing nothing but attending to the contents of awareness may lead, like the ingestion of a psychedelic drug, to a self-rewarding contact with reality, or to intense discomfort. When left with nothing but the obvious, our attitudes towards ourselves and towards our existence become apparent. This is particularly true of the negative ones. We may feel embarrassed, awkward, needing to explain ourselves, or to make fun of the situation; we may feel silly, uninteresting. If so, we do not have to wonder why we spend so little time in the present and so much in fantasy and speculation. If we have experienced the exercise of awareness as uncomfortable or painful, we will not have difficulty accepting the realization that our tendency to live in the past, future or abstraction, constitutes an avoidance of such discomfort.

There is one particular experience to which the suppression of avoidances frequently leads and to which the Gestaltist assigns particular importance— the experience of nothingness.

To speak of the experience of nothingness is, to some extent, a contradiction in terms, for an experience always entails a "some thing." "Nothingness" constitutes a limbo where the surface games of the personality have been dropped and self-awareness has not taken its place. There is an illusory quality in this "nothingness," just as in the negative feelings mentioned above. Shame, guilt, and anxiety, for instance, are not pure *experiences* of a reality, but the outcome of attitudes in which we stand against that reality, denying or resisting it, fearing to perceive it. Likewise, the experience of nothingness, or emptiness, is one in which we stand in judgment above ourselves and pronounce the verdict, "Not enough." Nothingness, emptiness, meaninglessness, triviality, are all experiences in which we have not relinquished the expectations, or standards, by which we measure reality. They do not stem from pure awareness, but from comparisons.

The importance of this experience of nothingness derives from the observation that it constitutes a bridge between avoidance and contact, or, as Perls expressed it, between the phobic and explosive layers of personality. Perls assigns so much importance to this phase of the therapeutic process, that he even defined Gestalt therapy in its terms: "Gestalt therapy is the transformation of the sterile void into the fertile void."

How can we understand this? "Nothing" is a nothingness only while we are under the compulsion of having it to be a somethingness. Once we *accept* nothingness, everything is added unto us. Nothingness then becomes a screen against which we can see all things, a "ground" against which every "figure" freely emerges. Once we do not *have* to be creative, whatever we do is our creation; once we do not have to be enlightened, our awareness of the moment is enlightenment; once we cease being concerned with being this or that, and feel a nothingness with regard to such standards, we realize that we are what we are.

The suppressive aspect of Gestalt therapy involves both general principles and what may be regarded as individual (negative) prescriptions. There are requests that apply to every patient, and constitute rules for group, and requests to a particular patient that he stop indulging in a particular game that constitutes his main avoidance mechanism. I shall deal with the general principles and rules in this chapter.

I have mentioned the principal no-no's of Gestalt therapy already: story-telling, anticipation, aboutism, shouldism, manipulation.

I have already touched upon the issue of future and past in this chapter, and will examine the matter more closely again, so I do no more than mention it here for completeness. Of the other issues (aboutism, shouldism and manipulation), I will speak in greater detail, and consider, too, the matter of exceptions to the rules.

I. Aboutism

Aboutism is a name which Perls likes to give to the "science game," just as he regards *shouldism* to be the essence of the "religion game." In the therapeutic situation, the most frequent manifestations of this attitude are the offering of (diagnostic) information, the search for causal explanations, the discussion of philosophical or moral issues, or of the meaning of words. All these, along with the polite clichés, are tabooed in Gestalt therapy as "verbiage." As Perls has put it, "*Why* and *because* are dirty words in Gestalt therapy. They lead only to rationalization, and belong to the second class of verbiage production. I distinguish three classes of verbiage production: chickenshit—this is 'good-morning,' 'how are you?' and so on; bullshit—this is 'because,' rationalization, excuses; and elephantshit—this is when you talk about philosophy, existential Gestalt therapy, etc. — what I am doing now."

The term *bullshit* in particular has become in Gestalt therapy a piece of technical jargon because of its expressiveness. It indicates something to be *eliminated,* something unsubstantial when weighed against direct experience.

The Gestalt therapist's disregard for conceptualizations is frequently very frustrating to patients previously exposed to psychoanalysis or psychoanalytic literature, for *interpretation* is there regarded as the avenue to the truth. Furthermore, a tendency to seek relief from psychological tensions through casual explanation thereof seems to be a natural tendency in many people. Should we call these psychoanalytic and spontaneous attempts at understanding no more than a sterile "fitting game," as Perls proposes?

I am personally convinced of the value of withholding expression of intellectual statements as a *psychotherapeutic technique,* though I do not agree with the contemptuous attitude of many Gestalt therapists toward the patient's desire to understand at an intellectual level. I believe that the respect for both is not only perfectly compatible with the employment of the technique, but more effective. We do not have to believe that "the Aristotelian why-because game" is *always* another avoidance technique (phobic behavior) to account for the usefulness of the rule under discussion. It is enough that we believe that *sometimes* explanations are avoidances. If so, when the patient must play the Gestalt game where the rules do not allow for "why" or "because," he will sooner or later come to the point where he feels uncomfortable without the habitual crutch. In other words, some of his explanations will be functional, others phobic. Yet, when he is asked to relinquish explanations altogether, he will find that *some* of these he cannot give up easily, and will feel guilty, empty, afraid, and will talk *about,* rather than experience the discomfort of the moment, or his "having" to explain himself.

If my view is correct, the technique of tabooing intellectual formulations may be seen as something like what the developer is to the photographic film: a means of bringing into light what otherwise would have remained invisible. I think this is one thing that may be said of suppressive techniques in general.

An appreciation for the effectiveness of the technique of omitting interpretation need not, on the other hand, be based on the assumption that all interpretation is sterile, and that the desire for intellectual understanding either constitutes a symptom or the missing of a point. It is enough that we see that interpretation *sometimes* is sterile and that the expectation of the patient that this type of understanding will change him is *generally* his choice of an unnecessarily long detour.

I see the matter of no-interpretation, again, as one of preference for the more effective technique—a matter of comparative efficiency, rather than as the outcome of a sacred injunction according to which all interpretation is intrinsically "bad."

Gestalt therapy is essentially a non-interpretive approach because its goal is experience, awareness, and not intellectual insight. Psychoanalysis is based upon the finding that intellectual insight may lead to emotional insight. Gestalt therapy rests upon the belief that, possible as that may be, intellectual insight more often than not becomes a trap, a substitute, or crutch, and replaces forever the experience *about which* it speaks. At any rate, awareness may be stimulated by more direct means than intellectual formulation of its probable contents. Aside from the indirectness of such a "computational" approach, the Gestalt therapist objects to it in terms of the "I am telling you" game that it implies a relationship not favorable to the development of self support or responsibility.

I think that if we ask our patients to follow the rule of no self-interpretation and accept our own rule of no interpretation, knowing this to be a technique and not a moral issue, we will be in better contact with them than if we implicitly regard their "becauses" as avoidances, or "sabotage." In my own practice, I generally make a statement to the effect that the need for interpretations may be based on erroneous assumptions, and I invite my patients to experiment with a situation where interpretation has no place. When a patient fails to abide by a rule that he has already accepted, we may infer that:

1. At that point he is experiencing something that he must avoid.
2. His desire to play "see how clever I am," or a similar game is stronger than his desire to share his experience.
3. He dares not trust the therapist and/or the method employed by him.

In any of these instances the failure of the patient to persist in the prescribed behavior (of merely verbalizing his experiences) is at least as important to the therapist as his successes. If he stays away from intellectualizations, he will sooner or later:

1. Realize that he does not need them in order to gain self-knowledge.
2. Stumble upon the "holes" in his personality— the areas of impotence, paralysis, inability to accept experience, etc., which give rise to the experience of emptiness. As we have seen, this is highly desirable.

If, alternatively, the patient explains or seeks explanations from himself or the therapist, the therapist may follow one or two courses of action.

1. Insist on the rule;
2. Direct his attention to his experience of the moment: the need to avoid a hitherto unacknowledged discomfort, the compulsion to explain away, or justify in terms of past events, his wish to feel accepted as an insightful patient, his choice of his own approach, rather than one suggested by the therapist, etc.

In instances such as these, the patient's failure to stay with the rule is *taken as a clue*, and the rule, indirectly, has then served the function of making the clue apparent. Part of the success of the therapist in any approach depends on his ability to pick up, in the patient's train of discourse or stream of awareness, the cues to meaningful issues, the expression of such aspects in his personality that require confrontation. The suppressive rules of Gestalt therapy constitute a valuable means of detecting those moments in the patient's experience that need to be brought into light. These are, in general, the moments when, in spite of the structure set up by the therapist, the patient chooses not to express his ongoing experience, but to talk *about* himself or others.

The rule of no *aboutism*, comprising the rules of no explanation, or search for explanation, no philosophizing, or search for a truth other than evidence, no personality diagnosis or gathering of information conducive to interpretations (plus discussion of the weather, the morning news, and so on), not only applies to the individual patient, but also is particularly effective in situations of group interaction. In individual therapy, explanations represent occasional losses of time. In a group situation, one explanation leads to another and another and another, so that such a level of discourse is established that nothing meaningful can happen. The simple rule of suppressing the voicing of opinions, ideas, opinions about other members' feelings, and so on, on the other hand, is, by itself, a guarantee that something meaningful will happen in the session, for the sharing of experience triggers experiences, and in an atmosphere of non-avoidance, the expression of "minor" feelings is likely to evolve, as sparks growing into fires—into dramatic involvement.

Nor does the rule of no intellectualization apply to verbalization only. In both individual and group therapy, this may be a useful exercise to carry out privately, extending it to all our thinking. This, again, does not imply that a thought-free state of mind is an ideal valid for every moment of life. It does imply that most of the time we are choosing to calculate, rather than being aware of ourselves, and are not even aware of our choice to do so. The technique of turning the "computer" off can make us more available for contact with our ongoing experience, which may involve the desire to prefigure the future, or not. Indeed, much of our thinking is in the nature of a rehearsal, and bespeaks a need to control the future. In search of this "safety," we may avoid losing and hurting, but if we have become computers, we are not fully alive, either.

II. Shouldism

Telling ourselves, or others, what *should* be, is like *aboutism*, another way of not experiencing what *is*. Fritz Perls tells a story to illustrate this: "Moishe and Abe are playing cards. Moishe: 'Abe, you are cheating!' Abe: 'Yes, I know.' "

Fritz is an *about*ist, a storyteller. Moishe is a *should*ist. Abe is an *is*ist.

Evaluating is a step removed from experiencing, for in the former we are attempting to *fit* a pattern borrowed from past experience into the present or extrapolated into the future. If, according to our judgments, the degree of fit is sufficient, we "accept." Yet, this acceptance is not a discovery of the intrinsic values in the given. It is not love for the uniqueness of the experience at hand, enjoyment of it for itself. Also, there is no discovery—only a stamp of approval based upon the matching of pre-established standards. There is safety. The status quo may be maintained. Whenever the degree of fit between standards and actuality is not enough, however, we attend to *what is missing*, rather than what is present. Much of what we call our "experiences" are the unpleasant feelings elicited by the frustration of our expectations, rather than by the awareness of what there is to grasp. There is not the experiencing of something, but the "experiencing" of nothingness.

We may be able to relinquish temporarily our judgmental stance towards reality, as we may do so in regard to our computing activity. To do this means, for instance, to stop playing the "self-torture" game or the "self-improvement" game. If we are able to do so, we may discover an unsuspected range of true feelings that our simplistic acceptance-rejection mechanism was covering up.

Anyone who has known the transient bliss of the psychedelic experience knows what it is to live without the "topdog." Once the monster of *should* is put artificially .o sleep, everything is what it is. A "comparing game" has ceased. Everything offers to us its matter of goodness, and is the most perfect example of itself.

I discovered something of the difference between true experience and shouldism through an awareness of tasting. Years ago, I had been in a Gestalt therapy session throughout the morning and had come out of it feeling open to the world, not needing to defend myself against anything, anybody—unafraid of meeting death itself. I came into the dining room to find clam chowder for lunch. Since childhood, I had detested the taste of seafood to the point of nausea. How ridiculous it seemed to me, thinking that I was ready to die, to have to reject a bowl of soup. As soon as I saw, too, that I could carry the sense of openness and unguardedness that was still with me into the soup-drinking situation, I really *tasted* clam chowder for the first time, and it was nothing like what I had "tasted" many times before. On previous occasions when I had a similar substance in my mouth, I was so busy experiencing rejection that I could not pay attention to the information given by my taste buds. I was "tasting" a fantasy, plus my own activity of setting up a barrier

between my food and myself. Now, open at last, I
realized that clam chowder was nothing like my
"memory" of it. Trying to describe its taste, I was only
able to say "good old protoplasm."

It is a *goal* of Gestalt therapy to be able to live so
much in the present (at least when we choose to) that
no standards from the past dim our awareness, that
we are so much what we are, that no sense of *ought*
clouds our identity. Yet, can we do this now? If not,
the rule of "no shouldism" is likely to be unrealistic.

Yet, something typical of Gestalt therapy is that
it tells us to do now what we would like to achieve
tomorrow. Just as its prescription toward the ideal of
present-centeredness is: "Live in the present, *now*,"
its prescription toward the ideal of freedom from
shouldism is: "Stop self-blaming and self-praising
now."

Though typical of Gestalt therapy, this approach
is not unique to it. We may do well to remember
Ferenczi's statement to the effect that analysis may
be terminated when the patient has achieved the
ability to free-associate. Free-association is in
psychoanalysis the goal and also the means. Furthermore, the same may be said of any skill. We learn
swimming by swimming, not by reading books
about it, or by analyzing our "swimming blocks."

In the specific instance of non-evaluation, the
practical expression of this injunction is to be seen in
a *simple acknowledgement* of experience, without justification or criticism:

> T.:   What do you experience now?
> P.:   I feel good. I am not tense. I feel warm towards
>   you (smiles) Great! (pauses)
> T.:   I think that you are doing propaganda for
>   yourself.
> P.:   Yes! I would like everyone to see that I am
>   okay. *That* is what I experience: wanting your
>   approval, and I feel afraid if I show you any of

my shit—if I show you my shit once more,
you will not stand me any longer.
T.: What do you experience *now?*
P.: I see you. I feel my hands on my thighs. I feel
poised. I hear the sounds of the ocean
(pause)—I could go on listening forever.

My statement, "You are making propaganda for
yourself," in this case, rested upon a debatable guess,
and to that extent, it was on the verge of being an
interpretation. My grounds for believing that this
was the case were:

1. The negative statement, "I am not tense." We can only
be aware of what we are. Negative statements involve
the "comparing game" and are generally evaluations.
"Am I up to this or that standard?" "Am I incurring this
or that sin?"

2. The predominance of evaluative terms over content.
"Good," "Great," "Warm," versus no perceptual or
descriptive information. The patient seems more interested in reporting his well-being than that which, in his
well-being, he is in touch with. Conversely, at the end
he is in contact with me, with his hands, with the ocean,
and I could see his well-being without his having to
report it.

The turning point in the patient's experience, in
the example above, was his willingness to examine
and express what he was experiencing but had
chosen to cover up under his "well-being." The
awareness of his fear of rejection, of his compulsion
to be comfortable and of his action of withholding,
i.e., pretending—all of which was clear to him—were
at first replaced in him by a scotoma. When he ceased
avoiding this obvious reality of the moment, he
started to be open to the environment, as well.

The rule of no evaluation is more difficult to
follow than the related rule of no thinking, and this
is partly due to the greater subtlety of judgmental
activity. In the illustration above, the patient believed
that he was only *expressing* his experience, while he

was, in fact, *defending* himself. Before someone can stop evaluating, he must clearly see how he is doing it, and this may require preliminary work. In Gestalt therapy one of the ways of bringing about this awareness, as we shall see in greater detail, is that of exaggerating the very shortcomings we want to overcome. In order to live in the present, we may find it useful to give the past its due, or to deliberately pursue our fantasies of the future. Likewise, before we stop judging, we need to judge in such a deliberate manner that we realize how we do it. Above all else, we need to realize that we choose to make judgements.

P.:   I feel nothing special. I see you sitting on the log. I feel the breeze on my face. I feel: "So what." All this that I perceive is fine, but I am not satisfied. I am missing something. I know that I can feel differently. I remember better times...

T.:   The game you are playing is called "This is not enough." From now on add "This is not enough" to each of your statements.

P.:   I see you, and this is not enough. I smell the fragrance of those bushes, and this is not enough. I am wanting for the next thing to enter my awareness and report it—and this is not enough. Now I am looking at the sky, and this is not enough. I am feeling "This *is* enough!" Ha! I am laughing, and this is not enough. I am enjoying this game, and this is not enough. Of course, I am doing it all the time, and it is a silly game!

T.:   Very well. Now I want you to spend some time doing the opposite; after every bit of awareness, add "This *is* enough," or "more than enough."

P.:   I am sitting here, and this is enough—sure it is. I am aware of your presence, and you are giving me your time, and that is enough. I feel grateful to you. I see the eucalyptus against the sky. This is enough—it is a marvelous tree.

> I see its bark, so venerable. It is precious to me.
> I almost feel that I *am* the eucalyptus. The
> breeze brings me the smell, and that is more
> than enough! It is as if the tree answered my
> thoughts, and that smell is so dear to me. Now
> I am aware of the atmosphere, the summer
> heat. I feel the air as a form of golden bees,
> busily buzzing one sustained note. Sweet and
> warm as the sunshine... There is nothing else
> I want right now.

If we are strict enough in our assessment, we will
find that feelings such as anxiety, guilt and shame,
are not direct experiences, but the outcome of evaluation: a mind-created curtain that we interpose between ourselves and the world. Behind every
instance of guilt is the ideal into which we are failing
to fit; behind every instance of anxiety, the desire to
manipulate the future as we think it should be. When
we tell somebody to express his *experiences,* and nothing more, we are ultimately asking him to go beyond
this *maya,* and describe *how things are given to him
when he ceases to color* them with these attitudes. We
are saying anxiety, guilt, and so on *are something that
you make yourself feel,* or *that you choose to feel*—they
are not your experience *of the world.*

In a more restricted sense of the word, however,
guilt, anxiety, and related feelings are not only "experiences" but those that lie closest to the
individual's awareness.

How far to push the rule of no evaluation in
these instances is a matter about which I have not
found any definitive statement, though it is easy to
see the possibilities of either alternative; going *into*
the guilt, dissatisfaction, fear, or conversely, not allowing these underlying games to interfere with the
experience of the obvious. Perls laid great stress on
the latter approach: seeing, rather than imagining,
and realizing that what we are missing is not mother
but, perhaps, a pencil. On the other hand, as with
aboutism, the failure to stay with the rule of no

evaluation may be taken as a cue for further work and for the application of other techniques.

The rule of no evaluation, as that of no computation, raises the question of its own extension. Is this to be taken as mere technique, the value of which is restricted to the therapeutic setting? or *should* we make our non-judgmental attitude one more "should," a rule for living? ("We should not should.") The latter question cannot be answered properly without some clarification as to differences between *shoulds* and ideals, or goals.

An ideal is a conception of the desirable, based upon either belief or experience. A goal is a target for purposive behavior, a landmark for our orientation, which may be an ideal or not. Gestalt therapy, as I understand it, does not seek to eliminate conceptions of the desirable or purposeful activity, though it does seek to counterbalance an excess of future-orientation with a good anchorage in the present. If Gestalt therapy aims at the elimination of goals and ideals, this is proof enough that it does not: the aim of aimlessness and the ideal of idealessness are still an aim and an ideal.

A "should" on the other hand, is different from either a goal or an ideal; "shoulds" constitute a psychological activity of being at odds with a reality that cannot be other than what it is. When we blame ourselves for something already past, for instance, we are indulging in a disfunctional feeling that neither improves the wrongness we incurred in the past, nor provides anything necessary to do better in the future. Perhaps the only benefit of our guilt is that, at some level, it makes us feel "better."

The same may be said of our stance toward the present. Our experiences and actions here and now are what they are and could not possibly be otherwise. Self-blame or self-praise do not make them more or less. And they certainly do not make *us* better. If there is a way towards the fulfillment of ideals, it is clearly not the practice of turning them into *shoulds*.

Yet, "shoulds" exist to the extent to which we do not believe the foregoing statement. We believe that we must "push the river"—that if we do not *make* things right, they will certainly be catastrophic. In this sense, *shoulds* are an expression of our control-madness, of which I will be speaking in the next section. Our catastrophic expectation usually takes the form, "What would become of me (or the world) if it were not for my (our) *trying?*" People should *should*, to keep out of trouble.

The standpoint of Gestalt therapy is, in this, as in other matters, that *awareness is enough.* Or better: awareness and orientation are enough, the latter being an aspect of awareness itself. If we have a conception of the desirable, and we know where we stand, that is all that we need for our movement to proceed in the desired direction. Perhaps a good analogy is that of the child learning to walk or to climb. Warnings of danger and criticisms, however accurate, will only detract from his attention to the task at hand and make him tense. If chronic, such "help" will make him less secure and not more skilled. Just as the adult in overprotecting the child lacks trust in the child's potential for learning and developing, we, in our self-manipulation, through prodding or blaming, lack trust in our psycho-physi-cal organism.

In saying that "pushing the river" (in the form of trying or striving) is unnecessary, Gestalt therapy is not seeing an *awareness of limitations* as an expres-sion of irrelevant shouldism. On the contrary, a realistic appraisal of where we are in terms of our aims or ideals is only possible when our evaluation is not biased by the self-punishing game or counteractive defenses. The put-down mechanism in which we invest so much of our energies is altogether different from the serene perception of our failings, just as hate for others differs from realistic love. The sane attitude toward self-failings may be best personified in the case of a good teacher of a concrete skill. "That was too high," a tennis coach will say. "That was good." "You did not get ready in time, now." "You can relax your shoulder more." All these are statements of facts, not moral statements. They take for granted that the student wants to use these *observations.* He does not coerce, or control him. He does not demand that he improve, but serves *his* desire.

What Gestalt therapy calls the *topdog* is the opposite: topdog imposes *his* wants upon underdog, manipulates, controls him.

It would be too simple—simplistic rather—to say that topdog is something to do away with, disfunctional as "he" may be. I think that the attitude of Gestalt therapy is best expressed in the statement that the topdog must be *assimilated.* His "helpful" control of underdog, to keep him on the path of righteousness, may be seen as a *projection* of underdog's own desires. "Duty," when experienced as a *should,* is one instance of disowned responsibility. "My duty calls for it" has taken the place of "I choose," "I must," that of "I want to." When we push the river, we do so with the river's energy. The river of our life plays a bad game with itself, pushing itself, rather than flowing.

III. Manipulation

The question of manipulation is closely related to that of evaluation, as evaluation is related to the fitting game of computation.

Aboutism refers principally to a misuse of intellect (i.e., use of intellect for avoidance), and shouldism, a misuse of emotional life. Manipulation constitutes a similar activity in the sphere of action. The rule of no manipulation is not usually formuated by the Gestalt therapist in its most general form, which is that of not acting out. Even so, I think that the *ideal* of no manipulation is so much a part of a therapist's actions that this is a point worth dealing with in this exposition.

Just as with thinking and feeling—which can be both positive and negative—action may constitute an avoidance. If this sounds paradoxical, it is in the measure to which we behavioristically equate phobic attitudes with the *avoidance of actions,* or "real life" situations. The Gestaltist's notion of avoidance, in contrast to this, is principally that of a *phobia of experience,* and *avoidance of awareness,* and it is not hard to see how many of our actions are directed to the minimization of discomfort, to the avoidance of the inner states we are not ready to accept. In a very broad way, it could be said that *most* of our actions are an avoidance of experience. Perhaps we will see most of our lives as variations on the common theme of running away from something, if we look at them with the eye of an enlightened contemplative. Anyone who has been involved in the Zen practice of "just sitting" knows how unbearable not-doing can become, and how the simplest of all practices can serve to reveal all that the agitation of overdoing conceals. Boredom, anxieties about the future, emptiness, sadness—all these will have to be confronted by him who has committed himself to sit and cease all trying.

To say that most actions in the common person are rooted in avoidance, which in turn is an avoidance of emptiness, is equivalent to saying, in Maslow's terminology, that actions are deficiency-motivated. If we bring to mind our peak experiences, past moments of exceptional fullness and openness to the world, we will probably find that these were moments when *being was enough,* moments when the ecstasy of the given was such that there was no desire for anything else, no need to act or bring about change.

Such statements from those for whom peak experiences are more or less enduring states—mostly
mystics—have frequently given rise to a response
much like the prospect of no-shoulds: "What would
the world become if everyone were to be so satisfied
with existence? Could the world have progressed as
it has without its discontent? Acceptance of suffering, as the Sermon on the Mount or passive Hindu
mysticism would have it, could only lead to exploita-
tion or stagnation."

Statements such as these stem from the assumption that change can only arise from the desire to
change, and action, from the desire to bring about
effects, or result. This is an assumption parallel to the
one previously discussed, according to which we
would not do good unless we "try to." Both are, in
the Gestalt view, expressions of a lack of trust in
organismic self-regulation.

The view of Gestalt therapists is, once more:
"Awareness is enough." In contrast to actions intended to avoid experiences, there are those actions
which stem from *and express* experience. These do not
intend to produce an effect, in the same sense that
great art is not intended to arouse certain feelings in
an audience, but points at its own existence.

In contrast to action stemming from deficiency
motives, which wants to put an end to dissatisfaction,
there is action which says *yes* to existence, action
rooted in the intrinsic worthwhileness of itself.

The work of a real artist or poet, who replicates
in form or words the beauty that he has perceived, is
such a yea-saying, much like the action of a lover who
moves his hands along the contours of his beloved.
Actions that are life-affirming rather than life-deny-
ing, self-revealing rather than concealing, expressive
rather than suppressive, are, in a way, like no action
at all. Since they proceed *naturally*, with no violence
to our tendencies, with no need of self-manipulation,
they may be experienced as a path of least resis-

tance—the simplest way to be at the moment. Perls remarked that such actions are not based on *choice* (a fitting game), but on *preference.* I think that the experience out of which he spoke was of the same nature as that which inspired Sengtsan, the third Chinese patriarch of Zen, to open his *Hsin-Hsin-Ming* with the verse: "There is nothing difficult about the Great Way, but, avoid choosing!"

Action, in contrast to manipulation (of self, or others), is experienced as flowing from within, rather than accomplished in order to meet extrinsic standards—whether internalized (as topdog), or not. To the extent that we identify (and call "I"), the self-manipulating function in us, we may experience such action as something that "we" do not bring about, but brings *itself* about.

It is a dirty word in Gestalt therapy, since it is employed often as a substitute for "I," or "you," as a means of avoiding directness or responsibility. We normally stress, in Gestalt therapy, that "it" does not "happen," but *we do* whatever we do. However true this may be, when most true—when applied to moments of extreme spontaneity—"it" can become a term most expressive of the experiential quality of such action. The painter may feel that the work does itself, the writer feels his characters escape his intentions, the dancer feels "inspired." I am certain that Perls, for all his insistence on avoiding "it" language, agreed to this exception, for in his painting workshops, he frequently used expressions such as: "Don't decide, don't hurry, just attend to the tip of your brush and let *it* go where it wants."

At the technical level the idea of relinquishing manipulation finds expression as the other do-nots, in the practice of the awareness continuum. For, to verbalize the experience of the moment, we must be open to the moment and what it brings, rather than being engaged in the production of our own program. The way in which manipulation sets in during the awareness continuum exercise may be predominantly that of self-manipulation, or a manipulation of others (therapist, group), though both are ultimately inseparable.

Manipulation of others, which we can also understand as a self-manipulation directed at manipulating others (as, for instance, in the predicament "Smile back at me so I can feel good") comprises the whole gamut of "game" behavior. A "game" always involves the hope of a goal, and may be seen as a manipulation for advantage, rather than an act of expression.

Perls saw games as an outer layer of personality: "The phony layer," "the Eric Berne or the Freudian layer"—and whenever he came across them, he would either withdraw, or (an exception to his rule) interpret: "You are playing helpless." "You are playing deaf." "How many therapists have you defeated before coming to me?" "You are bear-trapping."

Yet, these interpretations (global interpretations, rather than causal explanations) were not meant so much to be observations, as much as warnings: "If you want to work with me, better quit doing that."

No-manipulation was with Perls an *implicit* rule—part of a demand for authenticity, which he took for granted that it was within the capability of his patients to respond to. Or, at least, he set that as an admission test. His function was to pierce through the layers of personality to the level of explosion, but this first part of the job—that of transcending games—he took to be an elementary step for which the patient could be made responsible: "To work successfully, I need a tiny bit of goodwill. I cannot do anything for you, my smart-aleck."

"In this short weekend, I will not open up to you, if you are a poisoner who will leave me limp and depleted."

"If you are a bear-trapper, sucking me in with 'innocent' questions, baiting me, waiting for me to make the wrong move that will allow you to decapitate me, I will let you bait me, but avoid the trap."

"If you are a Mona Lisa smiler, and try to hide from me your indestructible 'I know better' and expect me to wear myself out to get to you, I will fall asleep on you."

"If you are a 'driver-crazy' I will soon stop following you and arguing with you. You are a relative of the poisoner."

The manifestations of manipulation that a person directs mainly at himself may be harder to notice than that involved in interpersonal games. For in the latter, the therapist can feel the pushes or pulls, the tacit demands or coaxings that want to limit his freedom, or bring him out of his own center. Yet, self-manipulation is perhaps the very factor that distinguishes the genuine practice of the awareness continuum from deceit, or from the pseudo-practice that the "good patient" can carry on for long periods of time without arriving at anything significant. These ways of controlling the flow of experience turn the awareness continuum itself into a game played by mere attention to the rules. The outcome may be a long enumeration of objects in the room, bits of physical awareness, sounds, etc., resembling more an inventory than a self-exploration. What happens in these instances is that the rule of "express your experiences" has been equated with "describe sensations," which is only superficially the same task.

This issue may be clarified if we think of an extreme example: a person sets out to give a detailed account of his visual percepts. The outcome of such an endeavor may be a catalog of impressions, useful for specific experimental purpose, perhaps, but not necessarily leading to enhanced self-awareness. The same may be true of enunciations of impressions of other sense modalities: olfactory, kinesthetic, and so on. Some patients, in fact, do something not very different from a shuttling back and forth from one inventory to another. The difference between the task above and the practice of the awareness continuum lies mainly in two factors: one, the question of *self-awareness*; the other, the question of *attitude*. I will comment upon both. One thing a patient undertaking a listing of percepts generally is not aware of, is his own activity: "I am *enumerating* things that I perceive." That is his most immediate experience, what should be most obvious to him, and yet it remains as invisible to him as his own face. If he could become aware of his own feelings and actions, the report might develop into something like the following:

> I am looking at the rug. I think I should move on and say something else. I turn my gaze to the right and now I see the lamp. Now I have been looking at one thing and then another for quite a while, and I don't think I am getting much out of this. I feel bored now, and somewhat tired. I wish you would help me get over my boredom and my shallowness, etc.

To the extent that the exercise in awareness remains shallow because of a scotomizing, such as the one commented upon above, it may be corrected by pointing out what is happening ("You are enumerating objects"), or by drawing the person's attention to his own activity, physical or mental. Once the patient notices what he is *doing*, other than expressing his experiences, he can take a step toward finding out what his natural experiences are. Before that, he might be likened to one who stands on one foot and wonders why one of his legs feels tired, or to one who reads aloud from a book he carries in his pocket and later wonders why the session was of little personal significance to him.

I think that the subtlest point in the practice of the awareness continuum—and because of its subtlety, impossible to formulate as a clear-cut rule—is the distinction between being *open* to experience and fabricating experiences.

One of the most common reactions of patients on the "hot seat" is self-consciousness, and along with it, the compulsion to *perform*.

Performing is necessarily a form of manipulation—making something happen, rather than seeing what is there. The way beyond performing, as with more obvious games, must start with the awareness of performing, which may then lead to the more subtle awareness of having to be productive, interesting to the therapist, creative, in fear of being trivial, in fear of emptiness, nothingness, and psychological death.

> P.: I feel that I am trembling (pause). I am waiting for something else to say, and am scanning for something to report.
> T.: Do you believe that you would be empty of all experience if you don't look for one?
> P.: I feel relieved at that thought. (pause) I see things out there, and I see you, and I feel that I am sitting here—and nothing of this interests me much... now I feel blank... I feel at ease... I don't have to avoid feeling blank! I feel like on vacation, not trying to do anything... and now I really see you. I had forgotten who you are... I feel very alive.

There are elements particularly relative to the issue of manipulation that arise mostly when Gestalt therapy is conducted in a group setting, and which are so common that they serve to be made the object of recommendations. Here are the main ones:

Questions

Questions are an important part of conversation in any session of group therapy that allows for them. Yet, few questions are genuinely such. A great proportion of them (phony questions) constitute a diplomatic way of exhibiting the questioner's views, a way of expressing doubt, a manner of exposing lack of basis in someone else's statements, etc. In general, a question is a form of manipulation directed at the elicitation of an answer, and does not express the questioner's experience. The questioner, rather, *needs an answer to better avoid the experience* from which the question stems.

Why are you angry with me? = Now it will become clear that you have no good reason to be angry = I am right = I can cease worrying.

Why don't you do this and that? = See how I am being helpful to you and see how I am better than you = You need me = I need your need of me. This weakness I must hide in order to appear as I need to.

Do you feel attracted to him? = I am itching to know whether I have a chance with him, but I will appear as free as possible from any personal interest, etc.

Questions do not only serve to mask the experience of the questioner, but also, by "sucking in" the addressed person to answering and satisfying the questioner's manipulative need, they deviate the content of group interaction away from what is therapeutically functional. For this reason, a rule of no-questioning (and particularly one against *why* questions) is likely to enhance the density of experience-sharing in the group. However, precisely because a question conceals an experience, it is a useful rule, too, to make a point of sharing the latter. One way of doing this is to re-word questions in the form of statements; for example:

What are you thinking? = I am worried how you feel towards me and would like to know.

Don't you think that you were right? = I feel supportive towards you. I would like to avoid your feeling badly.

Answers

A great many answers constitute passive compliance to someone's manipulation and are of no service to the answerer or the group. Moreover, they are most likely to be of no use to the questioner himself if his was a phony question and an expression of avoidance. This is not the case, however, with *responses;* that is, the experiences elicited by a question. More valuable to all, therefore, is the following two-fold rule:

1. The questioned one will feel free to answer or not, according to his general preference.

2. Regardless of whether he does answer or not, he will communicate his response: "I imagine that you are coming out with that question and I do not care to join you," or "I am excited by your question and afraid of answering," "I admire your perceptiveness in asking that, and would like to have an intellectual discussion with you at another time," and so on.

Asking for Permission

This is a frequent situation in the context of individual and group therapy. The request may be explicit, or somewhat implicit, in which case it deserves to be reflected, or explicated. In asking for approval for some intended action (taking the group's time, screaming, crying, etc.), the individual is so manipulating the situation that others will take responsibility for his action and he will, thus, avoid the possible impasse of a decision. "Asking for permission" is different from seeking information as to other persons' feelings or expressing the desire for this information in order to take a step. Because it is a behavior contrary to the promotion of risk-taking and responsibility, most Gestalt therapists only point out to the individual, when it occurs, his need for support, and in this way confront him with his own freedom and fear.

Demands

The attitude of the Gestalt therapist with regard to the expression of demands will vary according to the individual and occasion. He may frequently encourage the expression of demands, either in his work with a given individual, or as a group exercise, as a way of counteracting the inhibition of wants that was part of our conditioning as children. On the other hand, a demand is something more than an expression of a want. Even though the therapeutic ideal would be one in which the individual is free to make demands, it is also one in which the individual is free enough not to need his demanding; for, in the action of demanding, we are frequently unable to let others be, or to be open to them.

Our need for others to do or stop doing something is proportional to our precarious balance, in virtue of which we feel comfortable only when the environment is "just right" and nobody presses our pain buttons. We cannot let others be to the extent that we cannot let ourselves react to them as they are, or experience the impact of their being. They have to fit our ideals, for instance, for if they do not, we would be angered, and we cannot allow ourselves to experience such a bad feeling. Or we must act in such a way that our inner image of the world does not have to change and we do not feel sad, and so on. Because of this implication of demands, the therapist may sometimes insist on the Golden Rule of "expressing experiences" (in this case, desires or discomforts), rather than voicing imperatives, positive or negative. Otherwise, he will regard demands as cues to the areas in which the person needs to manipulate his own experience by means of manipulating others, and he will act upon these cues as he deems appropriate to the situation.

Chapter Five

Expressive Techniques

Awareness may be enhanced through suppression or through expression. Opposing an impulse may lead to increased awareness of it, just as we feel the push of a stream most strongly if we resist it with our hand than if not. Also, in suppressing the clichés—conditioned responses, games—that constitute some of our reactions, we become aware of what we are beyond these automatic responses.

Exaggerating the expression of an impulse, however, is an equally effective approach to enhanced awareness. Moreover, suppressive rules discussed in the foregoing pages may be seen as a means of revealing an individual's true expression (just as the suppression of noise reveals the message).

We are aware of our "selves" largely through our expression. Our notion of what we are is affected, if not completely determined, by what we fail to do, and what we have done. (Some existentialists would go further, saying that we *are* what we do: there is no essence divorced from our existence.) Yet, even if we are what we do, we only experience as if "through a glass darkly" the concrete actions and physical states that manifest our being.

The place of intensified expression in a discipline in awareness might be compared to what the contrast control does to the vision on a television screen or the volume control to the listening. In this analogy, the pure practice of attention, which is the ever-present background of Gestalt therapy, would correspond to the action of concentrating upon the screen, and deliberately watching or listening to the show. The suppressive aspect of Gestalt therapy, on the other hand, might be compared to turning off the light in the room, or closing the windows to eliminate distracting noises from the street.

By means of suppressive requests, the therapist discourages in the patient what he is not; by inviting his expression, he stimulates what he is. When the patient becomes able to express what hitherto was unexpressed, he will not only be revealing himself to another, but to himself, much as the true artist gains self-knowledge through his work. Not only is self-expression a way to self-awareness, but a means to itself: the capacity to express himself, like consciousness, is part of the fully developed person, and therefore an aim of psychotherapy. To express oneself—that is, to translate one's feeling and understanding into actions, forms, words—is to *realize* oneself, in the literal sense of making oneself real. Without such realization we are phantoms, and feel the frustration of not being fully alive.

To express (and thus actualize) ourselves would be as natural a process as the germinating of seeds or blooming of flowers, were it not for the fact that early in our lives we experienced friction, anxiety, pain, and we learned to manipulate through "strategies" rather than risking openness to the world; and this has served us—to a point. The sum of these strategies, however, in the form of a "character" became, to a greater or lesser extent, an end for itself, an "identity" to which we cling, which we justify, which we promote, while we alienate ourselves from what we truly are, and fail to express our nature.

In behavioristic terms, Gestalt therapy might be viewed as a program of positive reinforcement of self-expression, coupled with negative reinforcement of manipulation and inauthenticity. Every act of self-expression, in its context, is not only an occasion for self-awareness, but an opening up of an avenue to action—a corrective experience in which the patient learns in some measure that he can be himself without his catastrophic expectations being confirmed, one in which he takes risks in breaking his phobic patterns and learns that to express himself is satisfying and the basis of true contact with others.

> A man reported a dream in which he was a bear. Asked to become the bear, he felt at first very inhibited. Urged to imagine himself in this role, and do whatever—as a bear—he felt inclined to do, he started giving "bear hugs" to other group members, tentatively at first, and then with much feeling and delight. At last he exclaimed: "I much prefer to be a bear than myself." Someone else commented: "There is no more effective way of changing behavior than changing behavior."

Expressive techniques in Gestalt therapy may be regarded as instances of one or the other of three broad principles: the initiation of actions, the completion of actions, the pursuit of directness. Or, in other words: expressing the unexpressed, completing expression, making expression direct. In what follows, I will deal with these three groups of techniques under separate headings.

I. Initiating Action

Gestalt therapy sees much of current behavior as phobic: patterned in such a way that all of it may seem fluent and yet it avoids true contact and suppresses true expression. Beyond the almost universal avoidances of pain, of depth in contact and of expression, some of our phobias are individual, and are related to the disowning of specific functions that are part of our potential.

The idea of initiating action or expression has, accordingly, two forms of technical application in Gestalt therapy: one universal, the other individual.

A universal technique is *maximizing initiative,* risk-taking and overt expression in word or deed. A technique for individual application is a "prescription" based upon individual diagnosis, of something in the doing of which the person will be forced to overcome his avoidance.

A. Maximizing expression

This principle is applied in Gestalt therapy in various forms. One of them, of indirect relevance, we have discussed already: *the minimization of non-expressive action.* After clichés and verbiage have been suppressed, all that will remain is the choice between emptiness and expression.

A second technique leading to the maximization of expression is the *providing of unstructured situations.* To the extent that a situation is unstructured, the individual is confronted with his own choices. To the extent that no rules of interaction are laid out, or behavior expected of him, he must determine his own rules, be responsible for his own action. Lack of structure requires of the individual that he be creative rather than a good player of a predetermined game.

Absence of structure is, like many other aspects of Gestalt therapy, a component in its basic exercise: the practice of awareness continuum. Moreover, I believe that only through an appreciation of this aspect of the exercise can the therapist be in a position to respond effectively to the patient.

At every turn of the awareness continuum, the patient is either following or not following the dictates of his desires, impulses, leanings of the moment. Whichever he does, *he* does. He is *choosing,* and one of the functions of the therapist is to make him aware of his decisions, to help him realize that *he* is choosing—i.e., that he is responsible, as in these examples.

> P.: I am holding my jaw very tight. I also feel like
> clenching my fists... and I would like to stamp
> my feet.
> T.: And that, you are *not* doing.
> P.: Yes, I am holding back from stamping my
> feet...

To the extent that a person is not integrated, being confronted with his own choices will inevitably expose his inner splits in the form of conflicts:

> P.: I feel like standing up and roaring at all of you!
> T.: I see that you are not doing that.
> P.: I am afraid that it would be ridiculous.
> T.: *It?*
> P.: I would feel ridiculous doing such a thing.
> T.: So here you are in conflict: to roar or to fear
> the group's opinion. Let us do some work
> on this... etc.

The conflicts most often manifested during the awareness continuum practice are between the organismic needs, on the one hand, and the social rules of behavior and consideration of other people's reactions. This might be summarized by the dilemma of

"whether to belch and bear the shame,
or squelch the belch and bear the pain."

I think it is worth pointing out how important lack of structure is in dealing with such conflicts. In this situation, where the rule is "no rules," the patient cannot fail to acknowledge conflict as *his own.* In other words, the interpretation of conflict as one between self and external world (or social rules) would only be here a disowning of responsibility. The rule being "be yourself," he must meet the challenge of his freedom. This does not necessarily mean that on another occasion in his life he will not meet a conflict from the environment or that he *should* in every situation act upon his desires. That will be a matter of his mature choice. All that lack of structure does is provide an emptiness that he will fill with his expression, or, alternatively, with the awareness of his inability to do so, an awareness of his conflicts and their nature.

In the group setting, lack of structure takes on an additional dimension, and the rule of "no rule" may deserve being pointed out explicitly.

I generally make a statement to the effect that our session(s) will be in the nature of exploration into truth—our truth, and we can benefit most by risking not only the verbal exposure of our feelings, but the expression of ourselves in non-verbal actions. What we say or do may turn out to be very relative truth or carry an admixture of self-deception, yet even that we can find out only by sharing and acting upon the extent of truth we are in touch with at the moment. The rule also has exceptions, which will vary with the therapist. One, for instance, is that of the suppressive techniques outlined in the previous section. Another sometimes is a request of not interrupting the therapist's work on a singled-out individual. My own formula is *to restrict* interruptions to expressions, verbal or other, of intense feeling (no imperatives or comments), and when no single individual is on the "hot seat," maximizing spontaneity.

The other major component in the maximization of expression is a direct prompting to express, in words or actions. This prompting is implied in the description of the basic exercise, again, since the patient is urged to *express* moment by moment what he experiences. Furthermore, verbal expression is often requested by the therapist when the patient fails to verbalize:

T.:   What do you experience now?
P.:   I feel angry at Joe's remark.
T.:   You apparently stopped expressing your
      experiences at the point of feeling angry.
P.:   Yes, I was also feeling afraid.

In the group setting, verbal expression may be stimulated in various ways. Fritz Perls used to say: "You always have the alternative of interrupting somebody else or interrupting yourself. I want you to interrupt others more than yourself." A useful procedure is to take the time more than once in each session to request from each group member a brief statement of his experience at the moment. This serves as an awakener to feelings or reactions that might otherwise have been bypassed, points out something or somebody deserving attention, and contributes to keeping the channels of communication open.

A technique in which lack of structure and the injunction to express come together is that of a patient relating to the members of the group one after the other—frequently called "making rounds." This may be done verbally or otherwise; it is most effective, as a rule, as a one-way act of expression, without the expectation of a reaction or the obligation to carry on the exchange. An instruction leading to this may be: "Tell each person something," or, "Say to each what you want to say," or "Tell each person here how you feel about him," and so on. Or, to emphasize non-verbal expression: "*Do* something to each one of us," or, "Do to each what you feel prompted to do, acting on your impulse of the moment."

These procedures, like most others in Gestalt therapy, should not turn into stereotyped forms in which each participant in the group is asked to engage, but are most useful when employed as part of an organic development, and according to the needs of the individual at the time. Their function is mainly that of overcoming the individual's inhibition of expression or lack of expression in the inter-personal domain. The catalytic effect of others is here used as a stimulus to elicit what the continuum of awareness does not elicit spontaneously.

The active form is valuable in the case of risk-avoiders, with a marked split between verbal-intellectual responses and their emotional-impulsive behavior. In such cases, the prescription of *doing* something may either bring the individual to an impasse or reveal an aspect of himself altogether inaccessible through verbal terms.

Aside from the requests of saying or doing something, whether to other group members or not, there is a form of expression which deserves to be singled out because it brings together unstructuredness and initiative: unstructured vocalization, or gibberish. Gibberish is one of the few actions that cannot be programmed or rehearsed. Willingness to "speak" gibberish may be seen as willingness to say the unknown, the unthought. Yet the nature of the task is not only unpatterned, but expressive. Anyone who has experimented with gibberish will know how it reflects, for each one of us, something of our individual style and feelings of the moment. In its lack of structure, there is something predetermined to gibberish: it obediently molds itself to our inner reality, as an artwork.

The technique of requesting expression in gibberish can be valuable, as random actions are, to stimulate initiative and risk-taking in general, but has a more specific use too. Gibberish has the uniqueness—at least for some individuals—of allowing for a spontaneity of expression that their words or other actions would not allow. In this way, the message conveyed through these seemingly meaningless syllables can serve as both cue and seed for self-awareness. Sometimes the person may censor all anger from his statements, voice and awareness, and yet produce gibberish that he acknowledges as angry beyond doubt. Or, his ordinary voice and stance will become collected while his gibberish will be pleading, and this may inspire further work on his suppressed needfulness. Whatever the patient has said in gibberish he may experiment in saying in words later, and this is most likely to lead to expanded awareness.

B. *"Individual Prescriptions"*

Whatever the basis for the therapist's intuition or perception, it is a fact that he may sometimes see the "holes" in an individual's personality, as Perls described in this passage:

> ... every one of us has holes in his personality. Wilson Van Dusen discovered this first in the schizophrenic, but I believe that every one of us has holes. Where something should be, there is nothing. Many people have no soul. Others have no genitals. Some have no heart; all their energy goes into computing, thinking. Others have no legs to stand on. Many people have no eyes. They project the eyes, and the eyes are to quite an extent in the outside world and they always live as if they are being looked at... Most of us have no ears. People expect the ears to be outside and they talk and expect someone to listen. But who listens? If people would listen, we would have peace[1].

He may develop a notion of what the patient is avoiding in his life and behavior, what he is failing to acknowledge, allow or express, and yet is part of himself. In helping him to express the precise aspects of himself that he is suppressing, the therapist is helping him to know himself, to take responsibility for what he is and thus to become whole. The type of intuition or perception referred to above, which in ordinary psychotherapy would originate in interpretation or comment, the Gestalt therapist is most likely to put in the patient's mouth rather than his ear. Perls' formula, "May I feed you a sentence?" has become standard technique, whereby the patient experiments with the possible truth the therapist has seen, making it his own statement about himself. Most often, this action will elicit a sense of truth or falseness, or another reaction more significant than either intellectual agreement or lack of it.

[1] From *Gestalt Therapy Verbatim* by Frederick Perls, 1992 edition, The Gestalt Journal Press, Highland, New York. Reprinted with permission.

The therapist's invitation to the patient to do something avoided is generally more effective when it entails actions rather than statements or words that have the value of actions.

T.:   I see that you avoid looking at her.
P.:   Yes.
T.:   Experiment with the opposite: look at her directly.
P.:   I do not feel at ease when I do so. I feel I do not want to communicate with her.
T.:   Tell her.
P.:   I do not feel drawn to you. I feel like being far away from you. I would not want to see you at all. (More assertively) I do not like being around you. You are sucking me in all the time with your demands. (Loudly) And I hate you!

In this instance, the therapist's role is somewhat that of a midwife helping to bring into expression what otherwise would be left unsaid. In other instances, he may take greater leaps: he may request a complying "good boy" to express anger, he may direct a superman type to ask for help, an arrogant intellectual to repeat "I do not know." In many such instances, he will be acting upon his intuition of the "killer" in the "good boy," the insecurity in the know-it-all, or the superman's need for affection.

At other times, prescriptions such as these may be based upon a formulation other than intuition or perception of cues: the principle of reversal.

One of Perls' original ideas has been the application of the figure-ground distinction to the question of self-perception and personality functioning in general. To the extent of our neurosis, we inflate the magnitude of some of our traits, which we regard as virtues, and we scotomize those that we call vices. Similarly, we filter down our spontaneity, fostering some manifestations, inhibiting others. What if we shift our point of view, and choose to see as figure what we have been regarding as ground? What if we carry out an experiment of living upside-down in the world for some time? If it happened that we are upside-down in it now, without knowing it, the experiment may reveal to us a better possibility.

The idea of reversing habitual self-perceptions and actions may take different forms, all of which may be seen as a means of eliciting the expression of what is postponed, bypassed, or suppressed in terms of an incompatible gestalt. The assumption here is that the opposite to the person's attitude is likely to be a part of him too, yet a less-developed side of his personality.

The principle of reversal can be applied not only to feelings but also to physical attitudes. Opening up when in a closed posture, breathing deeply as an alternative to restraining the inhalation or exhalation of air, exchanging the motor attitudes of left and right, and so on, can eventually lead to the unfolding of unsuspected experiences. The following is an example of this kind:

> The therapist notices that while expressing his ongoing experiences the patient often interrupts what he is saying and feeling, and in such moments he swallows or sniffs. The therapist suggests that he do the opposite of sniffing and swallowing. The patient engages in a forceful and prolonged exhalation through the nose and mouth, that ends with what he reports as an unfamiliar and surprising feeling " ...somewhat as if I were sobbing, but also pushing against a resistance, and my muscles are tense, as when I stretch in yawning; I enjoy this tension when trying to exhale to the very end of my breath, which also feels somehow like an orgasm."

> Later, he discovered that he had been living with this feeling for a long time without being aware of it: "It is like wanting to burst, wanting to explode from the inside, tearing down a sort of membrane in which I am wrapped and limited. And I am at the same time this strait jacket and I am squeezing myself."

This short experience was the starting point of a spontaneous development which took place in the coming months. The muscular tension and concomitant feelings were always very much in his awareness from then onwards, and he felt more and more inclined to do physical exercise. He then discovered the pleasure of dancing and becoming much freer in his expression, both in movement and general attitude. Finally, he could sense the anger implied in his muscular contractions until he would be aware of it in his reactions to people to a degree he had not been before.

Still another guideline for the initiation of action or expression that has been withheld is the person's own sense of lack of "finishedness," or in Gestalt terminology, lack of closure. Words unsaid and things undone leave a trace in us binding us to the past. A considerable part of our daydreaming and thinking is an attempt to live out in fantasy what we fail to live in reality. Sometimes, as we shall see, the therapist invites the patient to make fantasies more real by acting them out; at other times he merely inquires about his sense of unfinishedness, and invites the patient to carry out what he has postponed or avoided. This idea may apply in different forms: finishing in fantasy an unfinished dream, saying to parents what was not said to them during childhood years, saying goodbye to a divorced spouse or a dead relative. In group therapy it is a common practice to inquire at the end of sessions or days about unfinished situations between group members. Most frequently, "unfinishedness" is created by withholding the expression of appreciation or resentment, and such expression may be required directly as a group exercise.

II. Completing Expression

We are always expressing ourselves, to a point. The true novelist will portray the most anonymous character in such a way that the lack of anything special may be revealed as an expression of himself, after all. There are moments when we are all artists, and we have the insight to see the miracle of every individual's uniqueness through his seemingly insignificant actions. Yet like awareness, self-expression varies in degree from one person to another. One of the things a Gestalt therapist does is to *intensify* the person's self-expression. This he does, first of all, by recognizing the moments or elements of true expression in an action, and inviting their development.

T.:   What do you experience now?
P.:   Nothing special.
T.:   You shrugged your shoulders.
P.:   I guess so.
T.:   There, you did it again (shrugs shoulders).
P.:   I guess it is a habit.
T.:   Please do it again.
P.:   (Complies)
T.:   Now exaggerate that gesture.
P.:   (Shrugs, grimaces, and makes a rejecting gesture with elbows and hands.) I guess I am saying "Don't bug me." Yeah, leave me alone.

For the sake of clarity, I think we can distinguish at least four types of procedures leading to an intensification of action:

1. Simple repetition.
2. Exaggeration and development.
3. Explicitation or translation.
4. Identification and acting.

I will deal with these four in turn.

A. Simple Repetition

The purpose of this method is to intensify the person's awareness of a given action or statement, it goes a step beyond the therapist's action of simply mirroring or reflecting. The example of shrugging shoulders, above, may serve to illustrate the point.

Sometimes verbal repetition may have a dramatic effect, in that the person brings himself to see more and more wholeheartedly something that he was minimizing or not weighing fully, or was covering up under a mask.

P.: (Talking to her mother) I don't want anything from you any more. I just want you to keep away from us. Don't intrude on us. I am not your daughter any more. I never was, really. You never understood me. I resent that you never did. I resent you and I hurt because you don't understand me. You don't see me. How I would like you to see me!

T.: Repeat that.

P.: I would like you to see me, Mother. See me. Here I am for you to see. I want you to be able to see me. Don't look away. Don't form theories about me. *This* is me. Take me as I am; no more, no less. Can you see me?

T.: Can she?

P.: I think she can. (melts into tears)

Sometimes repetition results, not in an intensification of meaning, but if the original statement was contrary to the patient's true self, to *increased meaninglessness,* and to a reaction against the original statement.

The technique of repetition can be adapted to the group situation by addressing the repetitive statement or action to different members. In these instances there is room for several variations of the exercise:

1. Strict repetition (for instance, saying "Goodbye" to each).

2. Strict repetition followed by elaboration according to the way the statement applies to the person in question.

3. Repetition of *content,* adapting the *form* of the statement to each person.

4. Repetition of *attitude* with variation in *content* (i.e., expression of anger in whatever way seems fit according to the individual encountered).

As in the case of other techniques, these cannot be expected to effect miracles by themselves, but afford an occasion for discovery when applied with the right attitude. It is the therapist's role to oversee the procedure and rescue the individual from slipping into a mechanical procedure, a performance or an avoidance. If he is stimulated to remain aware of what he is feeling and doing, something real is likely to happen.

B. Exaggeration and Development

Exaggeration is one step beyond simple repetition, and frequently takes place spontaneously when a person is asked to do or say something again a number of times. A gesture will become broader or more precise, a statement louder, or more whisper-like, more intensely expressive of whatever its feeling-tone initially was.

When a person is asked to exaggerate and does this a number of times, he may discover something new in his action. Perhaps this is not a completely new quality, but one which lay in his original behavior like an invisible seed, so that only exaggeration could make it obvious.

In the following illustration (which I am reconstructing after several years) Fritz Perls plays the therapist's part and I am the patient:

T.: I have brought a gift for you. Here.
     (Produces a bowl with sand.)
P.: (Takes the bowl.)
T.: *Eat it.*
P.: I feel perplexed. I don't know whether you really want me to eat it or whether there is another message that I am not getting.
T.: Eat it.
P.: (Takes a pinch of sand between two fingers and puts it into his mouth.)
T.: What do you experience?
P.: I feel the grains of sand in my mouth and between my teeth, and I hear the sound of

the grains when I chew them. I notice more
saliva coming to my mouth and I feel the desire
to get rid of the sand. I start spitting some
grains out but they still stick to my tongue.
I take my tongue between my fingers to clean it
—and now the sand sticks to my fingers.
I'm rubbing my fingers with each other
—while I continue to spit.

T.:   Exaggerate that.
P.:   And I rub my hands with one another, and
against my pants and keep throwing away
sand, throwing it away, away, away! (with
broad rejecting movements of arms and hands)
Yes—that is what I feel—I have been swallowing
down too much that had nothing to do with me.
I'll get rid of you now. Out of me!
Thank you very much for your sand!

Exaggeration constitutes a form of development
of an action, but development does not always involve exaggeration. Sometimes, if we stay with an
action or statement through repetition, emphasis will
result in a modification of the said action, in such a
way that one movement leads to another, one feeling
or thought to a different one. The instruction
"develop that" is an invitation to the patient to explore the *trend* of this movement, gesture, posture,
vocal sound, or visual image. In this way the urge,
only imperfectly expressed in a fleeting action, may
reveal itself fully in a sequence which may at times
constitute a piece of dance, music or poetry.

P.:   I don't have any marked feeling. I don't see the
point of enumerating my physical sensations...
T.:   Please go on speaking with the same voice but
without the words.
P.:   Da da da da da da da da da da da.
(with an expression of hopelessness)
T.:   Exaggerate that expression in your voice.
P.:   (Goes on; this time with more apparent
sadness.)
T.:   Still more. Exaggerate it and see what develops.

P.:   (His voice becomes a melody, sad and
       majestic, and with increasing potency.) This is
       what I wanted to do all my life! To sing! (tearful)
       That was truly *me*, more than in all my words!
       How wonderful! I don't want to stop!
       (Goes on singing.)

C. Explicitation or Translation

I'm giving the name "explicitation" to one of the
most original techniques of Gestalt therapy, which
the therapist generally introduces with statements
such as "Give words to your nodding," "If your tears
could speak what would they say?", "What would
your left hand say to your right hand?" or "Give a
voice to your loneliness." In doing so the patient is
being urged to translate into words a piece of non-
verbal expression—a gesture, visual image, physical
symptom, etc.—and he is thus requested to make
explicit a content which was only implicit.

T.:   What do you have to say to Martha?
P.:   (With a very dead voice) I don't have much to
       say to you. I like your expression and what
       you have said today but I am a little afraid
       of you...
T.:   Speak to her in gibberish.
P.:   (Turns very animated while doing so, leans
       forward, smiles and gesticulates with his hands).
T.:   Now translate that into English.
P.:   Martha, you're lovely. I'd like to caress you,
       kiss you, take care of you. I feel very tender
       toward you. You are like a beautiful flower
       and I always like to be near you.

In the process of explicitating the patient must
necessarily empathize with that aspect of himself or
his perception that he tries to put into words. He
must, so to speak, experience the event from the
inside rather than as an external onlooker; the result
may be surprising when applied to the perception of
persons or dream images, both of which are screens

for our projection. In these instances the projected phantom may grow and become explicit in its fantastic quality; alternatively, a true perception that was covered up by a projection may come to light:

P.:   I hated him, and I still do. He was a dirty old
      man. He always liked to touch me or kiss me
      and I was so scared of him...
T.:   Let him speak. Imagine what he would have
      said if he had been able to talk to you in
      complete honesty about how he felt.
P.:   He would have said, "You're a beautiful little
      girl. You're so much as a little girl is meant
      to be: so healthy, so pure! It's like drinking
      fresh water in the middle of a desert. I feel so
      lonely and cut off from life, and all my loneliness
      vanishes when I'm with you."
T.:   How do you feel about him now?
P.:   I feel compassion. I wish I had not been so
      mean to him. There was nothing to be
      scared about.

The process of explicitation leads to the desired end of interpretation through a radically different approach. In the first place, it is not the therapist who tells the patient the supposed "meaning" of his action, gesture, voice; but the patient is urged to *contact* his message for himself. In the second place, there lies the great distance between "thinking about" a piece of behavior or symbol and empathizing with it.

The implicit first step in explicitating is *experiencing* the feeling-content of the action to be explicitated. The second step is translating that content into the alternative medium of words. This process is similar to that involved in poetry or in the figurative visual arts. Attempting to draw, for instance, is, above all else, learning how to *see*.

This process of contacting an experience and then expressing it in words may be seen as one more instance of exaggeration and development of an expressive act. The difference is that, in explicitation, development does not remain within a single domain of experience (movement, voice, words) but flows from one domain into another.

When a message (hitherto invisible as such) is translated from actions, sounds or images into words, the process rightly deserves to be called one of explicitation, since ordinarily motor-visual activity is closer to our automatic and unconscious processes, whereas the verbal or conceptual, linked to the "secondary process," is part of our wakeful activity. The process of translation need not be from action to words, however, in order to serve the general aim of amplifying alone:

T.: What are you feeling now?

P.: I feel restless. I am impatient at myself for not coming up with anything important. And I'm very aware of the group as a captive audience.

T.: I see that you're stamping your left foot.

P.: (exaggerates the movement) Yes.

T.: Now do with your whole body what your foot is doing.

P.: (gradually develops movement until he is stomping forcefully with both feet while he slaps his thighs with his palms and bares his teeth)

T.: Make some sounds, too.

P.: Ah! Ah! Ah!! (forceful exhalations preceded by glottal stops which turn more and more into laughter)

T.: Now *do* something in the same attitude.

P.: (uncrosses somebody's arms and straightens out his posture) Wake up, man! (walks around stomping his feet and motions with arms and hands as if to indicate standing up) Wake up, everybody! Let us get out of this sick, dark place! (Opens the door and pushes somebody out of the room) Or *you* get out. I'll clean up this house and throw away all your shit. (drags somebody by the arm.) Be clean and joyful or get out of here!

D. Identification and Acting

Acting is an important part of Gestalt therapy, both in the external sense of going through the motions that fit a given role and in the inner sense of experiencing oneself as another, imagining oneself as possessing the attributes or actions of other beings or things.

In the sense that acting gives motoric expression to an idea, feeling or image, it may be regarded as one more instance of *translation* from one expressive modality to another. Indeed, it is the converse of explicitation: in explicitating we give words to our movements; in acting we give movements to a thought. Acting, therefore, may be understood as one more way of *completing* or implementing expression. The private behavior that we call "thinking" might be regarded as incomplete action or symbolic action. In embodying or carrying it into the medium of flesh and bones, we carry out that action to its full expression. The same may be said of anticipation and remembering. What the Gestalt therapist is doing when he asks a patient to act out his memories or expectations is equivalent to asking him to carry out physically an action which he is carrying out, repetitiously sometimes, in fantasy. While doing so the patient may discover that he is hanging on to that particular memory or fantasy as a consequence of its very "unfinishedness"—an urge to take action, chronically prevented and substituted for by halfhearted rehearsing.

Aside from the principle of completion there is still another sense in which acting expresses the attitude of Gestalt therapy. In an inner sense, acting entails a process of identification, of becoming one with the part that we act or recognizing "its" experience as our own. The instructions *"be* him," *"be* your hand," *"be* your voice," and so on, are one step beyond the empathy required by explicitation. Between "give a voice to the cry-baby in you," and "be the cry-baby" there is a difference in the degree of identification with us as actor. The task will probably be harder for the patient when it amounts to identifying with an unpleasant side of himself that he is trying hard to disown. On the other hand, to the extent that he is able to identify with all that he is—good or bad—he will be taking responsibility for himself.

Not only do identification and acting shorten the distance between "I" and its processes, but they are major avenues to awareness. We can know by being something or somebody more than by reasoning about it or him. Acting calls for the holistic understanding that is the function of intuition more than of any other single task. What is specific to the Gestalt employment of acting, however, is that the injunction behind every task is a variation upon "Be what you are." Scenes and characters are not the gods of a religious ritual or the creations of a classical author, but aspects of our own lives which we might be prone to regard as accidental or trivial, sometimes meaningless: a favorite figure of speech, a gesture, a fantasy.

The main applications of acting in Gestalt therapy are the enactment of dreams, the acting of anticipations of the future (which lie behind most real-life conflicts), the representation of the past and playing the different parts that are in conflict in personality. With the approach of Gestalt therapy to dreams, to the past and to the future, I deal elsewhere in this book, so I will speak here only of the enacting of personality traits.

Some of the most dramatic moments in Gestalt therapy sessions are those in which the patient takes sides with the different parts that constitute non-integrated aspects or conflicting sub-selves within his personality: the good boy and the spiteful brat, the bully and the philanthropist, the caring person and the selfish one, the masculine and the feminine, the active and the passive, parent and child, topdog and underdog and so on.

I think that much of the artistry of the therapist lies in his ability to indicate to the patient the key roles to explore through acting—a matter which requires, like all else in Gestalt therapy, sensitivity to the moment. The assumption or knowledge that practically everybody wants to feel special, for instance, is not enough for telling a given person "be special" or "act special." In order for such role-playing to be successful the patient must have been coming into contact with this region of his psyche by gradual steps, so that acting "special" crowns an organic development during the session.

Here are some of the cues that may reveal to the therapist the presence of an attitude eligible for enactment:

1. Psychological symptoms such as anxiety, guilt, shame. Most instances of anxiety involve either:

A. The imagined judgment or reaction of another (as in stage-fright) who may then be chosen as a subject of role-playing and eventually recognized as one's own attitude towards oneself; or

B. A catastrophic fantasy of the future, which may be similarly acted out: failure, disgrace, death, etc.

In guilt there is always a self-accusation or projected self-accusation that may be likewise dramatized by playing guilty to the fullest measure and then by playing accuser. In both instances other members of the group may be used as targets by seeing them as being judges or underdogs.

In the case of shame or embarrassment the sense of exposure implicit in such feeling also implies an onlooker or a judging witness, the attitudes of whom may be explored by acting him (or her) out.

2. Conflicts. Even micro-conflicts such as smiling or not, looking at the therapist or away from him, and so on, are usually the expression of a broader split than that which is apparent in the specific action under consideration. By explicitating or exaggerating both alternatives in this conflict at the moment, the patient is likely to arrive soon at two broad aspects of his psychological functioning.

3. Exaggeration and reversal. The amplification of virtually any feeling or expressive act, gesture, posture, voice inflection, verbal statement may soon disclose a broad attitude worthy of further exploration by enactment. Once this is defined, the converse attitude may be explored as well.

4. A discrepancy between verbal and non-verbal expression may be the avenue of investigation of another split. A patient, for instance, was reporting anxiety and trembling while his voice, posture and demeanor conveyed great poise and security. I asked him to act overtly afraid and poised, alternatively, matching in either case verbal and non-verbal behavior. In doing this, he soon discovered that he was *always playing* poised, that he did not feel free to show his weakness, and that he had a topdoggish compulsion about being the master of the situation and so forth. In another instance the patient spoke with calm collectedness, reporting pleasant feelings, while at the same time he obviously writhed in his chair and rubbed his sweating hands. An indication similar to the one above, to the effect of *being* anxious and *being* a person who "feels fine" alternatively, revealed to him his own pretense and the fact that he played "a cool role" not only when asked to do so, but always.

5. Total behavior. At times the therapist may become aware of a patient's role through the style of his total behavior rather than by any precise cue. To the degree that the game so spotted by him is subtle, he will rely on his intuitive apprehension of the behavioral gestalt. After reflecting his observation (i.e., "You seem to be playing innocent," or "I think you are looking for the limelight") and if this observation is acknowledged by the patient, he may move on to suggest an exaggeration or the acting out of the relevant characteristic.

III. The Question of Directness

A. Minimization

Self-expression is frequently blunted by actions such as minimization, roundaboutness, vagueness, etc. In such cases an increase in directness will amount to a greater message-to-noise ratio in an individual's communication.

> P.:   I feel rather tired and a little bored. Perhaps I am a little irritated at you, too. It might be that I don't enjoy very much being here at the moment.
>
> T.:   I notice that you use many qualifiers: "*rather* tired," "a *little* this or that," "*perhaps, it might* be"...
>
> P.:   I think that you're right.
>
> T.:   (ironically) You "*think*," *perhaps* it *might* be true.
>
> P.:   Yes. I use a lot of qualifiers. It is... kind of a habit.
>
> T.:   "Kind of?"
>
> P.:   It is a habit.
>
> T.:   Please tell us again of your feelings, this time omitting *perhapses* and *maybes*. Could you repeat what you said a while ago with this change.
>
> P.:   I feel tired. Yes, I do. And I feel irritated and bored. I would like to go to bed rather than being here. No. I do not prefer that. I intensely desire to rest and yet I am interested enough to stay.

A frequent source of minimization is related to the use of the conjunction "but," and therefore the very occurrence of the word may be taken as a signal. Aside from valid meanings that require the existence of the word in our language, "but" is all too often introduced to disqualify a statement or take away some of its weight or validity. At any rate, "but" is an audible reflection of conflict. "Yes, but..." "I would like to do this, but...", "I like you, but..." By means of this ambiguity the individual avoids taking sides or fully experiencing either half of his statement—each half invalidating the other. Aside from the indications that the therapist may give him at this point to the effect of taking sides with or exaggerating either one of them, he will sometimes discourage the use of the word "but" and suggest, instead, "and."

P.: I am holding back from you but I like your
     peacefulness.
T.: Try "and" instead of "but."
P.: I'm holding back from you *and* I enjoy your
     peacefulness. Of course! This is much
     more true.

"*It.*" Another turn of language intimately related to the issue of directness is the use of "it" instead of a specific content.

P.: He wanted us to do something that I couldn't
     agree to. And he insisted so much on it that
     it became the object of endless fights between
     us...
T.:   Could you tell us what the *it* is?
P.: (a long pause) He wanted us to take a
     psychedelic trip.

Frequently the real meaning substituted by "it" is "I," or "you," and in this way "it" acts as a buffer to dampen the directness of an encounter.

"My hand is doing this movement . . . "
"Is *it* doing the movement?"
"I am moving my hand like this . . . and now the thought comes to me that . . . "
"The thought 'comes' to you?"
"I have the thought."
"You *have* it?"
"I think. Yes. I think that I use 'it' very much, and I am glad that by noticing it I can bring it all back to me."

"Bring it back?"
"Bring myself back. I feel thankful for this."
"This?"
"Your idea about the 'it'."
"My idea."
"I feel thankful towards you."

Perls first suggested the use of *I* instead of *it* in *Ego Hunger and Aggression* and he gave much importance to this seemingly trivial detail of language in his work. He says, in the above-mentioned work, "Every time you do apply the proper ego language you express yourself, you assist in the development of your personality." As with many techniques, though, I prefer to regard this particular one as a useful prop, the value of which will be determined by the appropriateness of its use at the moment. I have seen therapists picking at words and accomplishing little, for that was seemingly a wrong choice at the moment. I am personally willing to let many "its" pass when the request of rewording would interrupt a feeling, disrupt concentration on an image, distract the patient from identifying with a dream-character, and so on.

Avoidance of "I" is not always paralleled by the introduction of "it." Here are some alternatives:

P.:   We are all feeling nervous and I don't think
        that we like what is going on.
Other P.:   Speak for yourself.
P.:   Well, I am nervous . . .

In this case, "we" serves as the forest that hides the tree and entails an unwillingness to take responsibility for an experience. Another screen is "one."

"One does not do this easily."
"One?"
"I have trouble expressing myself to all of you."

Impersonal statements are frequent and pass as scientific.

P.: I see your eyes are looking at me... There is perspiration in my hands... And there is a quavering in my voice. There is fear...

T.: Your manner of speech is that of a very detached observer: "there is" this or that, never "*I* feel afraid," or "*my* voice quavers."

P.: Yes. That is so true. That is what I want most, *to be able to say I.*

B. Retroflections

One instance of indirectness that is the object of a specific technique in Gestalt therapy is the undoing of retroflections: the redirecting of an impulse that has been displaced in such a way that, instead of meeting its intended object, it reverts to the agent.

Perls has given the name of *retroflection* to the behavior by which a person "does to himself what he originally did or tried to do to other persons or objects." Instead of directing his energies to actions upon the environment which will satisfy his needs, he "redirects activity inward and *substitutes* himself in place of the environment as the target of behavior." To the extent that he does this, he splits his personality into "doer" and "done to."

Retroflection is a consequence of environmental obstacles to the expression of impulses, which have led to an active holding back on the part of the individual. In holding back, the person does to himself what originally was done to him by the environment (he introjects) and uses for this activity the energy of his own impulses (retroflects).

Retroflection, according to Perls, may be quite functional: "Do not jump to the conclusion that we imply that it would be fine if we could all, without further ado, release our inhibitions! In some situations holding back is necessary, even life saving—for instance, holding back inhaling while under water. The important question is whether or not a person has *rational grounds* for presently choking off behavior in given circumstances."

Many of our retroflections, however, are dysfunctional and unconscious. To Perls *repression* is "forgotten" retroflection.

I think that the concept of retroflection is of particular value to the psychotherapist, for it brings to his attention the *active* aspect of repression and inhibition. As Perls has said, "Psychoanalysis has stressed recovery of awareness of what is repressed—that is, the blocked impulse. We, on the other hand, emphasize recovery of awareness of the blocking, the feeling that one is doing it and *how* one is doing it. Once a person discovers his retroflecting action and regains control of it, the blocked impulse will be recovered automatically. The great advantage of dealing with the retroflecting part of the personality—the active repressing agent—is that this is within fairly easy reach of awareness, can be directly experienced, and does not depend upon guessed-at interpretations."

The content of retroflections may vary, and so its outcome: self-hate, self-pity, greedy self-squeezing and so on. Even introspection is considered by Perls as a retroflective peering at oneself: "This form of retroflection is so universal in our culture that much of the psychological literature simply takes it for granted that any attempt to increase self-awareness must of necessity consist of introspection... The observer is split off from the part observed, and not until this split is healed will a person fully realize that self-awareness, which is not introspected, can exist. We previously likened genuine awareness to the glow produced within a burning coal by its own combustion, and introspection to turning the beam of a flashlight on an object and peering at its surface by means of the reflected rays."

I think that by far the most common type of retroflection with which we deal in psychotherapy is the retroflection of aggression. Just as aggression toward others may constitute a projection of aggression toward self, self-aggression may well constitute a retroflection of an impulse originally directed towards another. In this way, a person may turn resentment into self-accusations and guilt, sarcasm into a feeling of ridicule, hatred into a feeling of having no right to exist, and so on. In general terms, retroflected aggression becomes depression, as psychoanalysis has established long ago.

The possibility that a person's feeling toward himself may constitute a case of retroflection is tested out in Gestalt therapy, not through interpretation but through experiment. When a person is directed to do to another what he is doing to himself, he *may* find out that this is what he really wanted to do. If this is so, he will have regained some of his directness of expression.

The prospect of reversing a retroflection frequently meets considerable anxiety, shame or guilt, and when the retroflection is finally undone, this may lead to socially inappropriate or childish behavior. However, this is one of the instances in which acting out may be the quickest road to insight upon the repressed as well as toward a redirecting of impulse. Perls, Hefferline and Goodman give us the following example:

> A religious man, for instance, unable to vent his wrath on the Lord for his disappointments, beats his own breast and tears his own hair. Such self-aggression, obviously a retroflection, nevertheless *is* aggression and it *does* give some satisfaction to the retroflecting part of the personality. It is aggression that is crude, primitive, undifferentiated—a retroflected childish temper tantrum—but the part of the personality that is attacked is always there and available for attack. Self-aggression can always be sure of its victim.

To reverse such a retroflection in one fell swoop would mean that the person would then attack others in ways just as ineffectual and archaic. He would rouse the same overwhelming counter-aggression that led him to retroflect in the first place. It is some realization of this which makes even the imagined reversal of retroflections productive of so much fear. What is overlooked is that the change can be made in easy stages which gradually transform the whole situation as they proceed.

One can, to start with, discover and accept the fact that he does "take it out on himself." He can become aware of the emotions of the retroflecting part of his personality—notably the grim joy taken in administering punishment to himself. This, when he achieves it, represents considerable progress, for vindictiveness is so socially disesteemed as to be most difficult to acknowledge and accept even when one supposedly spares others and directs it solely against oneself. Only when accepted—that is, when it is reckoned with as an existing, dynamic component of one's functioning personality—does one reach the possibility of modifying, differentiating, redirecting it into healthy expression. As one's orientation in the environment improves, as one's awareness of what one genuinely wants to do becomes clearer, as one makes approaches that are limited try-outs to see what will happen, gradually one's techniques for expression of one's previously blocked impulses develop also. They lose their primitive, terrifying aspect as one differentiates them and gives them a chance to catch up with the more grown-up parts of the personality.[1]

The step by step approach to which Perls refers is not a matter of technique, properly speaking, but of what I am calling *strategy*—that is, the organization of techniques in the context of a session. I will turn to such matters in Part III of this book.

---

[1] From *Gestalt Therapy: Excitement and Growth in the Human Personality* by Frederick Perls, Ralph Hefferline, & Paul Goodman, 1992 edition, The Gestalt Journal Press, Highland, New York. Reprinted with permission.

Chapter Six

Techniques of Integration

In a broad sense every expressive technique is a technique of integration, for expressing means bringing into awareness what was disassociated from awareness, or bringing into the domain of action something that the person was carrying in his mind as a disassociated—and therefore ineffective—thought, image, or feeling.

There are more specific ways, however, in which we promote an integration of personality in Gestalt therapy. Sometimes the therapist will indicate a resource adequate to a specific situation—as in suggesting a role to play that will constitute a synthesis of elements now in conflict in the patient's psyche. Most often, however, he will encourage the integration of conflicting inner voices by means of one or another of the two teachings that I am discussing below: the intra-personal encounter and the assimilation of projections.

Intra-Personal Encounter

One of the most original techniques of Gestalt therapy is that of bringing the sub-selves in a person into *contact* with each other, by instructing the person to play their parts in turn and have his "characters" talk (or relate in some way) to one another. So much is this a part of Gestalt therapy that Fritz Perls humorously stated that all he needed was his skill, the patient's collaboration, kleenex, the "hot seat" and an empty chair. This, because in these inner dialogues the patient is encouraged to switch from one chair to the other to reinforce the reality of his identification with alternating sub-selves.

The idea of intrapersonal encounter is simple enough: having two or more sides of a person relate to one another so that a dialogue is established. Perls frequently gave the instruction: "Make a skit." In this way a conversation of increasing depth and meaningfulness may develop between, say the good mother and the little girl that needs attention, or between the person's purposefulness and his inclination to improvise, or between his reason and his heart. What determines the effectiveness or success of this procedure, however, lies in factors which may call for a therapist's subtlety to assess. I'm listing some of these below:

> 1. An encounter must not be premature. Before selfish Joe may talk with selfless Joe, for instance, it is necessary that Joe become aware enough of these two sides in himself and contacted their way of experiencing.

> 2. The encounter must not degenerate into an intellectual discussion or the ping-pong game of mutual accusations and defense; contact between the sub-selves must be pursued at the feeling level. When Underdog is pleading "not guilty," for instance, the therapist may have to step in to inquire, "What are you experiencing in the face of this accusation?" Then the dialogue may continue with the underdog's expression of shame or rage.

Here are some examples of intrapersonal encountering which I am borrowing from an earlier publication:

> 1. A lady explains she would like to remember last night's dream. She is instructed to call the dream, to address it directly, and she says in a very low, monotonous voice, "Come, dream, I want to remember you." When her attention is drawn to the lack of feeling

in her calling, she tries again several times with no success. In doing so, she is able to experience the fact that she really does not feel an urge to remember. She feels rather indifferent towards the issue and has been misinterpreting herself, assuming she had such a desire. She can now see that she has been playing the "good patient."

2. A woman had a dream in which she saw herself crawling across a room. Somebody asks what she is doing, and she answers: "I want to have a confrontation with that wall." "Why don't you rather have it with a person, then?" She answers, "People are walls."

Not only was the person replaced in the dream by a wall, but the wall itself was never reached and "confronted." When told to do so in a session, the woman did so in the same position as in the dream, on her knees and bowing. "I want to go through you, wall." Taking the role of the wall, her reply was distant, hard and disdainful towards her meekness and docility, her posture and weak complaint. After several role reversals, she stood up; and further, she adopted the attitude of the wall herself—firm, erect and hard—so she was visualizing two walls in front of each other. This felt to her like the confrontation she was seeking. A week later she reported that she had for the first time been able to confront a man in the same attitude.

A great many (perhaps the most) significant encounters are particular forms of the widespread split in personality: the "I should" versus the "I want." It may take the form of a dialogue with an imagined parent, with a disembodied self-accusation, with "people in general," etc., but the parties appear again and again with the distinctive feature that inspired Perls (in his inclination for a phenomenological nomenclature) to call them Topdog and Underdog.

Topdog can be described as righteous, bullying, persisting, authoritarian, and primitive.

Underdog develops great skill in evading Topdog's commands. Only half-heartedly intending to comply with the demands, Underdog answers: "Yes, but...," "I try so hard, but next time I'll do better," and "mañana." Underdog usually gets the better of the conflict.

In other words, Topdog and Underdog are actually two clowns performing their weird and unnecessary plays on the stage of the tolerant and mute Self. Integration, or cure, can be achieved only when the need for mutual control between Topdog and Underdog ceases. Only then will the two masters mutually listen. Once they come to their senses (in this case listening to each other), the door to integration and unification opens. The chance of making a whole person out of a split becomes a certainty.

The following encounter (actually written by the patient during a therapeutic session) does not lead to full integration, but nevertheless illustrates the procedure:

The therapist suggests an encounter between the monk and the beast.

Monk: Terrible, terrible, the pains of the flesh.
New I: No pain necessary right now—listen to "Trout" and grok the sunshine, grok the trembling, which is for opening the Door, man.
Monk: You make me feel so lonely, Charles.
New I: Thanks for naming me. Now I can proceed to fuck or at least *feel* something down *here* between the legs.
Monk: That is a dog, that puts his tail between his legs.
New I: Then you are a dog, sir.
Monk: *How dare you!*
New I: Now you're acting like Miss Henrietta. Reach down there, man, and feel your balls for a change.
Monk: Don't use such vulgar language.
New I: Just for that, sir, I sentence you to 90 days and nights of extreme pleasure.

Monk: *Anything,* so long as you don't play the
          Japanese music. (Just the mention of that
          makes me tremble clear up to the armpits.)

New I: I am going to play that, man, exactly as
          soon as this fucking "Trout" quintet peters out.
          (This Japanese music is very pleasant—
          rather innocent.
          Well, that's the way to start, in innocence.
          Puer aeternis is thyself and every other
          beautiful person.
          Yes, it's cruelty of myself, to my body.
          The monk tortured and killed my body.
          No wonder I put the Crucifix above the bed:
          "the man who died.")

Monk: I became what I am because you left your
          playmates behind in Minnesota.

New I: Makes no sense.

Monk: "Lose your mind and come to your senses."

New I: You're getting pretty sharp, man.

Monk: Thanks for calling me that, son.

New I: I'm not your son, thank God.

Monk: I see you recognize me.

New I: You mean, I presume, that every man who
          oppresses the body is my mother. By the way,
          are you aware of the fact that we have reversed
          positions?

Monk: Wasn't so important as we thought, was it?

This last sentence sprang from the feeling that
the two characters were not in antithetical roles any
more. Both have changed to the point of sharing the
same traits (the "New I" does the torturing, the monk
feels victimized), so that now it does not make much
difference who is called by what name, or who is in
what position.

Assimilating Projections

When we say that "It feels good" rather than "I
feel good about it," "It feels uncomfortable" rather

than "I feel displeased," "It feels right" rather than "I approve," we are projecting ourselves into "IT." Sometimes this may be a true matter of language or little more than that: perhaps a certain preference to dissimulate our personal involvement, to minimize our assertiveness or mask our responsibility for our reactions. At other times, however, the projection may amount to a complete disowning of our part in the experience: a certain person *is* good—not that we personally like him—or that person *is* bad— not only does he make us feel bad.

Various forms of projection are well documented in the psychological literature. The one that interests us here is the type of projection that psychoanalysis regards as a "defense": the process of attributing to some person or thing in the environment qualities or feelings of our own that we are not willing to recognize as ours. Frequently this amounts to "seeing the mote in someone else's eye rather than the beam in one's own."

To the extent that we disown part of our experience or do not acknowledge some of our traits we do not see reality about us as it is, but distort our perception of reality with the attribution of all that we reject in ourselves. This is particularly true of person-perception (perhaps more so in the measure of our personal involvement with another person). In Gestalt therapy we also treat dream images as projections of ourselves— not onto the real environment but onto the imaginary environment of the dream-state.

Projections constitute an illusion, but also a reality. They are illusory in that they frequently do not belong to the person or thing to which we attribute them (though projection and reality *may* coincide). They are a reality in that they are images of our inner life, and avenues to ourselves.

The main technique for the assimilation of projections is one already discussed—that of *identification* with the projection by means of acting its part.

T.: What do you feel now?

P.: I feel under scrutiny. I don't think you like me.

T.: Be me, for awhile. Imagine yourself in my place and give words to the feelings or thoughts that I may be having.

P.: "She is a bore. I would rather be at home than listen to her. She's just uninteresting and I'm stuck with her because I am supposed to help her."

T.: Please repeat this now as your own statement about yourself and see whether it fits.

P.: I am a bore. I'm uninteresting and I cannot believe that you like me or that you like to give me your attention, since I cannot give you anything worth it. Of course. It is exactly what I think.

In the foregoing example, acting served as a means for the patient to experience the content of her projection, but was not enough. What brought about her contact with her own experience (her self-judgment at being uninteresting) was the suggestion of *reformulating the projected experience as her own*. This is equivalent to the substitution of "I" for "it" and may be done in different ways. Sometimes a question will be sufficient: "Is this your own feeling? Do you recognize this as part of yourself?" and so on. At other times, a complete reformulation of the experience substituting self for other may be necessary. When applied to short statements, the procedure has been called in Gestalt jargon "trying it for size."

P.: I dislike your deviousness. You withdraw and gossip and I never know where you're at.

T.: Try that on for size.

P.: I dislike my deviousness. I withdraw and gossip and people never know where I'm at. Yes, I think that is true.

At other times the assimilation of a projection may be effected by turning an interpersonal dialogue into an intrapersonal one:

P.:   You make me feel uncomfortable, Jane,
        because you look like you are expecting
        something great from me and I am always
        afraid of disappointing you.

T.:   Imagine you are Jane and talk to Henry
        making him feel uncomfortable.

P.:   (Henry) You are such a gifted guy and yet you
        say so many stupidities. Use your talent,
        Henry. You cannot afford being one more
        ordinary guy. You know you can do better.

T.:   OK, now put Henry on that chair and you tell
        him what Jane just told you.

P.:   You're a genius, Henry. You are not living up
        to it. You're wasting your life. You act like one
        of the guys and we know that your potential
        is much greater. You should take yourself more
        seriously and show the world who you are.

T.:   Good. Be the underdog now and answer to
        what you just said.

P.:   Fuck you, man. I'm fed up with trying to be a
        genius just to please you and to be what my
        mother expected of her wonderful little boy.
        I am *me* and that's it. I am here to please myself
        and I don't care a shit about your expectations!

T.:   Go on with the dialogue.

P.:   Careful, Henry. This new philosophy of yours
        sounds very appealing and right but it's only a
        fashion. If you stop listening to me and just
        do what you please, you will just fool around
        for a while and end up feeling empty. You're
        somebody now because I have taken good care
        of you. You have grown so much in these
        years and now you're about to fuck it all up.

As in the illustration above, projections frequently correspond to the aspects of the personality
that we call in Gestalt therapy "topdog" and "underdog." In the latter instance the individual feels
criticized, inadequate in meeting demands, guilty or
ashamed, etc.; in the former instance he stands in
judgment over others and adopts the demanding
role. In both instances, the projection may reveal

what simple introspection or premature intrapersonal encounter would not, and the therapist may
want to spend some time encouraging the expression
of the projections (for instance, by means of making
sounds) and their explicitation or development
before any attempt at reassimilation.

According to Perls, Hefferline, and Goodman,
the neurotic fear of being rejected is a consequence of
projection of the individual's own rejection of others.

> Neurotics talk much of being rejected. This is, for the
> most part, a projection onto others of their own reject-
> ing. What they refuse to feel is their latent disgust with
> what they have incorporated in their own personalities.
> If they did, they would have to vomit up and reject
> many of their "loved" identifications—which were un-
> palatable and hateful at the time when swallowed
> down. Or else they would have to go through the
> laborious process of bringing them up, working them
> through, and then at last assimilating them.

Castration fear, too, of which psychoanalysis has
made so much, Perls, Hefferline, and Goodman interpreted as a projection of aggression:

> The *vagina dentata*, the frequent fantasy of castration
> anxiety, is the man's own unfinished bite projected onto
> the woman. Little can be accomplished in working on
> castration fantasies until dental aggression has been
> remobilized, but once this natural destructiveness has
> been reintegrated into the personality, not only the fear
> of damage to the penis but also the fear of other
> damages—to honor, property, eyesight, etc.—are
> reduced to proper size[1].

As a consequence of disowning both disgust and
aggression—his healthy mechanisms of rejection—
the individual must "swallow down" everything

---

[1] From *Gestalt Therapy: Excitement and Growth in the Human Personality*
by Frederick Perls, Ralph Hefferline, & Paul Goodman, 1992 edition, The
Gestalt Journal Press, Highland, New York. Reprinted with permission.

that the environment "feeds him" whether adequate to his needs or not. The person remains a child at the sucking stage, unable to "chew up" his experiences, bite through obstacles or exercise selectiveness. The consequence of this attitude is the introjection of what may be regarded as psychological foreign bodies. An introject in Gestalt therapy is regarded as an unfinished situation: something incorporated into the personality without proper assimilation, which would entail an action of psychological chewing, analysis, and selective incorporation or rejection of the component parts or aspects of the object. Perls saw a close correspondence between the process of assimilation at the psychological level and at the physiological level of incorporating food. More specifically, he saw a correspondence between fixation at the passive oral stage and the inability to chew properly. Because of this he recommended a number of exercises involving the practice of awareness while eating and the remobilization of oral aggression.

> Because of scheduled feedings and other "scientific practices" applied to you as an infant, the blocking of oral aggression as described above is probably in some degree present in your own case. This condition is the basic prerequisite for tendencies to introject — to swallow down whole what does not belong in your organism. We shall, therefore, attack the problem at the source, namely, the process of eating. The solution involves remobilization of disgust, which is not pleasant and will rouse strong resistances. For once, therefore, in stating the following motor experiment we do not propose as something to try out in a spontaneous fashion to see what happens, but we appeal to your courage and charge you with it as a task.

> During each and every meal, take one bite—remember, just one single bite—and liquefy the food completely by chewing. Do not let one morsel escape destruction, but seek it out with your tongue and bring it into position for further chewing. When you are satisfied that the food has been fully liquefied, drink it down....

...As a functional counterpart of the task of chewing up a single bite of food, give yourself the same training in the intellectual sphere. For example, take a single difficult sentence in a book that is "tough meat," and analyze it; that is, take it apart thoroughly. Get the precise connotation of each word. For the sentence as a whole decide on its clarity or vagueness, its truth or falsity. Make it your own, or else make clear to yourself what part of it you don't understand. Perhaps you have not failed to comprehend, but instead, the sentence isn't comprehensible. Decide this for yourself.

Another profitable experiment, one which makes full use of the functional identity between eating physical food and "stomaching" some interpersonal situation is the following:

When in an impatient mood—angry, upset, resentful—and thus inclined to gulp, apply the aggression in a deliberate attack on some physical food. Take an apple or a tough heel of bread and wreak your vengeance on it. In accordance with your mood, chew as impatiently, hastily, viciously, cruelly as you can. But bite and chew—do not gulp![2]

[2] From *Gestalt Therapy: Excitement and Growth in the Human Personality* by Frederick Perls, Ralph Hefferline, & Paul Goodman, 1992 edition, The Gestalt Journal Press, Highland, New York. Reprinted with permission.

Part III

STRATEGY

Chapter Seven

Strategy as Meta-Technique

The description of techniques that I have presented in the foregoing chapters is to the practice of Gestalt therapy what the bricks are to the house. The various types of brick displayed show a family resemblance or common style that derives from their being conceived as expressions of a single view and they may be seen as parts of a single structure. Of the structure, however, I have said nothing.

Seen from without, the structure of a psychotherapeutic session is determined by the sequence in which the therapist employs the different tools or techniques available to him through inheritance or personal inventiveness. It is probable that, notwithstanding some general validity to every technique, there is also, for every individual at every mo- ment, a particular direction that may be of greater promise—a path of least resistance. Though the therapist evaluates the timeliness or appropriateness of a technique through a combination of intuition and emotional responses to the ongoing encounter in addition to reasoning, I will refer to his choices as strategy. It is certainly at this level of strategy that the therapist's intuition is most decisive, and where his creativity consists precisely in meeting a unique situation with a unique response. The notes of the scale are few, and yet the number of tunes unlimited. The number of good performers, too, is greater than the number of good composers.

As in the more general case of art, the learning of strategy seems to derive mostly from personal experience and from the observation of skillful performance. The background of Perls' California disciples was essentially a combination of personal psychotherapy and observation of the master at work. Of course, in addition to these elements (and of course supervision) it can be helpful not only to observe the therapeutic process but to reflect upon it, and I think that a specially valuable contribution to the understanding of strategy can be access to the retrospective spelling-out, by a therapist, of his interventions. Consequently, I have sought to enrich the transcripts in this section through self-commentary. Except for the comments on the first of these (Len) which I added when I rewrote this book in 1987, these observations were recorded a short time after the sessions themselves (1970) in the course of meetings with a small group of students.

In addition to the sharing and reflection on my therapeutic activity, I have attempted to implement clinical material with some theoretical remarks. In Chapters 8 and 9, I outline two specific strategies which, I believe, constitute an ever-present background for the choices of a therapist. Just as, at the technical level, the Gestalt therapist can emphasize suppression or expression, at the level of strategy, he can require the patient to work against his symptoms (by being direct or truthful for instance), or urge him to "ride with" his symptoms—exaggerate his psychopathology, or brag about it—as an alternative way of understanding, assimilating, and transcending it. This choice involves, in particular, the alternatives of staying in the present or of dealing with the past or the future, and also those of owning or disowning experience. Past and future, as well as the present, have a place in Gestalt therapy, and a "strategy of irresponsibility" along with the pursuit of responsibility—as I will be discussing further.

Chapter Eight

Here and Now with Gerald: An Annotated Case

GERALD: I am producing sinus drainage and I am also producing... I want to know what's *behind* the sinus drainage, what I'm doing to myself. Munson triggered this off on me last night when he said that every symptom or complaint is a brag.[1] So I turned it back on myself, and said "There goes your sinus drainage; what the hell are you bragging about?" The other thing is that I have a stare, and sometimes I try so hard to see that I blind myself,[2] and I'm aware of

---

[1] Here is an issue on which Gestaltists might differ. He is talking about something that is not happening right now, and yet, I think that symptoms are, like dreams, such important cues that no matter whether they belong to the here and now or not, they are a very valuable starting point. I never discourage a person from reporting symptoms at the beginning of a session, in order to be able to choose whether to work with them or not. Though sometimes the symptom may be part of a game that the person is playing ("see all the problems I have," or "pity me"), it may also be that it constitutes material that would not come up otherwise. If dreams, that are not here and now, can be brought into the present and worked with, this can be done with symptoms, too. I generally leave that open, or sometimes request from the patient a statement of what he wants, what he has come for.

[2] Of the first symptom, the sinus drainage, he already has a preconception about: he is bragging. Because Munson said that symptoms involve bragging, or because Fritz may have said so, I think that he is being a "good boy" and feeling that must be true. My symptom reflects something wrong about myself, and I should set it right. It would be a possible line of action to explore this self-improvement zeal, confronting him with what he was doing at the moment. I was more interested in listening further, however, now he goes on with a second symptom: staring.

my throat, kind of dry in back, and I seem to need moisture. I'm aware of my voice getting softer and I am scratching my nose on my right nostril, which makes me get a little analytical about the whole thing. I'm aware of my eyes closing, sighing a little heavily, possibly saying I want to slip away into a kind of sleep or fatigue. I'm aware that you're looking at me quite intently with your right hand on your beard. Again I feel myself trying to stare and I end up not seeing as much of you as I want to see.[3] I'm aware of sucking my lips. I'm aware of wanting to ask you to say something to me, too, by saying "Hey can you tell me anything about what I just said?" with my seductive smile. I don't know if it's really seductive, but some kind of smile, the waving of my hand, the weight of my right arm on my legs, the movements in the wrist, the pulling in of my shoulders, the eye movement downward. Some anxiety about this, there's a slight moisture in the palm of my hand. My voice is getting softer. Licking of the lips again.

I: You feel moisture, several times you've been licking your lips, and there is your sinus drainage.

---

[3] I think it is desirable to have in mind what the alternatives are in the continuum of awareness. There can be focusing on the inner world and upon physical feelings; there is also the possibility of concentrating on the external world — what Fritz called the "outer zone" — and there is the possibility of concentrating on fantasy and thoughts — Fritz's "intermediate zone." I am always suspicious of a person who does only *one* of these, unless something develops that justifies that. Otherwise, he may just be enumerating objects. Then I ask what he is feeling, what his mind is doing, or I may ask him to report actions, what he is doing moment after moment, so as to check whether he is not avoiding an area of experience. If so, then the difficulty will become apparent when he is confronted with the task. Such is not the case here. You can see that he shuttles between inner and outer world. Now, he is again aware of the staring: "I don't see much." I feel that he is *demanding* of himself "I *should* see much more; instead of just staring without seeing, I should be seeing more, myself: I should see much more; instead of just staring without seeing, I should be seeing more."

Experiment a bit with the licking, exaggerate it, see how it feels.[4]

GERALD: I'm aware of the feel of the salt on the hair, the pull on the back of my tongue, some pleasure in it, not licking as much as sticking out my tongue and feeling the pull in the back of my eyes. I feel like I'm just getting to know my lips. And my eyes feel a little freer, right up through the top of the cheek bones.[5]

I: If your tongue could speak to your lips, what would it say?[6]

GERALD: I am Gerald's tongue: Lips, I've missed you. You're always on the outside and I don't get out there very often. I wonder why you're afraid of me, why you keep me closed up so much? What is it about sticking out the tongue, what is it that keeps you from coming between us?[7]

---

[4]Here I made a choice. He seems quite fluid. He speaks of me, he speaks of the movements, he speaks of his feelings, and then I pick one movement, the moistening of his lips, which seems to be relevant, partly because he is doing it, partly because I thought he was not so much in touch with this action as with others, and also because it fits with what he originally reported as a symptom: sinus drainage — a symptom related to the mouth-nose area.

[5]I am struck by the fact that his *eyes* feel freer, while he has only exaggerated the licking of his *lips*. There was a forcefulness to his licking movement, which may account for the effect on his eyes. The two original symptoms were sinus drainage and staring, and from this, they seem to be related somehow. Also, I have the feeling that in doing intentionally what he was doing all the time naturally (something which was in the nature of a little symptom) he is satisfying a healthy urge. In other words, there is an organismic, corrective tendency behind his lip motion. It fulfills some need, whether symbolic or real.

[6]I first pointed out the symptom to him. Then I asked him to repeat the movement, which he did, exaggerating, as well. Now I am asking him to explicate it. The importance of verbalizing is not in the outcome of words, but, in order to translate from body language to verbal language, he must get more in touch with himself. When we try to express something, we realize to what extent we understand or not.

[7]The content of this has been, so far, a feeling of loneliness, a feeling of being kept out and wanting to be let in, and yearning for affection: a standard pattern, in psychoanalytic terms. The subject is in contact with his need, which he perceives in oral terms.

Why? I feel that I don't want to come out any more. I feel closed in on the bottom and I'm so tired I don't feel like coming up to the top. I just get tired of trying to come up because you just keep closing the entrance.

I: Could you repeat the same thing as Gerald, imagining that you are expressing these feelings about you?[8]

GERALD: I want to come out. I want to come between you. I've missed you. I'm tired of trying to come out when you're keeping me closed in. I can't remember what else I said.

I: You said you feel tired; you said something about getting sleepy, I think.

GERALD: Yes. Heavy eyelids, and a pulling down. I want to fall asleep. I want to withdraw.

I: I'd like you to go all the way. Go on and withdraw. Close your eyes. Let yourself withdraw.

GERALD: It makes me anxious. I feel perspiration.[9] I feel grinding my teeth, biting, not wanting to let go.[10] Coming back slightly. Grin and bear it.

---

[8]Now, I am asking him to *assimilate* the experience, which he has been projecting. What he has reported was his tongue's experience, not "his". Yet, most likely, *he* feels closed-in, he feels a yearning to come out and meet somebody or something. The prop of introducing a grammatical change and repeating his tongue's statement as his own may serve as a means for him to discover whether they are truly his feelings.

[9]I think this is interesting. As soon as he withdraws from communication, he gets anxious and perspires. My impression is that his withdrawal is for him anti-life: is a symptom; that is where he betrays his own deeper impulse, his organismic needs, his need for life, his truth: he is unfaithful to himself in the moment of withdrawing, and he feels immediately the signs of lack of life—anxiety. He makes a bad choice, and he gets an extra symptom, a punishment in terms of life. Life does not let you fool around with your nature.

[10]I am tempted to make a psychoanalytic interpretation here. He can't suck, he can't reach out, he doesn't allow for a natural train of behavior to proceed, and then, he needs to bite. In strict psychoanalytic terms, the biting would be understood as oral aggression, taking the place of earlier oral receptivity. It can also be true in a very general sense that if you block an impulse, aggression takes place as a corrective mechanism: biting to right what is wrong.

I: Go with this a little bit more, and see where it takes you.[11]

GERALD: (After a silent period, with eyes closed) I felt myself wanting to smash, and I felt myself warding off blows. I am holding myself up. (As though coming back to "reality" after a measure of trance): I thought I was warding off blows. And then abdicating, submitting to it. Still refusing to be pounded into the ground. And I hear some hurt in my voice. And I was aware that there was a release, a discharge.

I: I see a lot of contrast between your expression, your movements and what you say *now*, and your ordinary style. There is in your usual voice and attitude a lot of good-boyishness and concern about saying the right thing. Possibly this wanting to smash and ward off blows is the opposite that wants to come out. Maybe you could find some way of adding sounds now to this thing, bringing it more into your throat. And also express this attitude, relating— maybe with just gestures and sounds; go to somebody else.

GERALD: I'm afraid of hurting someone. I pulled back because I thought I wanted to ask permission to hurt. But I don't know that I would hurt them. But I found myself pulling back when I said it. I pulled back. (sounds) Gagged. Nauseous. Something here. Flashing heat. Difficulty in swallowing. Warmth. Some sudden flushes of some kind.

I: When you come up with anger, you make yourself feel sick.

GERALD: Gags me.

---

[11]Again, I do not want to interpret, so I tell him to exaggerate, to do again with more forcefulness *what he has been doing* (i.e. biting) so that if there is any truth to what I am imagining, this truth may have an opportunity of becoming apparent for itself. I am asking him to *exaggerate* the biting.

I: You have kept your eyes closed. Let's move one step further into communication and try doing it with eyes open. Face the person you're doing it to.[12]

GERALD: Don't! You hit me and I'll hit back. (sounds)

I: There's no doubt, there's a lot of strength in that side of you. Now can you think of somebody who's being a target for these feelings at this point in your life?

GERALD: I'm aware of my hand on my throat like I want to choke myself. I'm getting an image of my mother, but it's not a visual image, it's just the word "mother".[13] And I want... I don't want to see it. My eyes are closed. And it's painful now, very hard. I'm looking at something ugly, something I don't like, something I don't understand. And I don't want to see it.

---

[12]This is still another step in the direction of a more complete expression: first he exaggerated, then he made sounds, but then closed his eyes. People will frequently close their eyes in moments of unusual intimacy. What we are after, however, is intimacy with others. Now, in asking him to do the same with his eyes open, I am asking him to bring his feeling into his relationship with the world. Even if he cannot still direct his feeling at others, he must be free to experience what he is experiencing in the face of others; to take responsibility for his feeling in spite of the presence of others, rather than as a private act. I am trying to make him feel more at home with what he was expressing in his gestures and sounds. My assumption is that his good- boy role is closely related to his social behavior, and his awareness of others, whereas he allows his aggression and his bad-boy pattern to appear only in the form of physical sensations, or when he is by himself in privacy.

[13]My first observation of him was a good-boyishness in the way he reported his symptom; then, his way of doing the continuum of awareness was fluent, but there was an eagerness to *produce* and do what is right. I never mentioned this at the time. I did not find the attitude clear-cut enough to reflect profitably while it was happening, and had another choice. Now, I see that, for the first time, he is out of that; his voice sounds different, and his whole style is different now, so he can probably sense that to be a distance from his earlier role, and see it in retrospect. I mention, now, what I see, just in case it falls into receptive ground. I don't push him into talking about it, but again, I ask him to develop further his aggressive movements by exaggeration.

I: Now do the same gestures you were doing to this ugly something. You feel that you are communicating with this something ugly by doing this warding off? (sounds)

GERALD: I feel very warm, sweaty, I feel like I want to look again. I was momentarily concerned with the fact that it was unfinished on my left, and feminine, side. And it was more of that which I was undoubtedly pushing away, and I'm still doing it.

I: Did you have an image of what you were pushing away?

GERALD: I have a word again, "mother", but no image.

I: See if you can become that which you were pushing away. See if you can experience yourself as being pushed out. See if you can describe yourself, and see if this image will take on some shape.

GERALD: Verbally or non-verbally?[14]

I: Verbally.

GERALD: I feel more comfortable about this. I want to. I need you. I need to lean on you. Don't injure me. I have been injured. This sort of thing.

And then if I were doing the pushing away it would be in great tears, bursts of hurt.

I: Be hurt and be her.

GERALD: There's some shame there, the lowering of the head, the lowering of the eyes.

I: Can you give more verbal expression to the shame?

---

[14]What is clear is that whatever it was that he was expressing, it was an expression that satisfied him. He feels better after doing it. He is apparently expressing something that is not part of his habitual self; something that he has been suppressing. And even now, he feels unfinished. He is still not sure of who this person is, aside from a vague association with his mother. Instead of pursuing the question intellectually, I am trying to facilitate his awareness of the mother by asking him to become it; that entity with a vague mother-quality. I am choosing not to direct him to encounter his mother specifically, for, after all, what he is pushing away is presumably not mother, but a part of himself, the imprint of his mother in his own personality.

GERALD: I'm ashamed that you have seen me weak. I'm ashamed that I can't cope with all your catastrophes that have befallen me and which have gotten transferred to you. I'm ashamed that I don't understand myself. I'm ashamed that I can't control more of the way we appear to others. It was not our intention. I would not have chosen these events. For us.

I: Who's we?

GERALD: My mother. And me.

I: Can you continue this dialogue with her?

GERALD: (as self) I understand that. Can't you see that I understand? My sinus! It's internal crying! It's a waterfall or something! What do I want to cry out?

I: See if you can give words to your crying without suppressing your crying.[15]

GERALD: My right arm is trembling. I see you hurting each other. I see you destroying each other. I see this is all so unnecessary. I see all these good intentions and I see so little know-how. I see you defeating the very ends you are trying to achieve. I don't understand. I feel helpless, because I, too, have these good intentions, these good desires, and I feel helpless because I don't know what to do about them. Leave each other alone. Leave me alone. Leave her alone. Leave him alone.

I: Now try directing this statement to your mother.

GERALD: I shook my head. I'm negating her or something. I don't know. Like I'm trying to rattle something from up here down to here. As though I

---

[15]I am afraid that whatever instruction I give might interfere with his experience. I don't want to interrupt what he is doing. On the other hand, I am afraid if I do not push him in the direction in which he is going, he may stop himself. So I compromise by saying "give words to your crying, without stopping crying." I want to make sure that he does not act as such a "good patient" that he loses contact with his feelings in order to comply with the instructions.

could get rid of a block across here. There's a block, and I thought maybe if I could shake my head hard enough, it would rattle down. Something would get through the block.

I: You look disgusted.

GERALD: I am. Yes. I felt hopeless at that going, so with that feeling of helplessness I felt rejected. Go away. You make me feel helpless.

I: A while ago you were expressing with your body, and then you turned to your mother. Can you imagine doing this to her, physically and with these non-verbal sounds? But this time put it together with your words. Say something like "Leave me alone." Only instead of just saying the words, do it with the warding off gestures; put the words together with your body.

GERALD: I'm experiencing a great dryness. I experience myself becoming somewhat intellectual, saying that's a trite emotion. I saw Carol do that last night. I judge myself. I judge my judging. I'm trying to go with it. Also I need moisture. I need air. Just to do something to get this dryness out of my throat. I'm aware that I don't want to see. My eyes are closed again. They are very tight. Short breath. My right arm... a pulling back. More dryness. More dryness. I can't swallow it. I can't make an opening big enough. The tongue won't come out far enough to make the opening in the back of my throat big enough.

I: Enough for what?

GERALD: I don't know.

I: You feel you're swallowing something? You had to swallow something?

GERALD: No. I feel like I have to. And I can't make the opening big enough. Now who's telling me what to swallow, and who's telling me you have to swallow it?

I: I now understand a bit more your having to gag. I want you to come back to this movement you

were doing before, anger and warding off, but directing it toward your mother.

GERALD: The dryness is coming back. It went
away for a while. Momentarily. It went away and
now it's come back.

I: It's the second time I suggest this, and on both
occasions, you have generated symptoms.[16]

GERALD: I guess I know I'm producing my own
symptoms. You're telling me something about how
I'm doing it. And I don't want to... and yet I do
because I'm here. I have something in my mouth
now. I mean the expression, I feel here, I'm not quite
sure what that means. Mother, if you were here, and
I said to you, did to you, what I did, I'd say "Mother,
stop your goddamn whining! Stop being hurt. So
much, so easily. Stop swallowing your pride, stop
swallowing the world, saying it's your fault. Come
down off the cross. Stop hurting other people. Stop
being so damn full of good intentions. Stop smother-
ing. Stop being so damn strong. Stop sucking us in.
Stop being so strong. Even in your weakness, strong.
You become the dominator in the family. You can
take center stage even when you're suffering
catastrophe. Stop being so concerned with my welfare. Stop demanding."

I: What do you feel?

GERALD: Some relief.

I: How do you sound?[17]

GERALD: Softer than anger. I don't think I felt
apology. It was more like... this is very much of what
I was aware of... grinding the palms of my hands into

---

[16]He has been holding back from this last step, and the session has
been at a standstill for a while. Before somebody can express objections, he has to become aware that there are objections. I only right
now mentioned this to him, mentioned his reluctance. My feeling is
that more would have been premature.

[17]I ask him how he feels and sounds, hoping that he would become
aware of his control, which has become more and more evident in his
speech and diminishing assertiveness of his voice.

the top of the chair, so I guess I was being the controlled, educated man. Making his point because, if I were addressing my mother, I'd say, "You've been hurt enough. I think I have to tell you this or someone does. I haven't been able to get through to you. And this was a way of grinding, trying to get through where I have not been getting through before." But it was still, I was still trying to be gentle enough.

I: Could you be less controlled and polite?[18] Try repeating some of the things you said, this time letting go more.

GERALD: It will add hurt to more hurt, and my throat is drying up again. I can't swallow that.

I: (again in reference to symptom generation) It's systematic.

GERALD: I can't swallow that, but I don't want to add more hurt to hurt.

I: You're just hurting your own mechanism, going against your limits.

GERALD: Maybe you're right. I feel like I need a hook.

I: Use the repetitive statement, "Don't smother me," or one of the statements you already made. And repeat it, but with gestures, with movements.[19]

---

[18]Now the situation is different. He has already become aware of his control, so now I am authorized to say "Can you become less controlled?" I can ask him to modify what he is well aware of doing.

[19]I am suggesting that he use the repetitive statement as a hook on which to hang the nonverbal affect. As we already know, he can express his feeling quite well in gestures and sounds, and he can also be verbally expressive. In no moment has he been expressing both verbally and nonverbally at the same time. When he uses words, he turns off his physical spontaneity. His talking and feeling selves are not united. So I am giving him already a set of things from which he can pick, asking him to pick a statement, and stay with it; which is not like telling him to express *more*. He has nothing to develop. His only task is integration: doing both at the same time, being in touch with both the verbal and the nonverbal elements in the pattern.

GERALD: Don't smother me! Don't keep insisting on all those tactics! Stop! Stop! Stop! Stop! Stop! What's the use of talking to her? I can't get through to her. I want to give up. Bury my head between my eyes. Rest a while. Maybe come off and try again some other time.

I: This is the same as you were experiencing before with your sleep and the tongue being closed in. Giving up.

GERALD: Yes. I felt like I wanted to sleep.

I: Can you withdraw again?

GERALD: I feel like I'm being beaten in this position. I had an image of flagellation on my back. And I wanted to come out. But I didn't want to come out fighting. I'm aware now that I'm saying "Pull me out. Somebody, pull me out." I'm aware that I'm supporting myself here, so I'm saying, "I don't want you to do all the work, but go first. Maybe you know a way of getting through that I don't, to stop the hurt. Some dryness here. I didn't want to stay there. But you see, I'm out.

I: My impression is that you wish that you get through, not to your mother, but to yourself. I don't believe there is an alternative to accepting.

GERALD: Accepting what?

I: This feeling that you convey with your body. From all that you have indicated, your mother and you doing this (demonstrates) choking, and squeezing, I don't think you have any other reaction but aggression.

GERALD: Let me see if I've understood what you've said. You see this is my jaw, my grinding of the teeth, and I don't accept that in myself.

I: You alternate between withdrawing and biting, and you don't get away. These are the two alternatives. The first time you withdrew, you ended up with (demonstrates biting attitude).

GERALD: Yes.

I: If you go all the way with this (gesture of aggression of biting) you end up withdrawing. You're not free in this motion.

GERALD: I see myself as a pendulum with no middle point.

I: Probably you would have a middle point if you had end points. If you could go all the way in your anger, but every time, for instance, that you entertain the thought of getting angry with your mother, your dryness comes back. And you withdraw.

GERALD: Yes.

I: So I still see you have to loosen up a little more.

GERALD: Now I'm thinking my father was a violent man.

I: You don't want to be like him.

GERALD: Not in that aspect. Because he did violent things with pokers and brooms. Intellectually I can say yes, aggression is different from anger and anger is different from violence, but I don't know where I would draw the line. I think it came out when I came to you and I said, "I don't want to because I would hurt you, or something like that."

MAN: You said, "If you hit me, I'll hit you back."

GERALD: Is that what I said? What did I say to you, Claudio? I thought I said to someone, I guess I said it to myself, "I don't want to add hurt to hurt."

WOMAN: "I don't want to hurt you any more." So you mean there are only two choices — you either become violent, crazy like your father, or you have to choke and have the tears dripping down. Those are the only two choices.

MAN: I'd be willing to risk a physical encounter.

GERALD: I feel like now I have to be goaded. I have got some head stuff going here.

I: I distrust your fear of hurting. I think the limits you are setting to yourself gives . . .

GERALD: Gives me more power than I have.

I: In order not to hurt, you have to let yourself be choked.

GERALD: How do I know that, though?

I: Experimenting. What is it like to lose control for a while? Finding out. Whether you can survive or not. Or how horrible it is. I don't know which is the case. I was just wanting to support your inspiration to get into a physical fight with him, and I suggest you find out how that feels.

GERALD: I'd have to try it. I don't know how it would feel.

I: Would this be a new experience to you?

GERALD: No, I've done push-downs before. I went for a man's throat once. And what delighted me is that . . . hey, it just occurred to me that what I did was to go for the throat. And the interesting part of it is that once I was out of control I found that he could carry me back. We had set some kind of limits non-verbally, and then he gave me something. He said, "You're beautiful when you're angry." So I don't know. I'm a little afraid of you. I think you're bigger than I am, outweigh me.

MAN: I suspect you probably are stronger than me. I don't think that's important. Do you want to start by grappling? What are you feeling?

GERALD: When you asked me that, a feeling was to let me pound on your palms to begin with. (noise)

MAN: You can't get me down!

GERALD: You're down! You're down!

MAN: Oh yeah?

GERALD: You're down! (panting) I very much felt you give up when I started to fight back. Did you hold back?

MAN: You were very strong as long as I was just protecting myself.

GERALD: Right.

MAN: When I started to wrestle, I felt all the fight go out.

GERALD: So I'm not afraid of hurting you. I'm afraid of something else. I'm afraid of being hurt.

When you had me down it was partly physical exhaustion. What was the surprise to me was that I was still biting. And I didn't have any alternative. So the feeling of helplessness returned. Okay, I don't know any other wrestling ploys.

MAN: Would you try to keep me down?

GERALD: Try to keep you down?

MAN: Well, just try to feel what it is to try to keep me down. (wrestling noises) Startling! (laughter)

GERALD: I wonder what the bite means?

MAN: The bite? I perceived it as a kiss.

GERALD: Yeah. I thought it was something else before. When I looked down at your face and you began biting and growling back, you . . .

MAN: Once again, I feel that you have a lot of strength that you haven't yet been able to use, that I haven't yet experienced being used against me. See, even in the holding down I was acting being unable to get up. Really all I had to do was to toss you over. You have all this muscle development which is just tense, one muscle tensed against another. I've never experienced the real strength you should have the use of — from looking at you.

GERALD: I agree . . . Because it came out as a slight headache at one point.

MAN: You turned it in on yourself.

GERALD: Yeah. What to do with it all now.

I: Where are you now?

GERALD: Experiencing various parts of my body. Feeling sweat coming off my forehead, my hands and my hair. The breathing in the throat which seems to be fairly open. Slight moisture on the lips. Kind of something's been taken away. Something's been loosened in here. Try to get some breath or come to a different rate of breathing.

MAN: Could you do the arm wrestling? It's just a simple contest of strength with no hurt involved.

GERALD: What do you think it could bring out?

I: You turn off immediately when you . . . well, the first time you disconnected was when you felt you were losing. All this movement against and away from, all has something to do with giving up. Hopelessness: Now you don't know what you will gain...

GERALD: That's pretty typical. I will push up to a point and then I'll abdicate. I don't know why I won't continue the fight, or don't continue the fight. That's why I suspected the possibility of hurt might have something to do with it. It sounds like I'm saying I've been hurt enough. I don't want to get hurt again.

I: So you might explore this with something where you can't get hurt.

GERALD: Now or later?

MAN: Now.

GERALD: Okay. You have to give me orders, don't give up, when I'm giving up. (laughter)

MAN: I might have to give myself orders at the same time.

GERALD: I'm going in with the feeling of fatigue right now.

MAN: Okay, you ready to lose? (wrestling noises)

GROUP: There you really did it. You didn't let him get up again.

GERALD: You see, there's the trouble, I really am strong. (laughter) I'm not going to lose again. I have more strength than the doctor realizes. (wrestling again)

MAN: Again, the same thing. You didn't give up. You're very different than you were before.

GERALD: I feel good. I feel like a dog that's been let out for a run.

WOMAN: I have an urge to have a contest with you on which of us can play the most hopeless. I can be more hopeless than you can.

GERALD: I don't think there is any wrap-up needed.

Chapter Nine

Psychological Judo

As I have stated in Chapter 2, the way of Gestalt therapy is frequently that of enforcing the therapeutic ideal (of authenticity and present-centeredness) and, rather than working towards a future fulfillment, pushing to bring about a healthy attitude in the moment through the confrontation of "games" and evasions. The way towards being genuine, seeking to be genuine—"deciding to be 'straight', quitting the bullshit"—is being genuine in this instant. The way towards standing for ourselves is taking the responsibility for our present actions and omissions. The way toward organismic self-regulation is letting go of the armor of conditioned personality this very moment.

This approach, however, is only one half of Gestalt therapy. We might call it "the direct way." In practice, many of the therapist's indications point in an opposite direction: he invites the patient, not to be genuine, but to exaggerate his phoniness; instead of encouraging his spontaneous expression, he may ask him to identify with his superego, or to play-act and put his whole heart into producing self-criticism, making demands upon himself; or to inhibit, criticize or sabotage himself. Instead of urging the patient to minimize his computing and fantasizing activity, the therapist may well ask him to follow his inclination to fantasize—much as in Desoille's guided daydream—or to preach, or to lecture. More generally speaking, the therapist will suggest to the patient that he exaggerate and take sides with his psychopathology, his avoidances, all the tendencies in him that conflict with the therapeutic ideal.

This attitude of siding with the symptoms might be summarized in William Blake's statement: "If the fool would persist in his folly he would become wise." Perls sometimes stated the principle entailed in such strategy as one of absolute validity: You never overcome anything by resisting it. You only can overcome anything by going deeper into it. If you are spiteful, be more spiteful. If you are performing, increase the performance. Whatever it is, if you go deeply enough into it, then it will disappear; it will be assimilated. Any resistance is not good. You have to go full into it—swing with it. Swing with your pain, your restlessness, whatever is there. Use your spite. Use your environment. Use all that you fight and disown. So, boast about it! Boast about what a great saboteur you are. If you were in the resistance movement in the last war, you would probably be a hero.

The principle may be regarded as similar to that by which the Judo or Tai Chi Chuan fighter manages to defeat the enemy without opposing him, but by deflecting his force or pulling him further along in the direction of his movements. Just as the fighter can be strong in his gentleness because he uses his opponent's strength rather than neutralizes it, the Gestalt therapist (or patient) may use the energy locked up in the form of symptoms or resistances by merely stimulating its expression and/or gently guiding its course, until there typically takes place a transmutation of neurotic into healthy emotionality with the character of an exorcism.

I am not sure that "you can *never* overcome *anything* by resisting it." I believe that much of Gestalt therapy can be seen as a *training* situation in which we resist the temptations to avoid, pretend, calculate, and so on, and in this process learn to feel comfortable without the crutches that have become part of our "personality." In other words, I believe that we are able to resist our deviances *to some extent*—and fruitfully. Each measure of success in this direction institutes a reliving and an emotional corrective experience. The indirect or roundabout way, however—the strategy of riding *with* the symptom rather than struggling against it—comes in at the point when we have reached our personal limit. I think that more effective Gestalt therapists know this implicitly and alternate between the direct way and the alternative or "opposite" way (opposite to the practice of the healthy attitude in that it entails a temporary surrender to what appears as opposite to ourselves). The therapist will typically stimulate the person to confront the challenge of the direct way, will regard his failures at this task as cues, and then proceed to work upon these cues by means of amplification, explication, development and identification. Much of the effectiveness of a Gestalt therapist, I think, rests on the ability to perceive neurotic character, to have a clear eye for deviations from the healthy self-aware and spontaneous state. Aided by his good nose for the fishy, the therapist suggests or directs the patient to become his opposite—what seemed furthest from the over-developed traits. In the strategy which pervades Gestalt practice, the therapist is leading the patient through a process similar to that through which a child that is learning to sit on a chair needs to discover that he can sit only by giving his back to the chair, not by moving towards it.

While this is a discovery that many make at a certain point in a typical session, a spectator may not share the insight. The patient discovers that his resentment was a diluted and devious form of healthy aggression, for instance, but this spectator may be frightened by what he sees as destructive loss of control; what the patient experiences as a rewarding and cleansing explosion of grief, brought about by the exaggeration of emptiness, the observer without familiarity with Gestalt may fear that the therapist, by urging on the patient's symptoms, may lead him to suicide. The therapist's ability to bring a patient to the turning point where his disowned destructive energies become *his own* purified strength will depend, in large measure, not upon technique alone, but on his *experiential knowledge that this is possible*, and in the consequent sense of *trust* in the constructive drives of which pathological manifestations are a distortion brought about by unhealthy denial and which can heal by itself in the presence of awareness. Such trust will enable him to pursue a given course of action to an effective degree, in spite of the patient's chaos, rage, or loss of control—and will be important, too, in eliciting the necessary trust in the patient for him to let go.

The fact that both the direct way and the opposite have validity presents the therapist with a choice at practically every step in a session. If the patient is not being direct, the therapist may either ask him to be so, or to exaggerate his indirectness; if the patient is avoiding contact, the therapist may ask him either to stop avoiding, or to exaggerate his avoidance. Here is an example, from a session of mine with Jim Simkin:

"I'm looking at the rug. Now I look at the ceiling. Now I am looking at the spot slightly above your head. And now at your feet. I'm beginning to feel at ease. I look at the rug again. It is very beautiful, with the sun's reflection on it. I hear a bird outside. I see the door. I'm looking between you both. I see the shape of the space between your heads and necks. I'm enjoying this very much—I feel so free not to look at you! All life long I was feeling guilty of withdrawing, and now I am giving myself permission to withdraw under the gaze of all of you. And I feel so warm towards all of you for letting me have this freedom! I don't want to look at you yet, and still I am beginning to love you!"

An instance of the indirect way that has not been pointed out and yet I suppose is implicitly perceived by many, is what I call the "strategy of irresponsibility." While the goal of Gestalt therapy is to bring the patient to a point where he may "stand behind" his actions and feelings rather than disown them, there are moments in the process which we can understand as a trick by which the therapist transitorily supports the patient's illusion of irresponsibility or encourages it. I think that this idea can be best understood if we first consider not Gestalt therapy but hypnotherapy. In deep hypnotic trance the therapist commonly (though implicitly) invites the patient to act upon the assumption: "This is not myself." "Whatever I say or do will not be my responsibility any longer, and therefore I am not responsible for it. From now onwards I will be in a 'trance,' and my unconscious, not me, will emerge. I don't know, and will not know what I feel or express while asleep. The therapist and myself know that all that will be my alter ego—not my self. He will not blame me for processes that are beyond my knowledge and control." The consequence of this attitude is that the person in the hypnotic condition may recall events too painful for "him" to recall, express feelings that "he" would have no courage to express, perceive things in a way that "he" was not open to, in his fear that "his" present views might have to change. Once he has experienced all this, however, he frequently discovers that all these feelings, views, memories, etc., which he thought intolerable or unbearable are something that he can easily bear. The trance state has had the function of a rehearsal before a responsible confrontation, or a screen upon which to project certain experiences before acknowledging them fully or rejecting them once more. Through discrimination, the patient finally achieves integration. By means of the illusion of irresponsibility, he has become more able to accept his reality and be responsible for himself.

What is true of the hypnotic state is also true of projections, and of the deliberate projective identification involved in the dramatization of expressive behavior. I suspect that even some of the explosive behavior that takes place when Gestalt therapy patients are acting out their conflicts may derive its intensity from the fact that they have entered a mild hypnotic trance in which they temporarily abandon the ordinary psychological center of gravity, their habitual role, and the corresponding control.

One instance in which the therapist protects the patient's psychological security by encouraging his projection is that in which he asks the patient to complete in fantasy an unfinished dream.

When a therapist does so, he is relying on the fact that the individual, in his wakeful state, may be able to "dream" what in the true dream—because of the sense of reality of dreams—was to him unbearable. The patient knows that at any point along his fantasy: "This is just a fantasy," and, like the spectator of a drama who knows his place in the audience, he is able to perceive and appreciate more than if he were totally involved. Once the fantasy is completed, however, the therapist will take him out of the spectator role, so that he may now actually experience the action (mostly through enacting) as his own.

The same may be said of interpersonal projections. In asking a person to share his perception of others and the feelings that he imagines others have toward him, he may be, in a measure, giving shape to aspects of himself projected onto others. While he is encouraged to speak of "them," he will be speaking of "I" and the psychological richness of his statements about himself may be proportional to his lack of awareness that he is doing this. Once he has described the "others," however, he has taken the first step to discovering that his description is a portion of himself.

One more example is that of non-verbal expression. A person may say in movements, melody, or gibberish something that he or she does not say in ordinary speech, precisely because he does not know well what he is saying. The censorship mechanism in us is well developed with regard to that which we can conceptualize and label, but our physical expression flows faster than our awareness of what we are conveying. After an action is completed, however, the meaning—part of the person's alter ego—may be brought into awareness, and the individual may assume responsibility for what he was hitherto only allowing himself to express as "not-self," or under the appearance of meaninglessness.

I think that the request of explication before total identification with an action or part of the body is an important step precisely because an individual may be more fluent before he realizes the total import of what he is saying:

T.: What would your left hand tell your right hand if it could speak?

P.: I am caressing you, I am comforting you...

T.: And what does your right hand reply?

P.: I like to be comforted. Please go on. I would feel very lonely without you.

T.: Now put Betty on that chair and tell her the same thing.

P.: I like to be comforted. I would feel very lonely without you, Betty. (Sobs) I must be nice to myself so I can forget that nobody else loves me.

What the therapist does in instances such as the one above is going along with the person's original estrangement from his act, so that "his hand" appears to do something by itself, not her.

Perhaps the most clear-cut instance of irresponsibility as a technique in Gestalt therapy is to be seen in some instances of acting. The individual, in acting, experiences himself as "merely" playing a role, he is "just acting," and this is

precisely what gives him the sense of freedom he
may need in order to express certain feelings. In the
process of expressing them, however, he discovers
that these feelings are his own.

> T.: Express your anger towards us.
> P.: That would only be artificial. I have no anger
>   towards anybody here.
> T.: Just pretend you are angry.
> P.: Well, I will pretend. I hate your guts, Mark, you
>   have been getting in my way all week. I don't like
>   the way you compete with me, and I am bothered
>   by you trying to seduce Linda. I am not your
>   friend any more since then. And I am not
>   pretending! I mean this!!

Because of the dual nature of the play-acting
situation—which is at the same time a deliberate
make-believe and an act of expression—the wording
with which the task is introduced may be very important. Sometimes, with the intention of bypassing
the individual's defensiveness, the therapist may un-
derline the "as if" character of the task at hand, and
postpone the work of assimilation. Perls frequently
used the expression "be phony," or "ham it up."

Parallel to the alternative strategies of promoting
responsibility vs. temporary irresponsibility or those of
directness vs. indirectness is the alternative open to the
therapist between the choice of actuality and the choice
of dealing with fantasy, the choice of attending to the
present (which is directly experienced) or to memories,
fantasies and anticipations.

From what I have said on present-centeredness
in Gestalt therapy, it would seem that the only technical response to the patient's production of
memories or plans is bringing him back to his present
experience. This is not so; in every deviation from the
ideal, Gestalt therapy is characterized as much for the
golden rule it perceives as the goal of life as by its
emphatic reversal of it. Wherever he chooses to "ride
with the patient's shift of focus to past or future," the

therapist seems to be implementing a strategy of: "When you remember, remember wholeheartedly by being absorbed in *memories* of the experience of your reveries; when you rehearse, rehearse fully even if it means suffering the perspective of your catastrophic expectations."

Given the importance of theories and anticipations in psychotherapy, I will devote the following two sections of this chapter to the specific issues of dealing with the past and with the future.

Returning to the Past

Our memories are *of* the past, but not *in* the past. Remembering is an activity in which we engage now, and one may be differently motivated according to the occasion. We may hang on to a memory for comfort, or cultivate a childish image of ourselves (and the corresponding childish attitudes) for fear of coping with the world in other terms. We may return to the past again and again, wanting to alter or to complete a situation that remained unfinished. We may be involved in understanding our past because we adhere to the psychoanalytic faith that tells us that such activity will change our present.

The Gestalt therapist often has the choice of inviting the patient to deepen his contact with his memories or of inviting him to let go of the past. Sometimes he will do both: ride along with the patient's spontaneous inclination to dwell in reminiscence, and once the tendency has been truly fulfilled in him (as not often happens in habitual remembrance), he will ask him to leave the past behind.

As in the case of dreams and fantasies of the future, the Gestalt approach to the past is through what I have proposed to call presentification.[1] By means of acting, the patient places himself once more

[1] I was pleased that Fritz adopted the term from my Festschrift paper.

in a situation the meaning of which haunts him, and deals with it as if it were the present. The therapist can help him toward being open and aware with regard to this imaginary situation just as he does when the patient is dealing with the real situation of the moment.

The acting out of past events is not new in psychotherapy. Reliving is spontaneous in the dream state and sometimes in hypnosis, and might be conceived as an instinctoid attempt at psychological restoration. Deliberately evoked reliving of childhood scenes or traumatic events in adult life is attempted in hypnotherapy, in narcohypnotic techniques, and in conjunction with other facilitating drugs, such as amphetamines, barbiturates, MDA, and the hallucinogens. Aside from hypnotic or pharmacologically induced states, every cathartic experience related to the communication of past events in psychotherapy entails some amount of reliving—and we might even say that all memory does up to a point.

In spite of the unavoidable observation, in psychoanalysis, that therapeutic effect of reminiscing parallels the degree of affective recall, and that this is in turn a concomitant of the degree of reliving (i.e., participation) as opposed to recalling, an obvious practical step toward maximization of effect was not taken in psychoanalysis: that of dramatization as a means of supporting feeling awareness—to relive deliberately, through role-playing, episodes of the past.

Fritz was influenced in this not only by his experience in drama and awareness of Moreno's work, but by the basic technique of Ron Hubbard's dianetics (as is clear from his preface to Dr. Winter's report on dianetics[2]). As described in Hubbard's volume, his technique of "returning" is a practice that involves recourse amounting to a training of sensory and affective recall in contrast to purely intellectual, abstract memory. To "be" the child again,

---

[2] Winter, J.A., *A Doctor's Report on Dianetics* (New York: Julian Press, 1951).

in such and such a situation of the past, and tell Daddy what failed to be said to him in reality, can be impressively more effective than pure description and reflection upon the remembered event.

To the technique of returning, however, Gestalt therapy adds two new elements: the technique of identification with significant others in the past, and the emphasis on the motor aspects of acting, beyond merely subjective identification.

The rationale for acting the part of others is that "others" in "reality" as in dreams, are regarded, to an extent, as our own projections. This is truest when it is the case of our childhood memories and parental images—as psychoanalytic literature has amply evidenced.

The importance of literally going through the motions of the recollected scene might be understood in terms of the close connection that exists between action and affect, and also in terms of the principle of completing actions, a principle that abstract recall satisfies only partially.

As important as the two foregoing technical points, however, is a point in strategy: when does the therapist invite the patient to dwell in the past rather than the present?

The answer may be expressed in this way, among others: when he sees that the patient's past is in his present, and that images of the past flow organically from the unfolding of the patient's present experience. When a patient feels ashamed of having said "something wrong," as she used to feel when her older sister ridiculed her, for instance, we may say in a very real sense that the patient is carrying her ridiculing sister with her as a foreign body in her psyche—an introject. If this is so, there is no need to embark on a childhood memory safari. By attending to the person's present experiences and concerns, all the past that lives in the present will naturally become explicit as such. In this, the significant past may be treated as a dream is treated. A dream is highly significant because it is natural. The activity of the dreamer constitutes a selection of what is significant among residues of experience precisely because "he" is not "selecting." In the same manner, the most significant reminiscences occur not when a person sets out to remember, but when his memories well up uninvited.

I witnessed a significant emergence of past experience in a session with a woman whose interest in therapy was that it might help her stop picking her fingers. Impressed by the self-reproach implied in this concern of hers, I asked her to scold herself and voice her objections to finger-picking.

"It is not mature," she said. "It is not pretty. Others don't like it. It is silly. You should have control over your actions. It is like masturbation."

Switching to the role of her own underdog, she replied, "I want to do so. They are my fingers, and I am bored. I get bored in meetings, or when I cook, and then I like to pick my fingers." Then she explained that before picking her fingers she used to chew them.

I thought that amplification might reveal more of the experience involved in the symptom, and asked her to extend the action to her whole hand. From picking she gradually shifted to massaging her fingers and hand, but she felt that this was less, not more satisfactory. The best was to pick the tips of her fingers, which were most sensitive. And then came a eureka: "I want to feel!"

Her picking her fingers and her struggle against it were the battlefield between her desire for selfish pleasure and the duty of pleasing others.

In order to have her take sides with what she perceived as selfishness, I asked her to make a round, acting selfish toward others in the group. She did, and asked for things: pretty clothes, gifts, travel. She realized then that she was asking for symbols of love rather than direct contact. She had not touched, or asked to be touched.

Her father had not hugged or touched her. He would only provide for her clothing, for her education. She talked to her father now, pretending to be a little girl. While she did so, she expressed a frustration that she had withheld for a lifetime, and wept. Father felt impotent, but she ended the session more in touch with a basic desire of hers. More wanting, less blaming and destructive criticism.

One more aspect of the Gestalt-therapeutic handling of the past is *variation*. Mere reenacting may be enough for the purpose of coming to terms with the past (or with the present as symbolized in the past and perhaps structured therein), but sometimes the individual spontaneously feels the need to relive something with amendments, to "rewrite" the past, or express something he had left unexpressed. Again, this is part of the natural process of dreaming, as well as of the phenomenon of screen memories. These may be regarded as expressive acts by which the individual assures himself of a freedom which he lacks and, like the fighter who tests his strength against a punching ball, he verifies himself to his resources in the medium of symbolic action. The Gestalt therapist encourages these acts of completion, acknowledging their natural healing value.

The following series of sessions which I will attempt to reconstruct after about two years not only provides illustration of work centered on the past and catastrophic fantasies more than on the present, but is one of the most dramatic in my experience as a psychotherapist. The starting point for the stormy therapeutic process that developed from a certain point onwards spontaneously was in the reliving of the past, even though the reliving of fantasies was here more significant than the reliving of actions. The substance of the events described below may be understood as a *completion* of the past. What the patient repressed in her behavior as a child, her fantasies expressed, and in developing, after many years, this expression, she found that part of her that she had disowned from her life.

The patient, a middle-aged woman psychotherapist, exposed for years to psychoanalysis, was attending a week-long workshop on Gestalt therapy at Esalen out of a professional interest. She appeared to be more mature and better adjusted than most of the other twenty participants.

Her individual session started with a dream. I remember of it only that the action took place in an arid, dry place, and that the other people in this place were also described by her as "dry." The whole scene was permeated by a strong sense of scarcity.

I asked her to become the scorched earth that she had described; in doing so she contacted very deeply a feeling of deprivation and intense dryness, that she now felt even physically in her face and mouth. I then asked her to experience, still as dry earth, rain pouring over her.

For the onlooker it seemed now as if rain began to pour from her eyes, as she felt the dryness dissolving in wetness and the waters quenching a century-old thirst. She became more and more ecstatic as she merged and identified with those abundant rushing waters of life. This was an experience of a different order than anything that she had known before. The immense "dryness" and the "wateriness" that she contacted in herself were self-evident aspects of her experience that she had never been aware of before in such a measure, in spite of years of self-examination and self-interpretation (and the best of analysts). Now, she merely experienced them, and felt little inclined to speculate on them.

In another session, the subject of dryness came up again and led her to the memory of a childhood feeling: the loneliness that she used to feel at night, in bed, in a room that lay far from her mother's room. Reliving these moments, she discovered a despair that she had forgotten. Her mother had difficulty in walking, and she, as a little girl, had learned very early to be considerate and not call her to her room at night. She would lie awake for hours, sometimes, terrified in the dark, and still not call out for help, so as not to disturb her poor mother. What terrified her so? In reliving her terror, she now remembered: fire. The thought that a fire might start during the night, and mother, unable to walk, would not be able to escape.

I asked her to be the fire, and burn the house down. Her identification with fire, which may have started as deliberate play-acting, soon took on characteristics of a possession trance. She was fire, and yet not fully so. She was still the victim of fire, at the same time, still in panic of letting go further, afraid at the same time of burning and of surrendering to be burned. She shrieked in terror and physically felt intense waves of heat.

This was the last hour of the last day in the workshop. The violent and surprising experience was, again, unlike anything that she remembered having experienced, and she felt an urge to pursue it further. We arranged for an individual session on the following day, after the workshop. This session, which we expected to be of one hour, lasted six hours. We went back to the burning. In the fire was her anger, her frustration at her mother, and a vindictiveness that she could not possibly tolerate in herself; but she had retroflected this anger, both in the childhood fantasy and the reliving of it, and instead of imagining the fire burning her mother's room, she feared that it would burn her own. She felt victimized, abandoned. Now it was she who became (like her mother) paralyzed and helpless. Being in touch with her fear, she now lived another fantasy that made itself present during these same nights: a fearsome snake lurked in a corner of her room.

Again in face of this aggressor, I asked her to become him: "Be the snake. What does the snake want?"

The snake wanted to crawl up to her mother's room, and so she (that is, the patient) did this in fantasy, identifying with the animal. Mother was afraid, did not want her there. The snake insisted— she wanted to be close. No—she did not want to hurt her—she only wanted to be with her, to touch her; but mother did not understand, and kept rejecting her. To mother, she was a horrible creature.

Urged on by me, she withstood her own disgust and fear, and managed to enact the fantasy of touching mother. She wound herself around her. To mother this was not as fearsome as she had imagined, but still very uncomfortable.

The snake wanted more; she wanted to be inside her body. She would feel more comfortable and warm in her womb—she wanted to do no damage to mother. But mother still would not understand, and panicked.

After a very long time of staying with this impasse, she (as a snake) finally entered her mother's body. Not through the vagina, but through her anus, which took, in her imagination, the character of a rose. Switching to the role of her mother, now, she had a serpent in her belly. And this was not a stable situation. She did not want it there. And the serpent, too, wanted to move.

The hours that followed were filled by the events related to a gradual ascent of the snake through her body as it lay on a couch. They were dramatic hours, in which the movements of the snake were perceived by the patient as a matter of life or death. The process could not be left unfinished. Whatever this weird fantasy "meant," she did not know or care, at that point, but she knew that this was an important process to pursue. All went very slowly because of her terror, which at times became so intense she would scream. The sensation of having a snake inside her body was, during most of the time, a true somatic hallucination, even though she was aware of ordinary reality and could maintain communication in it at the same time. The hardest step was for the serpent—which had become a cobra—to reach her heart. She feared so much that she would die, that perhaps over an hour elapsed in the transition of the snake from the pit of her stomach to her chest. Then the neck was difficult too. At last, however, the snake's head emerged from her forehead. It was a queen of snakes, at this point, and the patient now felt some sense of completion.

What was the connection of all this with the aims of psychotherapy? What would this "fantasy" do for the patient? Was it more than a fantasy, in some sense? She could not tell what value was in the experience, but did not doubt that the value was great. These hours had shown her another aspect of reality, she said; an aspect of life that she only vaguely knew had existed, from intimations during her early life that only now she could remember.

After the session, she returned from Berkeley to New York, expecting life to proceed as usual. After a week, however, she telephoned; she could live as usual, going about her ordinary business, working as a psychotherapist, but only at the expense of suppressing and preventing the development of experiences that she felt were important. If she opened up to them, she felt that this would mean psychosis: a condition of intense feeling relating to the unfoldment of fantasies that nobody would understand, and the desire to withdraw from the environment in order to give her undivided attention to the process that was knocking at her mind's door. After some deliberation, she chose to leave work and family for some time in order to see this process to its completion.

She moved to a room in Berkeley not far from my house, and for about three months surrendered to a condition truly incompatible with ordinary life.

She lived with a constant hallucination of one or two snakes in her body, hardly able to sleep at night in the midst of terror at the snakes crawling in her room. I saw her periodically, and trusted that, whatever time it would take, she would be a whole person when she could accept rather than fear her own "snakyness." The process was slow, and at times, seemed to be an interminable impasse. She would not give up the snakes, sending them to sleep in the underworld where they had been for years, before her Gestalt session. In the snakes were her vitality, her power. And yet, when she summoned up their image, this was more than she could tolerate, and sometimes she even physically ran away.

It was a slow process, but one with an end. She gradually learned to live among snakes, and while this happened, she became more of the woman that she had been. While she came to terms with images, the reality that was being expressed in these images came to life in her as her own instinctual foundation, her spontaneity, her wants and loves, her energies and assertiveness, her very identity—which she had for years mistaken for her role.

The process culminated, when, one day, she felt the snake again put out its head through the middle of her forehead; but this time it was not the snake who was the queen, but she.

Exploring the Future and the Possible

When a patient comes for psychotherapy, he frequently brings a "problem": a difficulty in relating to a family member or a superior, or a choice that he is not ready to make, or a psychological characteristic of his that he would like to overcome —such as a tendency to put himself down before others, excessive anger, delayed initiative, and so on.

Strictly speaking, any such problems belong to the past or to the imagined future. If the therapist chooses to stay strictly in the present, such issues may be found to be reflected in it or not.

Whenever a patient is concerned with a specific matter that has troubled him in the past and he foresees it may continue to trouble him in future similar situations, the therapist has two choices:

1. Insisting in the awareness of the ongoing situation, trusting that if the patient is able to be free, alive and whole here and now, he will also be able to be at his best in whatever other situation he must confront.

2. Bringing the problematic future into the present and exploring it by means of acting.

The possible advantages of the second approach are that: (a) By acting upon the patient's cue (i.e., the matter that is worrying him), the therapist is less likely to miss a substantial issue. (b) The patient's awareness of working upon an issue that concerns him may favorably influence his motivation during the therapeutic transaction.

To play-act the future means to act out a fantasy. For this reason, working on expectations or imaginations of what is to come may be regarded as similar to working on dreams. The difference is that those fantasies that we call dreams we experience as "mere fantasy"—whereas those that constitute our imagination of the future we take to be and treat as "reality."

I have called the following session "there and then" because of the extent to which my indications and the patient's experience during its course refer to the patient's imagination of the future. I think that it may serve to illustrate how work amounting to an explicit rehearsal of the future may be interwoven with the other resources of Gestalt therapy: rounds, repetition, exaggeration, and awareness of the present. I think that the session was rather successful in terms of outcome, for the patient eventually took in real life the step that his experience in the session anticipated.

Chapter Ten

There and Then (Len)

LEN: The thing I'd like to look at and work on is a very important thing to me which I've managed —which I have suppressed for about the last seven weeks in the encounter groups that I've been in. I didn't bring it up in the encounter groups and I didn't know if I was going to here because it is such a personal thing it might bore people and the rest of that. But on the other hand it's so important to me that I wanted to look at this and try to get some insight or some feeling for what I am going to do with this thing that keeps coming up—the necessity of having to make a choice, say, in the next year or so.

I: One of the ways to deal with conflict in Gestalt is to give a voice to each of the conflicting sub-selves. So imagine right now that you just want to leave the order. (*Obviously he had told me of his quandary since I didn't request his description of it in the group.*) Speak for *just* that point of view. Talk to us or to yourself, whatever.

LEN: This feeling of wanting to leave, that I have now, is a feeling that's like a tide that keeps coming in more and more, and I feel more and more pushed that way. I feel myself wanting to go that way. My life style is different than most of the other people's and I want it to be that way. I get criticized for the way I live, which is not standard or typical. I often ask myself why should I stay. Of course I can't come up with too many good reasons, and the reasons I should leave are that I could be more free to do the kind of work I want to do.

I: Make a case for leaving, now. Just say "I want to leave, I want to."

LEN: I want to *live.* I want to do the kind of things I want to do. I am disgusted and pissed off with so many of the things that are going on within the order. I feel a... (pause).

I: What happened right there?

LEN: I was starting to go to the other side and say "Yeah, but on the other hand... "

I: As soon as you say that "I'm pissed off with some things" you have to go to the other side. Could you emphasize your anger more?

LEN: Yeah. The anger is almost, it is the bind I get put into, with wanting to leave more and more and every time I get pissed off at something that happens the "powers that be" kind of reinforce me to . . . kind of keep me in just a little longer, in kind of a real subtle way. I get pissed off at them and I'll tell them I'm really angry at...[1]

I: Be pissed off at them now.

LEN: You people don't seem to appreciate, or you don't even seem able to live on a deep interpersonal level with other people—which I want to do and I have to do. And every time I bring this up, you say "Well, everybody can't do it, and so therefore it doesn't belong." And then I say "Well, screw you then." And just when I say that you'll come along and say "Would you be on this committee to help us change?", and you kind of suck me back in again.

---

[1]With the perspective of 17 years I am acutely aware of how the patient displaces responsibility for his actions to his authorities, choosing to be obedient and resentful over being non-resentful and free. He feels sucked in by "them" rather than experiencing his own self inclination and his excessive dutifulness. His last phrase seems to capsulize the insight he is offering in regard to the part he has just played: he is being seduced through an offer of power and in this way is kept bound, obedient and powerless.

And that's happened three or four times now, in the last couple months, where I just blast you. You had your big chapter meeting for changes and I sat through that and it was shitty and I told you so. And then you said, "Well, would you help us, criticize us at the end of each meeting as to what we're doing wrong and kind of conciliate it that way?" O.K. I just expressed that I feel shitty about what's happening and you kind of pull me back in by saying "Would you help us?" I just tell you that when I wasn't there the last three days were crap, and then you say "Would you be in a formation committee to help us change it?" And, I also feel the pressure from some of the other guys; that I'm kind of like the big hope or something, and if I don't stay and if I, if I leave, like I'm abandoning them.

I: Let's hear the other side—wanting to stay.

LEN: There's one more thing that's important on the wanting to leave. Besides this, all this crap with the order I've also been doing a lot of encounter group work, and one of the girls that I do encounter group with I love very much and she loves me. And she and I are both finishing our doctorate and that would be so easy for the two of us to get married and work together. That's for the leaving.[2]

I: Now convince us that you want to stay. (laughter from the group)[3]

---

[2] I am struck by the fact that he leaves what I imagine the most important reason till the end—even almost beyond the end, since it came from him as an addition that might have been easily bypassed. Today I would not have let him get away with this hiding of the chief emotional issue through the screen issue of ethics and reason.

[3] I feel like emphasizing the importance of this laughter to the ongoing therapeutic process. I think that in Gestalt groups, if not in groups in general, it happens that *vox populi* is *vox dei*: the majority of the group picks up where the individual's healthy next step lies. Such group perception in turn is clearly perceived, and does not need many words to be conveyed powerfully. In imitating his tone of voice as he says it is not so bad I seem to be emphasizing the contrast between his present wishywashiness and the vehemence of his anger while embodying his

LEN: I have a hard time convincing myself.

I: "I'm indispensable"... (laughter)

LEN: Yeah. I should stay because, some of the minor things are, if I leave what's going to happen? *Possibly* there is a chance to change this thing and make it good, make it worth while. There is a certain amount of freedom that I have inside here to come and go as I please, without a family and kids.

I: (Imitating tone of voice) "It's not so bad."

LEN: It's not so bad. Yeah. But probably the biggest thing—and this is the part I can't get to inside me—is that, ah... (a little hesitant) there's something about the whole thing that still is viable or there's worth or value in that...

I: So you are saying, "It's not so bad."

LEN: I don't even know what it is. (slight chuckle when saying it)

I: But all this "it's not so bad" can't be what's keeping you there.

LEN: (Fading in) Two things are keeping me there. One is the close friends that I have in the order that I feel I would let down, and I want to be with them also. And I wouldn't be able to be with them the way I am; as you know, living with them day by day, rubbing elbows, if I left. That's why, one reason I want to stay. And the other is, ah, it's a chance for me somehow to live out my ideals, whatever the hell they are.[4]

---

3 *continued...*

other side. Obviously he is not interested in a freedom that does not allow for his marriage, for the pursual of his love relationship and yet he continues to deceive himself into believing that it is freedom and that the love issue is only a secondary one.

[4]Notice he is creating a rift between his ideals and his wants or desires, so that his desired life style does not seem to him part of the ideal and the ideal continues to be upheld in spite of its non-inclusion of a love relationship. Today I might have smuggled in more interpretation in my invitation to dramatize his weak dependent self, that buys love through imprisonment, the obedient little boy that pays for love with imprisonment. Obviously and—not to interrupt the flow of his now self-directed process—I chose not to reflect the hesitation in his language as he criticizes his "good boy" and along with him the values of the authorities.

I: I think that you are paying with imprisonment for the feeling that you get when told that you're helpful, you're useful.

LEN: Yeah. That's very much it. Yeah.

I: Let's go on with this dialogue. Can you switch and tell him (pointing at empty chair) what you feel about him?

LEN: Yeah, I know I've, I know I've done a lot, and a lot of really good things. And I know that I kinda stand for a lot, a lot of things for, for a lot of you. But I have to, I have to live *my* life. I, I don't, ah, I feel more and more out of it all the time. I don't, I don't pray the way you guys pray; I don't, ah, I don't share your ideals; I don't, ah, I don't even share the same kind of beliefs that you have. And how honest is it for me to ah, to stay?

I'll switch. Yeah, but that's just what we need. We need your insights and we (laughs) we need your insight. We need, we need to hear this. Somebody's got to. You're J., you're the one that (group laughs with him although he is not laughing now) you're the one that, that can help us to see these things and to really make it important and to make it worth while and ah, if guys like *you* leave, what's gonna happen to the rest of us? (group chuckles) You're the one that's—Just look at all you've got and what you could, what you could give to us and what you could do for us. Mmmm, you're really powerful.

I: And how do you feel about that, being told that?

LEN: Yeah, I am. (laughter) This is *exactly* what happens to me. Exactly what happens to me. This is so much what happens that I'm just about ready to say "shit" on the whole thing. I'm gonna—And then I'll get a letter from somebody and then I'm back in it. Exactly, this is what's happening. (cut)

I: So there are two sides to you. One says: "I am full of insights, I want to be helpful, I want to be 'in' with you;" and the other says: "I want to live my own life." Now could you have a dialogue between these two sides of you, being the generous guy that likes to be told that he's good and the other who feels that this is not honest and says "I want to live my own life?" O.K. See what they have to tell each other.

LEN: I'm gonna take the other one; the one that says "I want to live my own life" first. I feel more and more out of it. And almost every day I get reinforced on how I really don't belong here. The whole thing pisses me off; not only the order. Just about two days ago we had this worship service and some damn priest, I felt, excluded some Jews who were there. That pissed me off. I had that host in my hand and I asked "Do I even want to participate in a kind of church that excludes people from worshiping together?" I get so pissed off at that and that whole system and that whole structure that I just don't want to be a part of any of that kind of crap and I just want to go do my thing and just be with other people in a real free way where I can be me. (changes seats) But ah, you just can't leave. You know, you got ten years investment with these people that you've lived with and you've worked together with, shared so much. Deep, deep friendship. Hell, I just can't leave those guys. It's, it's kind of not right.

I: "Right?" (ironically) Not for you, really. It's a question of *right* and *wrong*.

LEN: It would, it would tear me up to, ah, I'd, I'd have to live with bad feelings if I'd leave—I'd have to live with bad feelings about leaving you guys when you really needed me.[5]

I: Imagine you have.[6] Could you tell us more of those bad feelings?

---

[5]In view of the identification of Len as a "fear type" (see Book Two, Chapter 5) I would say that his duty not to abandon may be seen as a manifestation of a fear of being abandoned.

[6]With these words I am inviting him to live the avoided situation in spite of the associated catastrophic expectation.

LEN: If I had left? Or I did leave? The powers that be, which I think are shitty, gave me a lot—opportunities for education and lots of things like that. I feel I kind of screwed them a little by leaving. My friends, especially—that's the more important thing. They, they're working so hard and trying so hard to change a thing, and I'm so much a vital part or I, I *was* so much a vital part of that. And now that I've left everybody else is saying to my friends, "See, that just goes to show you what happens when you, when you start going that way."

I: Do you realize how much you always operate in terms of *duties,* and not *inclinations?*[7]

LEN: I'd get a lot of disapproval if I left. And people would say to me, "You could see it coming, the way he lived and the ideas he had." And everything that I said and that I stood for while I was in would just be washed away. And I don't want that to be washed away because I think what I said and what I did was valuable. And that would really hurt me to just have it all wiped away.

I: All your merits would be erased and all your demerits would be . . . Mmm. Yeah. (pause) How do you feel about this? Which side are you feeling closer to right now?

LEN: I'm feeling more and more I, I gotta do my thing. I can't be bound by rules. But on the other hand, just after the last couple of things I said I see how really bound I am, you know, by . . . And I don't want all that stuff wiped out. And I see even more the whole thing—I was ready to just wipe it out before but the more I talk the more I see.

---

[7]I think the most important thing I have done thus far in view of assisting the ongoing choice is a subtle irony pervading my interventions (an irony which may be missed without the tone when I speak of duties instead of inclinations, for instance, or the question of right and wrong). Though no explicit advice is given, I think my sense of the path of the healthy life was conveyed to him implicitly, in the same way as the group's sense of it was.

I: You get sucked in when you are threatened with demerits—all you did would amount to nothing, if you leave now.[8]

LEN: Yeah. Yeah, all the ideas and the program that I've set up would just be, could be wiped out. That's a good thing in itself. Even apart from me I think it's good.

I: Well, maybe we could move on to what's behind this specific problem. I see it as this need to live up to expectations, be good, helpful, etc., and your need to be independent and follow your impulses which *feel* "bad" and I'd like to experiment a bit here. To some people be as good as possible, according to all your views and whatever, and to other people be yourself, unbound. Show us both styles. (He makes a round in the group switching from one attitude to the other.)

I: Do you feel any difference in the satisfaction you get from both?

LEN: The feeling I had is, well I had a, they were somewhat sim—, both things were somewhat similar, but the other was condescending. You know, the guy bound by the rules or the right thing. It was a "Be sure you do this. Now do that. I'm telling you, be careful you don't do this." You know. I did that to you, too. And the other one was just real free. You know, "I feel threatened by you but" — you know. This kind of thing. I felt free to just tell you what I wanted to instead of ah, the nice guy kind of encourages you and that kind of shit. I am teed off with myself because I didn't realize how bound I was and also how, with the good-guy thing, how condescending that was. Even as I was saying it, you know, the encourage and the help—.

---

[8] I am being ironic again through my wording ("demerits") and implicitly conveying my values: approval should not be as important as feeling. While the path of the heart creates life, in the persistence of childhood obedience there is only the prospect of enslavement of the self and an abdication of one's true life.

I: Are you feeling disgusted? Your expression is one of disgust.[9]

LEN: That was crappy! . . . But I do, I don't think I usually act that way with rules. I take almost, I'll use the word childish delight in kind of being a bastard sometimes, in encounter groups or just coming on that—because I do that so seldom that I really like to do that if I feel it, you know. I really rejoice at expressing hostile feelings sometimes to people, simply because I'm usually the nice guy...

I: What's your experience behind the statement? What prompts you to say this now?

LEN: That I see myself more and more as a nice guy, of being a nice guy, and the expression of hostility is a way of saying I'm trying to move out of that.

I: I imagine that you are wanting now to be more like a bastard. Yeah. I agree that you could use some of that. (chuckle) I'd like you to do this a bit in the group now.

LEN: Be a bastard?

I: Be a bastard, with childish delight.[10]

LEN: (expresses some hostility to the group)

I: Now put in the next chair one of these friends that wants to suck you into staying. And be a bastard to him.

LEN: Why the hell don't you stand on your own two feet instead of always counting on me all the time. You are so sucked in by rules and regulations— Hell, you can't even see beyond, you know, like this much on what's on the outside. Maybe if you'd get out of the house once in a while and go do some stuff you'd see what the hell is going on in the world.

I: Are you still talking to these friends?

---

[9]This was a successful intervention in that my reflecting his expression allowed him to contact more of his forbidden anger toward his "nice guy."

[10]I notice that I often use this strategy of bringing a patient in contact with the feeling state and then have him bring to bear this released feeling to the problem situation.

LEN: Yeah. You spend your whole damned life sitting in front of the TV set sucking beer. (laughter) All this, all these people that are poor and starving and there's all kinds of stuff going on and you sit on your fat can all the time. You are so out of it. You know what I'm doing though? These aren't my friends. These are all the other people.[11]

I: Well, bring your friends here.

LEN: Bring my friends in. Hang on. I want to get some of the other stuff in first. (laughter) You sit all night working on plays for basketball or working out charts and stuff like that, and you're so god damn hung up on your charts and statistics and stuff like that, that you can't even talk to the kids, for Christ's sake. I really feel sorry for you. You were raised in a different age and you just don't understand what the hell's going on today. I feel sorry for you.[12] Now I'll try to do it with some of my friends because that will be harder.... Be a bastard, though.

I: Maybe you can get cruel?

LEN: That's the problem. I can be a bastard to them, but I can't be to my friends.

I: They won't know. (laughter) We won't tell them.

LEN: Mike, why the hell don't you just forget about it. You're young; you got so damned much talent. Why waste your talent on that kind of crap? (cut) Al, you are really stupid.

I: Imagine that you are your friends convincing you about staying in the order. And suppose they were to be very sincere with you as to how they're feeling about themselves and you. Take one of them—one representative—and see what he'd have

---

[11]Apparently at this point he has transcended his false friendship (i.e., his idealization of neurotic allegiance) and chooses to change his in-group into an out-group.

[12]He has changed considerably from his beginning idealization.

to tell you if he had been present here seeing what's in your mind.[13]

LEN: "Gees, I can understand that, Len, how you feel that way. But I just ah, I just have to stay. That's my thing. Now if you want to leave, I'd really like to let you be free to do that. And I mean that. I want you to, to be free and we could be, we could still be close if you would leave. But also consider (laughter)[14] what you could do if we'd get a group of us together and we could live together. We can really, ah —"

I: What does he feel when he makes this last statement, "but consider what you could do if we could live together"?

LEN: What does he feel?

I: What's in it for him?

LEN: He's hanging on to me.

I: Can you be him making a direct statement? "I need you," or whatever.[15]

LEN: "I'm hanging onto you. I really need you. There aren't too many people I can relate to on a kind of a deeper level and you, you're one of them that I can. I really need somebody like you. I'd be very lonely if you left."

I: Your answer to that?

LEN: Yeah, I know you would. And that's why— you, you're gonna leave me free but that's why I feel bound. That word "bound." Boy, I feel bound by my

---

[13]This is a technique that I have not borrowed from anybody and yet I see myself using now and then: that of helping the imaginary encounter by inviting the patient to imagine somebody as this third party, etc., as witness to the present session segment *a posteriori*.

[14]The group laughs at the now coming—because pervading—ambivalence of the patient: there is always "on the other hand" another point of view to consider, an insidious doubt.

[15]When I suggest to him a direct statement here my psychoanalytic mind is at work. I see him projecting his own dependency needs when he feels needed, and that just as he rather projects than acknowledges them in himself, even when he steps in the place of his friends he tends to be in touch with their patronizing advice rather than their contact needs.

friends and I feel bound by so many of the things I've been getting too. Like time off to get a Doctorate and stuff like that. I feel *bound* a little by that.

I: What I see as different now from when you started working on this is that now you are seeing the issue of the order as a matter of ideals, as separate from that of satisfying the personal needs of your friends.

LEN: That's the main thing that's keeping me, is the friends.

I: Now we can deal with these two as separate.

LEN: The first one—the order thing—I don't think bothers me that much. I can, in fact I'm so much out of it that I deliberately got a grant so that they couldn't say, "We paid for your schooling." So I can say I did it myself. Now the friend thing, that bothers me.

I: Tell him how it bothers you.

LEN: My friend?... Boy, I really feel caught. But you gotta understand that more and more, especially after this summer, with the freedom I felt and how I, and how I was, and about the only thing holding me back from a full enjoyment of it was this damn decision.

I: How do you sound now?

LEN: Apologetic?

I: Now try the same statement but like a bastard. No apologies.

LEN: That's hard. To my friends? Mmmmm. (softly) Boy, I really don't—After this summer it's clear to me I've had it. It's almost to the point now where I kind of feel sucked in by your friendship a little bit and that's the only thing that's keeping me.

I: It's *almost* to the point.[16] (chuckles)

LEN: I *do* feel sucked in and yet I kinda like wanted to be, also, because it makes me feel good... They experience an ache. A bit of it's loneliness now. They have to start making new friends. A bit of it is a god damned feeling of obligation inside me that I should not have, and that's that even though they

---

[16]Combination of support and irony.

said "O.K., you don't have to live for us." They're still disappointed in me. And that's me and not them.[17] That's the thing inside me. I still feel bound.

I: And the details of living. I'd like you to do one more thing now which is just to repeat "good person, good guy" or something to that effect, and share with us what you feel, what comes up in your mind.[18]

LEN: You mean the good guy; how he feels now?

I: Just repeating this statement or these words "good guy, good guy, good guy".

LEN: Good guy. You're a good guy. And you're all right. You're a good guy. Images of "Good guy, but I never did get to know you," come to mind from people like in encounter groups.

I: Good guy.

LEN: Good guy. You're a good guy. You know, you're a good guy. (chuckles) I was picturing myself walking in front of people and each one says to me "Good guy. Good guy." And about the third time I was saying to myself, "No I'm not. No I'm not." (laughter)

I: Try it once more. Good guy.

LEN: You're a good guy. You're a good guy. Oh you're a good guy. Good guy. Good guy. You're a good guy. Good guy. (Sounds like he's praising a dog for these next two) Good guy. You're a good guy.

I: Your expression has changed.

LEN: Disgust. It's such an empty, futile thing being a good guy.

I: O.K. We will leave it here.

END OF SESSION

---

[17]I see some progress in how he has shifted from the sense of *them* sucking *him* through their need to the recognition expressed in "*me* and not them" through which he is beginning to take his life into his hands.

[18]At this distance in time I do not remember my motivation here since he had already explored the good boy in him through dramatization. The indicating was useful, however, in that it served to put his approval need and dependency in further perspective and thus liberated him from identification with his "internal enemy."

Chapter Eleven

On Working With Dreams

The term "dream work" was used by Freud to refer to the process by which the dreamer's mind weaves together the residues of wakeful experience in order to (supposedly) conceal as well as express an unconscious meaning in cryptic symbolic representation. (Whether it is true or not that dream symbols actively conceal the message they half-reveal, or whether it is truer to say that we have only ceased to understand their language, I will not discuss). In Gestalt therapy the expression "dream work" is generally employed to speak, not of the encoding, but the decoding of the dream's message.

What is special of the Gestalt way of working with dreams is that it is non-interpretative in its approach to memories, physical actions or symptoms. We regard the dream as an existential message that may be eventually understood, and yet we do not seek to arrive at such an understanding through *thinking about* it. "Understanding," in this context, refers to the direct experience of the dream's content rather than to an intellectual inference, in the same way that "awareness" stands in opposition to intellectual insight. The road to awareness, in dreamwork as in other aspects of Gestalt therapy, is letting the experience speak for itself rather than thinking about it: "entering" the dream rather than "bringing it to mind." In accordance with this, it is important that the dream may be not only remembered but "brought back to life." Only by experiencing it *now* can we gain an awareness of what it is conveying. It is therefore advisable to begin by narrating the dream in the present tense, as if it were happening at the moment.

The mere change in wording implied by the use of the present tense instead of the past may be enough to bring about a great difference in the process of recall, which now, to some extent, may become a returning to the dream and to the feelings that belong with the fantasy. This may be an adequate moment to sense its metaphorical language by thinking or saying before every sentence: "This is my existence." I was present in a session of Perls when he first thought of asking somebody to do this. When I was asked to write a monograph on Gestalt therapy soon after, for Esalen Institute, I suggested this as a technique of general validity and I understand that it has since been taken up by many therapists as a standard practice. In repeating "This is my life," "This is my existence," "This is myself," or something to that effect after each statement in the dream, the patient may, at least *sometimes*, make a connection that he would have otherwise missed. Most often, some details fit the generalization less than others, but the total plot or central image reveals its significance beyond doubt.

Saying "This is my existence: I am rolling a peanut with my nose," suddenly made a patient aware of how in her life she was adopting an overly humble role, "kneeling down," and preoccupied with menial tasks instead of "standing up" and facing important issues. After the significance of her posture in the dream became thus clear to her, she engaged in a significant fantasy of standing up, first against a wall, later against an important person in her life. This fantasy was a spontaneous reversal of her dream's content, and was followed by a measure of reversal in her real life.

In another instance, after saying "This is my life: I am driving on a freeway and would like to pull up and sleep," the patient realized that he was caught in a conflict between a compulsive, stressful and lifeless race for power, and the wish to relax, enjoy and dream. This episode may have contributed in some measure to the action the person eventually took within the year, relinquishing his position of power and radically changing his life style.

Some persons may not be able to produce any more than a dry recall of dream images, in spite of the efforts to reexperience, and this only indicates the strength of the individual's tendency to alienate the dream from his "own" experience. This alienation is to some extent present in every dream, so the task of Gestalt therapy is that of reassimilating its content into the ego and helping the person to take responsibility for his unacknowledged forces, now projected "out there" as "strange images." When an attempt at the actualization and contemplation of the dream does not lead to more than verbal formulas, such reassimilation may be effected through the acting out of the different elements in the content.

The acting out of the dream necessarily entails a creative experience of interpretation or translation into movement; as such it involves an extension of the creative activity expressed in the dream itself. But this is not the only way in which the dreamwork can be expanded. It may be fruitful to fill in the gaps with fantasy or finish the dream where it was forgotten by waking up. In being faced with this task, the individual necessarily turns into a dreamer again, and becomes one with his dreaming self. Or he may give words to characters that only felt unspoken emotions in the dream, so that they now engage in the dialogue. This is only feasible if the individual really "listens" to his dream by becoming part of it.

The idea of dream enactment is not completely new or exclusive to Gestalt therapy. Just as the

principle of attending to the *here and now* constituted
a rediscovery by Perls of something known for centuries in the East as a form of meditation, the acting
of dreams or visions was a rediscovery of a practice
known to North American Indians. Consider, for
instance, the following observations of a Jesuit in the
seventeenth century:

> The Iroquois have, properly speaking, only a single
> divinity—the dream. To it they render their submission,
> follow all its orders to the utmost exactness. The Tson-
> nontouens (Seneca) are more attached to this supersti-
> tion than any of the others: their religion, in this respect,
> becomes even a matter of scruple; whatever it be that
> they think they have done in their dreams, they believe
> themselves absolutely obliged to execute at the earliest
> moment. The other nations content themselves with
> observing those of their dreams which are the most
> important; but this people, which has the reputation of
> living more religiously than its neighbors, would think
> itself guilty of a great crime if it failed in its observance
> of a single dream... he who has dreamed during the
> night that he was bathing, runs immediately, as soon as
> he rises, all naked, to several cabins, in each of which he
> has a kettle full of water thrown over his body, however
> cold the weather may be. Another who has dreamed
> that he was taken prisoner and burned alive, has found
> himself bound and burned like a captive on the next
> day, being persuaded that by thus satisfying his dream,
> his fidelity will avert from him the pain and infamy of
> captivity and death—which, according to what he has
> learned from his divinity, he is otherwise bound to
> suffer among his enemies.

The practice described by Father Fermin in the
preceding paragraph had its foundation in the Indian
belief that *dreams express natural desires*, distinct from
conscious voluntary desires. To satisfy these desires
was, to them, a religious duty and the basis for the
welfare of the community. Writing of the Hurons in
1649, Father Ragenau describes this theory in a

language that, as a modern anthropologist has commented, "might have been used by Freud himself":

> The Hurons believe that our souls have other desires, which are, as it were, inborn and concealed. These, they say, come from the depths of the soul, not through any knowledge, but by means of a certain blind transporting of the soul to certain objects; these transports might, in the language of philosophy, be called *desideria innata* to distinguish them from the former, which are called *desideria elicita.*

> Now they believe that our soul makes these natural desires known by means of dreams, which are its language. Accordingly, when these desires are accomplished, it is satisfied; but, on the contrary, if it be not granted what it desires, it becomes angry, and not only does not give its body the good and the happiness that it wished to procure for it, but often it also revolts against the body, causing various diseases, and even death....

When a person was sick as a result of ignoring his natural desires, the remedy for his psychic or psychosomatic distress was, as Wallace puts it, "to give the frustrated desire satisfaction, either directly or symbolically." The choice of direct or symbolical manner of expression depended greatly on the circumstances. Thus: "dreams in which hostility was directed at members of other nations were satisfied by acting them out both in pantomime and in real life; but bad dreams about members of the same community were acted out only in some symbolic form which had a prophylactic effect."

Some years ago, Professor Michael Harner and myself attempted to bring to life the ceremony of dream enactment as practiced among the Seneca Indians. The person would relate his dream in a group, a brief discussion followed in order to interpret the desires the dream was expressing, and finally the whole group took part in enacting the dream and satisfying the person's desire. The results were spectacular to some individuals, much in the same manner as the Gestalt therapeutic approach can be. A woman who had dreamed about being buried alive, for instance, was mourned, put into a box, and carried in a procession by group members, and while this was being done, she was able to re-experience intensely the dream feelings, remember a forgotten sequence to the dream and learn from it what she never expected to learn—without any attempt at understanding or interpretation.

What lent effectiveness to the procedure of acting out dreams, from one point of view, is the process of *assimilation* entailed in such activity. In the process of performing voluntarily what in the dream only "happened," the individual is placing *himself* behind his irresponsible dream actions and becoming responsible for them. He is implicitly saying: "This dream is *myself*, not *just* a dream"; and he thus integrates his hitherto unconscious activity into consciousness.

Working with dreams does not entail anything that we have not discussed already in the chapter on Gestalt techniques: attending to the ongoing experience, explication, development, repetition, identification, assimilation of projections, undoing of retroflections, integration of personality functions by bringing them into a relationship through an interpersonal encounter. What makes dreams special to the Gestalt therapist is the extent to which they constitute, at the same time, an instance of unusual spontaneity and articulateness.

With regard to spontaneity, there is probably no other activity comparable to that of the dreamer. Our voice, posture, gait and facial expression are far more spontaneous than our verbal behavior, but we can readily control them when we choose to. The dream, however, is something that—so to say—happens when we are not there. Yet in contrast to other types of spontaneous expression (i.e. voice and movement) the dream is most articulate, visual images being almost as explicit as concepts, though more expressive.

Even though the discrete techniques employed in Gestalt dream work are the ones that we have already discussed as of broader applicability, there is one point which needs illustration: the way in which dream work is integrated into the totality of the Gestalt session—the ongoing situation, group interaction, the patient's difficulties at the time of the session. This is a matter which can only be adequately discussed with reference to complete session transcripts. In the next chapter I am presenting an "undoctored" transcript of a Gestalt dream session along with comments on my interventions.

Chapter Twelve

Richard

R: We're confronting ah, an equal number of Gooks but they are about forty yards away on a fairly craggy sort of terrain. And ah, McFarlane is, well we're all standing up, and they're all standing up also, and they're all in nice straight rows, and we're kind of in our rows. And we're kind of confronting each other sort of like David and Goliath, sort of feeling. And McFarlane says something like—No, he opens fire on the, on the ah, on the Gooks; starts shooting at them with his rifle. And he t-turns as he's doing this and tells all of us to get down, to take cover.

So he says "Take cover," and he remains standing. And for a period of about four minutes he's taking rounds into his body and you can't s-s-see it, see or hear any sounds or any kind of thing, but he's taking bullets into his body. He remains standing there for about four minutes being shot at while the rest of us are taking fire, and I turn around and tell the rest of them to open fire. And so we start firing back into the Gooks and *they* all remain standing, during this—what seemed like about four minutes—period of time.

And, then, at the end of that time, everybody stops firing on both sides, for some reason. McFarlane topples over to the ground and—he's been dead since the initial barrage, but he's been standing there all the time, drawing the fire of th... of these Gooks and kind of sucking them in somehow. And so then, as soon as he falls, then the... some of the Gooks start falling in the, in the secondary rows, and some of them in the front row, and some of them just then just topple over on the ground. And ah, the, then there's a voice, and I don't know where the hell it comes from.

Somehow, where we're fighting, the scene of this battle is Plymouth Rock. And some voice is saying, "This is the fifth time Plymouth Rock has stood this country well." You know, presumably we had won the battle or something. Fifth time in U.S. history.

And then in the next scene—there's a break—and in the next scene there's a—I'm walking back with my troops—a smaller group of maybe six or seven men now—and we're in the headquarters area, and here are all these other Gooks, the remaining living ones—and these are three, four thousand of them it seems like—are standing in the big compound area. And as we start filing slowly by them—we're all bedraggled in our combat uniforms and everything and tired out from that big huge battle—it was only, it only lasted four minutes—and one of the guys—and the guy's name somehow seems like Kirby, who was a Kirby in a TV series, "Combat," that I used to enjoy—and he approaches the Gooks and he says, "Hey, they're women. Some of them were women, males and females."

And he says "Ah, let's tease them and scare them." And he says, "Some of you women aren't going to have any babies. Some of you women are going to die." And he's menacing them with his rifle. But they just stand there and they just giggle and laugh back—all the males and females—because they know he can't do it. They're prisoners of war of some sort.

And going up a stairway to a landing where there's a PBX system—a telephone exchange system—and there's a female receptionist there and she's in her mid-thirties or something—ah... Let's see. Before we get, excuse me, before I get to that, we walked through an office—a very large office—and there's a man sitting at the desk. He's the boss. But we don't look at him; we just kinda walk past him with our backs to him and don't look at him. But somehow I know that he's very, very proud of us and what we have done out there. And then I get to this landing— out of his office—and get to this landing ah, where the PBX is, and the, the secretary-operator there ah, says something about ah, "The boss is very proud of you." And I make some comment about ah, ah, "Mc-Farlane did a wonderful thing out there today."

And I'm standing there and I'm on this landing with my feet, feet wide spread apart and my rifle butt on the floor holding it by the snout with my helmet over atop the rifle butt. You know, very dramatic pose, you know, with the messed up hair and all of this business, and ah, saying that McFarlane did—didn't make it today. He got killed and he did a wonderful thing out there. And she says, "Yes he's... , he and Andrews said that they wouldn't be coming back," whoever Andrews was. And I don't know who Andrews was. Ah, and then I make some comment about, "They couldn't have done it without me."

And ah, then the boss's voice comes over the intercom system to the secretary saying, "Send him in as soon as he gets here," which seems kind of incongruous since I've already filed through his office. Ah, and so I start off the landing and to a stairway and down a long stairway which goes out of a doorway at the bottom, with glass in it, and it goes out to a sidewalk. And I get about one-third of the way down that stairway and that's when I woke up.

I: So what's unfinished?[1] (laughter)

R: Well, I think one of the things that's unfinished is something about the fact, whatever reason

---

[1]This was one moment of choice. At this point I had to decide whether to ask him to enact the dream, or pick a specific episode in it to concentrate upon, or do what I did. There are some dreams in which it is obvious that there is an unfinished situation. What I found incongruous in this dream was so much concern with winning and fame: Plymouth Rock, the term "Gooks" — with it simplified patriotism or ethnocentric distinction of "in" and "out" — and yet there is no winning. The theme of the dream appears to be his personal glory — the whole dream arises from this, and yet this glory he does not achieve.

I didn't look at, at the boss when I went through there or for whatever reason, I didn't go back and receive praise or something from him and that the secretary, you know, gives me the praise indirectly somehow.

I: Why don't you close your eyes and continue the dream. Finish it.

R: Go on down the stairs? I'm by myself and I'm going down the stairs, and I'm about a third of the way down right now. I'm walking down and I'm, hmmm. I'm kind of dragging my rifle and banging on every step as I go down, just letting the butt hang down... I'm going back up the stairs. (sounds a little surprised) And I'm puzzled because I don't know what the hell I'm doing that for.[2]

I: Let's find out...

R: (quietly, like thinking) Yeah. I'm going up the stairs. (normal tone) And now I can't decide whether now to go to the secretary or to the boss's office. So I'm standing in conflict right now at a juncture where I could go either way in the hallway. So I decide to go to the secretary—the PBX again. I go in the doorway to the, to the landing where she is, and I look up at her... And she doesn't look toward me. She doesn't acknowledge that I'm here. And then she does look around and she says, "The boss wants to see you." And I say, "O.K."

Where am I gonna go? I don't wanna go see the boss... Hmmmm. I'm just kind of standing, transfixed, right now on that landing. And the secretary's looking at me kind of quizzically, as though she's saying, "You better go on in. He's waiting." And all I can see is a picture of the boss at his desk but I'm not there. I'm still back on the landing. But I can see it, a picture of him at his desk, and he's just sort of

---

[2]It's interesting that he is really dreaming again, and not purposefully finishing the dream by saying, "O.K. What's missing here is my satisfaction, so I'll get it by deliberately daydreaming of going into the boss's office." He's really gifted in the capacity of letting the imagery form itself. So he is even surprised that he finds himself going back to the building. His fantasy is really spontaneous.

working doing something. And now's tapping his finger on the... the pencil on the desk. And now he's calling back on the intercom again and telling, "Send him in!" And I hear that, and I don't go.

And now the boss is coming out to find out what the hell's going on. And he's impatient—not really angry, but he's impatient. Then he sees me standing there and he comes in to where the PBX is and he says, "Hey, come on in here." And I kinda look at him, but I don't move. I just don't move! I turn my head a little bit to the right and look at him, but I don't move. I'm standing there with my rifle right up against my chest in front of me holding it tightly in front of me with one hand. And the snout's right underneath my chin, and I feel like I wanna pull the trigger and put myself out of my misery. But I really don't want to do that. I feel like it would be an easy way out for me... Hmmmm. Nothing happens.

I: You're stuck when it comes to this confrontation with the boss...

R: Yeah.

I: ...who appears to be proud of you.[3]

---

[3]First in the spontaneous dream he passes *through* the office. I see the dream as a spontaneous process in which he moves to his boss's office; and yet he is not able to finish the situation and get what he wants, and he passes through the office. Then the secretary says, "Your boss wants to see you." And he points out, in his first telling of the dream: "There is a contradiction here. I passed through already." And when the secretary says, "He wants to see you," he proceeds to the stairway and down to the street, which is a further contradiction. The contradiction starts manifesting in the dream from the moment when he avoids the natural end. And he doesn't even realize this contradiction when I tell him, "Go on dreaming and we'll talk about it." And he goes *down* to the street, and then, as if not knowing what he is doing, he comes back to the building. The first time he speaks of conflict he says, "I don't know whether to go to the secretary or to the boss." And finally chooses the secretary, thus avoiding direct confrontation with the boss. Then the secretary says, "The boss wants to see you," and he says, "I stand there transfixed, not moving." Finally, he says, "I can see the boss at his desk but I'm not there." He goes in without going in; without taking his body, he goes in his mind: a further way of trying to take the next step without taking it.

R: Yeah. But he never tells me directly. I see him as a symbol of my father right now. At least that was the relationship that I had. And my mother always gave me the indirect feedback if my father liked what I was doing. He'd never tell me himself.

I: Talk to your boss now, and imagine the boss in the dream there: he knows you have been reluctant to come in, and tell him about your reluctance to talk to him; what you feel about him.[4]

R: ...O.K. I'll put him sitting at his desk and I'll be in his office. Ah, I don't know. I just didn't want to come in. For some reason I'm afraid to. And, it isn't that I didn't want to. I'm afraid to come in and see you. I guess I'm afraid of bragging about myself; that I'm not supposed to do that... and I really can just guess about why I'm... Because I don't, you know, because I don't really think you *mean* it. I don't trust that you really feel it. And I feel that you're afraid of *me*... But I *did* fight a good fight today.

Footnote #3, continued:

If this thing had been a natural dream, he would have woken up or finished dreaming, dwindled out or gone in some other direction. But now I am pressing him, because of my very presence, implying: "Well, what now?" The whole group is waiting for him to do something and it is becoming obvious that he is not taking a step towards meeting the boss. He cannot avoid the situation any longer; there is too much awareness about the issue. So how does he resolve this in his fantasy? The boss comes to him. "What's going on out there?" But he cannot do it. By now he cannot avoid contact any longer. Because, remember, he cannot move. He is there with his rifle in his hand and speechless.

[4]Here I saw the need for a way out of the paralysis; he can imagine the situation well, but it is an impasse. No further action flows. He is stuck, wanting and not wanting, or not being able to do something. So he can only go on further with an extra push: "*Encounter* the boss." So the next step now is communicating about his predicament. Not communicating his desires to have a medal nor the natural confrontation which would take place in the real life situation—which he is avoiding—but to acknowledge: "I am paralyzed." In this way he at least acknowledges that he is avoiding, and communicates at the level of the obvious, which generally is the level at which a person doesn't think of communicating. If a person feels "I have nothing to say," he usually just doesn't say it, and walks away. So the most helpful thing to say in such case, is "Tell him I have nothing to say."

"Yeah. You did a good job. I just wanted to tell you so and ah, ah, let you know that ah, let you know that ah, that I've been watching you and that I like what you're doing. And ah, you're in line for a promotion. Ah, also ah, I got word from the big brass that ah, that they want to give you a special commendation. And I'm kinda pleased that you've ah, you know, done such a good thing for this organization. Yeah. For the organization. (this was parenthetical) Made a good name for us. Good for our reputation. Yeah. Good for our reputation. And ah, we're proud of you."

That sounds like my dad. Always concerned about family reputation.

I: How do you feel about it?

R: I don't *like* it. I don't like him for, for not seeing *me* as a person. That what I do reflects on his reputation; it doesn't reflect on anything that's *me* or something like that. It's just on the reputation of the family. I see him very much as my father.

I: Tell him about your feelings.

R: What the hell is a reputation? If you had any confidence in yourself you wouldn't be concerned about your damned reputation. What about me? I'm the one that did the job out there along with lots of other guys, but I did my part, too. And I did it because I wanted to; because I *wanted* to do a good job. So where the hell am I in all of this? I'm not a reputation...

I: There's a lot, in the dream, of reputation. Plymouth Rock...

R: Yeah.

I: ...and so on; and a desire to brag, and a reluctance to take in the praise. So I would like to experiment a bit more with the bragging side. So do some bragging about yourself here.

R: I'm glad you like my harmonica playing because I think I'm pretty damned good on it, too. I worked at it and I'm pretty good at it. Yeah, pretty good. Better than most. You don't know this, Joe, but I'm a hell of a good ping pong player. (laughter) I beat most people I play. You ought to hear me give a speech. I can really give a good speech; really turn people on. Ohhh... I was pretty gutsy the other day telling you about your stomach. That took some courage and that's pretty gutsy. I think I'm... I won't say strong; that's really not the word I don't think— pretty ah, *flexible* and ah, non-rigid about being able to relate to you since the start of this workshop. I mean pretty much of a perfectionist. And I'm probably the most screwed up perfectionist there is.

I: What kind of bragging is that?

R: I'm bragging about my . . .

I: Instead of saying you're a perfectionist, could you say you're *perfect?* (laughter)

R: Wow. (laughter) Yeah, I'm perfect. Wow. (more laughter) There just ain't nothin' like me. Ain't I cute?

I: Could you take that seriously for a while? Pretend you're perfect or make people believe you're perfect. You're doing it now in a joking way.

R: Mmmm. Yeah. Don't make fun of myself, huh?... Hmmm. O.K. Yeah, I'm perfect. I don't even need to be here. (laughter) Hell, I don't need you people here for this game. If I liked being here I'd be pretty stupid and that wouldn't be perfect, would it. Yeah.

I: Perhaps we need you.

R: Yeah. Everything I do, I do the very best way that I can, and that's perfect for me. Yeah. Other people don't always like what I do, but for me I'm perfect. And you can't expect anything more than that of me. It won't do you any good anyway. Wouldn't do me any good; so I'm just not asking anything more out of myself. Yeah, yeah. Yeah, I'm in pretty good shape. (laughter)[5]

---

[5]Which can be seen as a disowning of the responsibility for the honor. "You've done a good job for us." Not even his boss takes it as a personal thing; as a personal honor to have won that battle. It is the *country's* glory. Remember the earlier statement about Plymouth Rock: "The fifth time in the history of the United States." All this conveys a tremendous concern with winning, but all this concern with winning is not acknowledged as a personal feeling or a personal need; it is the country that takes pride.

I: Would you act out that part of the dream where you are with the rifle?

R: Oh yeah. Give me your crutch. (laughter) I'm standing on the landing talking to the secretary, and she's saying McFarlane did a wonderful thing out there today. And she says "Yeah, he and Andrews said they weren't going to come back." And I say, "They couldn't have done it without me." (in a bragging voice) And I'm very proud of myself and I'm intervening so that she doesn't have to tell me. I don't have to have her tell me that she's proud, so I say it first—which I do frequently. I'm saying, "Look at *me*. I'm O.K. I'm *great*."[6]

I: Tell us: "Look at me. I'm great." Add some... elaborate a bit on it.

R: Hmmm. O.K. Well, I'm still perfect so... (in a loud voice) Look at me. I'm pretty great. I went out today and did my job and... (laughter).

I: "*Pretty* great" you said, this time again. How do you feel when you say that word?

R: "*Pretty* great?" I think I'm leaving myself an out, so I don't have to be perfect. Yeah. Look at me.

---

[6]In this round he was very tentative at the beginning, but more serious towards the end, and I had the sense that he was really believing what he was saying. The last three or four statements had the quality of insights; not just playing at bragging but discovering; "Yeah, I *am* pretty satisfied with myself." As if his capability of acknowledging "Yeah, I am pleased with myself" had been suppressed; being pleased with himself he equates with bragging, which is taboo. Now, invited to say it as if playing, he discovers: "Yeah, I am." So he doesn't need the general to say it to him anymore. I would say that there is in him a knowledge of what he is doing, and a knowledge that he is doing his best at some level. And this is personified as the officer, who is wanting him to come in and who says, "I'm watching. I've been watching you and you have been promoted." That is *him*. But between him and him stands this need to suppress, the need not to face this part of himself, telling himself "You are O.K." He knows it, but avoids eliciting praise, even from himself. So throughout the game I had this feeling that he was really discovering: "Yeah. I *am* doing the best I can." And this would be the equivalent of the officers telling him "You're promoted," and his being able to really take that statement in saying "yes" without having to avoid the situation; so I am testing it out by going back to the dream.

I'm great. I did my job well, and I came back, and I'm ready to go again whenever they need me. Look at me. This is the greatest guy around. Does everything just right. Does the best job going.

I: Could you go on with this, and illustrate a bit with your life?

R: With my life?

I: Mmmm. Yes. Bring it from the dream into real life.

R: Things that I do, you mean?

I: Mmmm. "Look at me. I'm great."

R: I just did a lot of that. But I can probably find some more. (laughter)

I: I think you haven't gone into the important ones yet.

R: The important ones? I think I have. Ah, yeah. Look at me. I'm great. I'm the best father around. I do a real good job of being a father. I know what my kids want and what they need; I know how to respond to them and how to excite them and help them to be happy and grow and expand and be lively, open people. And they really are. And that's largely because of me, and because of what I am. Look at me. I'm great. I, ah, I'm articulate and intelligent... and I don't miss much. Look at me. I'm great, Bob. I do my job well; people respond to me well; they like me, and even when they don't like me at first they soon discover that there's some real substance there that they can respond to and they find out that they're responding to a real person and not a phony.

I: How do you feel while you do this?

R: Pretty good about it, this thing's...

MAN: I have a strong feeling that...

ANOTHER MAN: Let's see you try the other side, Richard, to use the crutch as a crutch. Do you think this would be relevant?

I: What do you mean use the crutch as a crutch?

MAN: To turn the crutch upside down and say, "I need a crutch to walk with."

R: No, I don't want to do that.

I: You are reluctant to accept praise and to let others be proud, so...

R: I always say it first, certainly.

I: So I'm interested in the other side of this: In what made you joke about this, say "pretty good" and let yourself have an out. Could you play "one of the boys?" "I'm not better than you: I'm like everybody else."

R: Oh yeah. O.K. Sure, I can do that, too.

I: So perfect you can do that, too. (laughter)

R: Right. Yeah, I'll do whatever we're doing now and get with it: dance, and it doesn't make any difference.[7] You know. I can move right in and get along with you on any level, wherever you're at I can be there, too. I can ah, talk politics, ah, just lay around and flop. Sing. Whatever, whatever you wanna do. I can ah, be casual, I can be very formal. Whatever you wanna do. Just one of the guys. Just relax, shoot pool, whatever. I'm a pretty good pool player, too. Pretty good. Pretty fair for a country boy.

I: Stress that you are not better than others.

R: I'm not better?

I: No.

R: That's hard for me to do.

I: "McFarlane did it. Not me."[8]

R: Oh yeah. Yeah, McFarlane did it. I'm pretty good as second in command. I'm not, don't really like too much being number one. I'm pretty good at being

---

[7]I generally try to do these two things in a session. I see one line of activity as a Socratic bringing out of leading forth; in this case, gradually coaxing him into being proud. First, inviting him to finish the dream, and then shifting from boasting to "I'm great," or even "I'm perfect." But then, since he obviously has a difficulty in this, it is not just a matter of training him in coming out with the suppressed impulse, but giving a voice to the obstacle. I hesitate in being satisfied with a session, even though there is a bringing out, or an explosion when I have not heard what is at stake in the opposite; because that opposite is alive in the psyche of the person. So now the issue is getting in touch with *what is at stake* in being just like anybody else, what is at stake in *not* receiving praise. Because in being just like anybody else there is pride, too.

second in command, you know, carry out orders. In fact I'm the best second commander there is. (laughter) Ah, yeah, I'm not any—not all that much different than you are or anything. I just do whatever there is to do. You do your thing and I do mine. Get along very well that way.

I: How do you like this role?

R: I like it all right. I do. Yeah. A lot more comfortable; just being more relaxed.

I: Somehow it's the first one in command that gets the bullets.

R: (smiling) Oh yeah. Sure, that's right. (laughter) Wow! Yeah. He did, didn't he. That's right. It's a lot safer—I'm a lot safer being second. I get a little bit more shit, but I don't get killed.[9]

I: And you get more joy in being first.

R: Yeah.

I: I'd like you to now do the part of the dream and act McFarlane. Be McFarlane standing there.[10] Just get into how it feels to be him, and let him speak of himself. What it feels like to be a commander and...

R: O.K., O.K. Now I'm McFarlane and I'm in charge of all these four thousand troops, and we're, and I've organized them and got them all trained and worked with my sub-unit commanders, and done everything needed to do to get a well organized, disciplined team. And so, ah, I'm taking them out to the battlefield now, and we know we're gonna fight. So, like we've got an appointment with these

---

[8]I am helping him in establishing the connection between dream and real life. Normally this connection is seen by the patient in the process of enacting, but an alternative is the one here; using dream images to speak of the now. In the former case the connection is from dream to life. In the latter, from life to dream.

[9]That is his solution.

[10]What I am suggesting is a reversal of his solution—which is also his avoidance. Being shot is probably the same thing as facing the officer; accepting being first, or the promotion. The willingness to be first, in spite of some catastrophic expectation. Without the fear of being first he would probably not even be stuck on being first.

damned Gooks or something like that. Ah, and we're gonna fight them and so here we are standing on the battlefield and I'm in front, and I'm ah, I'm standing right in the front row of the people, and I *know* that what it's gonna take, tactically, to win this battle is for me to sacrifice myself, somehow. And I'm quite willing to do that because I'm—that's my job. Yeah. As McFarlane I am. I'm not working for myself. And so they're all there and the time has come and I'm standing with my rifle, and—this wasn't in the dream but I feel it now—I take one step forward out away from the ranks, and I lower my rifle and I fire at the Gooks—just fire into them. It doesn't make any difference where I shoot because there are so many of them. And I'm not gonna get off more than one or two rounds anyway. Ah, O.K., so I'm—I'm at the point of making this sacrifice.[11] The tactical maneuver of drawing their fire. All of a sudden I've put a bulletproof vest on myself, but it won't stop everything. But I think that's not McFarlane. I think that's me again who put the vest on.

I: See if you can experience yourself as McFarlane receiving the bullets.

R: That's what I'm afraid of. O.K., so I lower my rifle and I shoot two rounds (is very quiet and hesitant) and I start feeling the rounds coming back, and I get right here—the first hits me right here just above the heart. Then I get one in my neck. And now they start all of a sudden coming very fast, and I feel like I'm just being struck all over on my legs, testicles, my feet, my head. But I just stand there. And what I'm gonna do is die so I won't hurt any more, but I'm just gonna stand there, rigid, and take the shells. And I'm leaning forward so that I won't be knocked over by the impact. And so I'm just standing there. And now they're just coming in and I don't feel it any more. There are just thuds there and there, clothing

---

[11]His notion of being first or to win is "a sacrifice."

being torn and flesh being torn and all that, but it doesn't mean a thing. Except somehow I seem to have, still have a mind or something, and I feel like I'm, that my leg bone might be shattered and collapse under me before the tactic is completed. And that would be disastrous for our troops. That didn't feel as bad as I thought it would.

I: A little exercise in being vulnerable.

R: Yeah. I sure thought that was gonna be hard to do.

I: Can you go through the telling of this in the present tense and trying it on, see how it fits you to say, "This is me. This is my life." See if it makes any sense to insert the statement, "This is my life" after the statements of the description.

R: Of the vulnerability sequence?

I: Yeah.

R: Hummm.

I: Can I interject? Drawing fire; does that mean drawing fire, drawing to yourself?

R: Yeah, it probably does. Like I'd asked for it or something?

I: Purposely.

R: Yeah.

I: Focusing it on yourself.

R: Yeah, I did it as a, ah, I'm *doing* it partly as an act of heroism but also because I really believe that that's my mission and this is the important way of doing it. O.K., so I'm from the point of my starting to shoot?

I: All of why you have said, like, for instance, "This is my mission. This is my life."

R: O.K. Yeah, O.K. I'm gonna shoot at these, shoot at these Gooks; not because I really like killing people, but this is my responsibility now. And I know I'm really not gonna kill many of them anyway since I'm gonna be dead before very long. Sacrifice myself; and this is my existence. (some laughter) O.K. I'm gonna sacrifice myself for the purpose of winning this battle. This is a very important battle and it's gotta be won for mankind or something, and this is my existence; this is my life. Yeah, that's what I wanna do, but I'm afraid to. In life that's what I want to do—make the big sacrifice.

I: As a pride to the institution?

R: No. For the glory of Richard. For some idealized values of the enhancement of mankind or something. So I'm—O.K. So now I'm gonna shoot a couple of rounds and I'm gonna take all of these bullets and I'm gonna stand right up and take it, because that's my job and this is my existence—to do that. I'm going to not even really feel the hurt, the pain. Because this is my existence, too, and I've gotta protect myself from that feeling so I'm not gonna feel the hurt. I'm just gonna do what I know I've gotta do, and this is my existence. Whatever the obstacles are—and this is my existence. And therefore ennoble my purpose in living or something. And this is my existence.

I: Tell the boss about this existence of yours. About your being a hero.

R: McFarlane, or myself, or what?

I: See if it fits as Richard. Richard has been avoiding him, and doesn't want to get praise. See if you can get yourself as Richard to—instead of avoiding the praise—tell him. Not just that you did *pretty* well, but that you're a hero.

R: Oh, well I think the "pretty well" means that I'm waiting for them to tell me "Yeah, it was great." Yeah. Or I was great. I did a good job, and I'm a hero. Or, I led all of those men—after McFarlane died then I was in charge and I led all those men and I did a good job, and I'm a hero. And I deserve the commendation.

I: Do you feel you want it?

R: I'm ambivalent... Yeah. I want the commendation as a symbol of what I have done and what I am. But I would be very humble about it and put it off—you know—put the paper off in a drawer somewhere and not show it to anybody, and like that... After I *get* it. And I do want it.

I: Well, maybe you could have a dialogue between the proud bragging Richard and the humble Richard. Take these two sides.

R: O.K., I'll be proud, bragging Richard, for the moment. No, I just bragged enough. I'll, I listen to him so I'll answer all this garbage.

Yeah, you think you're pretty great. You want everybody to tell you how great you are. And then they tell you how great you are and then they turn around and say to their friends, "He's an ass," you know. Is that what you want; to be called an ass all the time?

That's not what I want. I want for people to like me for me and to really be with me as a *person;* not as a damned symbol of greatness or a noble sacrificer, nor as a braggart. I want them to come to *me.*

You always reach out and try to take people in all the time instead of—instead of letting them come to you; you're so damned desperate. And, ah, you really screw *me* up that way.[12]

So that's my thing, you know. You just drag along and get whatever the hell's left over. Ah, I'm pretty great, you know, and I might as well let people know about it. I like doing that. There's nothing you can do about it. There's nothing you can do about me. You know.

(Almost in a whisper) Whew! (in rather sad tones) It's too true!... That's the way it's been, all right.

As usual you're very accurate in your analysis. And at the same time you're full of shit. Because I know that you're hurting for the same kind of thing *I* am, which is open, free affection and real liking from other people and being able to like other people. And you can't do it this way. You can't like anybody

---

[12]A logical step, at this point. He has explored both, so now we can think of integrating.

when you take the initiative and tell them how good you are. And they really can't like *you*, that way, because they don't have a chance to be themselves with *you*.[13] You push too much. You push too much for *your* own good as well as mine. As a matter of fact, there's hardly any place at all for pushing the way you do. It won't get you what you want. And I know you want. You might not want to admit that, but you want.[14] You're pretty weak acting the way you do. You're weak and you're out of control. You're neurotic, compulsive and desperate. And that's all a lot of bullshit the way you are. You're a lot of bullshit.

So what do you want me to do? Look ashamed? It's not my style. But you got to me. You never got to me this way before. And I have to admit you're right in your interpretation. So where do we go from here? I'll tell you what. I'm inclined right now to do something about what's going on. I'm not sure what I can do, but what I'm gonna do right now is maybe be more aware of when I'm doing this. Maybe you could help me do that. I'll make an effort to listen and when I'm not listening, just kind of gently remind me that I'm not listening. Can you do that? Because I *do* want that. (crying) That's what I want. I hope I... I don't want to be the shithead. I don't want to be perfect. (still crying) Shit! I don't know anybody this way. Nobody knows me! (really sobbing) Oh how I hurt! (convulsive crying during the next sentence) Oh shit, I gotta do something different! (pause, voice back to normal and pulled together again)

---

[13]I think that this is a therapeutically effective discovery: that he wants to brag so that others see *him*, but that bragging will not do that for him.

[14]Here there is a synthesis of the two. Richard II does not antagonize Richard I any longer, but loves him. He gets praise and it is like his father's praise. He knows that it is not acknowledgement of *him*. By dwelling upon his pride rather than suppressing it, he has contacted the source of his need of praise and discovered that it is not need of praise at all. The experience of wanting to be first has changed into the *experience* —not mere interpretation—of wanting to be seen and loved.

That's what I've been waiting for. You sure do test my patience, though. So let's do something about it. Hey, you know what? Don't worry about being reminded. (in comforting tone) That isn't going to work anyway. Just *relax.* Just let go. If you feel like being sad like you just were, just go ahead and be that way. Don't apologize t—to me or anybody else about it. I'll listen... Hmmmm. I like shaking hands with you. And so does he feel like that. (sighs)

I: Is there anything that *you* want to say to others here? Not to him but...

R: I guess I just want to say here I am. Yeah. Here I am. This is me.

Book Two

GESTALT THERAPY REVISITED

Chapter One

The Transpersonal Aspect of Gestalt

Without awareness there is naught.
Not even knowledge of the naught.
Fritz Perls

As with existential therapies in general, Gestalt therapy is ordinarily regarded as a humanistic approach. This is not all, however: as much as the Gestalt process differs from psychoanalysis, it carries a considerable Freudian component—and so it did, particularly in the work of Fritz Perls, once a psychoanalyst. Less apparently, and yet more significantly, the most distinctive features of Gestalt therapy are, properly speaking, transpersonal.

By "transpersonal" I mean that which lies beyond the "person" in the sense of a conditioned and individual personality. This was implicit in Jung's view when he applied the term to the contents of the collective unconscious, in contrast to the "personal" unconscious and ordinary consciousness. Yet the fact that Gestalt therapy is usually regarded a "humanistic" rather than a "transpersonal" approach in these days when both terms are dominant in our system of psychological packaging (each connected with a Journal and an Association) reflects a tendency to associate the transpersonal more with the visionary realm, altered states of consciousness and the paranormal than with the basis of all these: awareness itself.

The fact, however, is that awareness is transpersonal. Or, to use the earlier term, spiritual.

The most articulate spiritual traditions make this very clear. Buddhahood (from the root *bodh*, awake) is not a particular state of consciousness, but consciousness itself; enlightenment is not a state or a content of the mind, but mind as such, the container. Perhaps even more explicitly Sufism makes clear that the goal of awakening from the state of restricted awareness that is ordinary consciousness lies beyond "spiritual states." These are derivative manifestations of consciousness itself and the result of an impingement of the transpersonal on the personal (or, in traditional terms, of the spiritual on the ego)— which is the explanation usually given for the fact that "the novice gets drunk on little wine" (i.e., manifests an abundance of ecstatic and visionary phenomena on little *baraka*, or "spiritual force").

The beginner's usual tendency to get more excited about the productive phenomena of "spiritual drunkenness" than about the basic awareness that makes them possible is suggested by a Sufi story that tells of a young man who was guided by a dervish to a place where he conjured the earth to open, and instructed him to descend and fetch a candlestick of iron. As soon as he descended into the vault thus exposed, he saw such dazzling treasures that he filled his arms with jewels and gold. Then he saw the candlestick and decided that he might just as well take it along, too. When he came out, however, the dervish was gone and his treasure had disappeared. Only the candlestick remained. This is only the beginning of the story, which proceeds to tell how this was a magical candlestick which could be used in a certain way to yield treasures, and how the young man, due to his greed and lack of knowledge, lost it. Yet this bare outline can serve to illustrate the relations between awareness and the "glittering" states of consciousness. Awareness, like the

well-known hen of the golden eggs, is the ultimate
transpersonal treasure, but we are not likely to value
it for itself.

I think that a shift in emphasis from mental
contents to awareness itself may well be the most
significant feature of today's humanistic and
transpersonal therapies, yet this leap in
psychotherapeutic practice, as usual, has antedated
the corresponding leap in theory, and thus (in spite
of a growing interest in meditation) the transpersonal
nature of awareness has not been properly underlined.

That Gestalt therapy is commonly regarded as a
humanistic rather than a transpersonal approach is a
reflection of this lack of conceptual precision, though
a most understandable one if we consider that the
spirituality of Gestalt therapy is, in a sense, dis-
guised. With this "in a sense" I refer to Perls' rejection
of ordinary religiosity and his usual unwillingness to
use theistic language more than metaphorically. (I
once thanked him after a workshop for his inspired
work with myself and others and he commented:
"This is one instance where I could say 'thank
God'."). His usual practice of responding to
"spiritual" talk (and most talk anyway) as to a
neurotic symptom was generally appropriate, however, and even highly spiritual, in that it was a challenge to relate to him beyond symbolic and
ideological crutches. I well remember the perplexity
of a minister, for instance, to whose religious statement Fritz answered saying, "I feel separated from
you by your God." He clarified: "You're putting God
between you and me." Of course he was addressing
himself to the quasi-universal tendency to compli-
cate direct enlightened action in the moment with
patterns of relationship that are bound to constructs
and assumptions about reality. There were many, to
be sure, who failed to give him credit as a spiritual
authority as soon as they were wounded in their

sacrosanct beliefs, and this contributed to the view of the man and his work as "anti-spiritual."

Spirituality is not a matter of ideology, however, and the transpersonal nature of an approach is a fact that overrides statements about it. Perls' personal experience of satori (described in his autobiography) and his experience with meditation (he once told me, while living in Esalen, that he practiced at least an hour a day) undoubtedly served as a background to his shaping of Gestalt therapy—perhaps without knowing it—into a modern equivalent of Buddhist practice.

Buddhist practice is essentially awareness training plus morality, and so is Gestalt therapy, even though the word "morality" may seem as far from it as spirituality. Inasmuch as the therapeutic process in the Gestalt approach involves an attempt to debilitate what Karen Horney (Perls' analyst) called the "tyranny of shoulds" with which ordinary morality goes hand in hand, the approach may at first seem not only anti-spiritual but anti-moral. More deeply considered, however, it creates a context (particularly in its group form) for the practice of virtues such as courage and authenticity which are the gist of moral development—beyond specific rules of behavior. Indeed, as I have expressed elsewhere, the therapist's actions may be understood, from one point of view, as a systematic negative reinforcement of phoniness and support of genuine self-expression.

Morality may be understood as the interpersonal work of traditional spirituality. The early masters of different cultures must have clearly realized how mental development may be self-deceptive if contemplative practices are pursued without a foundation of a practice directed at the transcendence of such compulsive appetitive and aversive behaviors usually called "passions": no lying, no stealing, no killing or harming are in the Eastern ways of growth not mere morality, as they have come to be in our watered-down Mosaic tradition but, as in Patanjali, preliminaries to samadhi, and as in the Buddha's "Eightfold Noble Path," aspects of right livelihood and right effort, which follow from right view, and prepare the ground for right mindfulness and concentration. It is hard to imagine a successful attempt to lead a pure life in this traditional sense without a process of personality change involving a diminution of deficiency needs and a decreased reliance on deceptiveness. In the absence of an appropriate mental context, and in a climate of authoritarianism (both, conditions of our cultural background), morality becomes moralism, however, which leads, not to increasing transcendence of deficiency (i.e. non-attachment), but to repression.

The greening of our once puritanical America has been characterized by a breakdown of repression, and the many therapies conducive to this—heralded by psychoanalysis—are characterized not by the control of behavior but by the surrender of control; not by inhibition, but by expression.

Gestalt therapy is, to a considerable extent (like other contemporary therapies) a way to awareness through expression—not only verbal but motor-gestural, imaginal and, broadly speaking, artistic. What is often forgotten, however, is that the Gestalt approach involves a no less important but subtler and less explicated element of voluntary inhibition: inhibition of the obsessive conceptualization, of manipulation, and of inauthentic behavior ("games"). True, "everything goes" in the Gestalt framework as far as experience is concerned, and its expression, but acting out, dramatic as it may be in the context of a guided experience, is not anything that we might call a Gestalt rule. Precisely because the manipulative and inauthentic behavior characteristic of the neurotic modes of being-in-the- world involves an attempt to *avoid* certain experiences, the attitude of the therapists is to invite an undoing of such avoidance, a "staying with it," however painful or confusing. In Perls' view, our awareness is constricted because we have not accepted our suffering, and thus the therapeutic process necessarily involves (like in the spiritual traditions, we might add) an element of austerity. The basic austerity, we can say, is the non- indulgence of what the spiritual traditions call the ego, and Perls called "character" and equated with a system of obsolete fixed responses that interfere with organismic function. To him (and this was an unpopular view at the time) the ideal human being would be beyond character—a statement that we can translate into: "would function at a transpersonal level."

Since Perls was a fervent non-dualist—in the sense of denying "the superstition that there is a separation, yet interdependency of two kinds of substance, the mental and the physical," he preferred the word *organism* to terms such as *soul* or *Higher Self*. To him "matter-mind as unity is truly organismic." His choice of terminology (borrowed from Smuts and Goldstein) has no doubt contributed to the generalized impression that his view was materialistic rather than spiritual (i.e. transpersonal). This assumption is easily dismissed if we consider his view of awareness (together with space and time) as intrinsic to a tri-une universe throughout its different levels of organization. Furthermore, he adds in *In and Out of the Garbage Pail*[1]:

> "*Thus matter seen through eyes of mine*
> *Gets god-like connotation*"

and

---

[1] *In and Out of the Garbage Pail*, F.S. Perls (New York: Bantam, 1971).

> *"The triple God is ultimate*
> *He is creative power*
> *Of all the universal stuff."*

If the morality of Gestalt therapy is one of authenticity and non-manipulation (of self or other), its awareness training may be summed up in the statement that J.S. Simkin proposed as a capsule definition of the approach: "I and thou, here and now." In other words, it is a practice of awareness in relationship (though this may at times be an internalized relationship). In this it differs from the Buddhist practice of insight meditation or Vipassana, which is in its basic form a practice of awareness in isolation. Just as this awareness training (the seventh item in the Buddhist Eightfold Path) is a transpersonal process, the practice of awareness in relationships may be characterized, like Gestalt therapy in general, as a bringing of the transpersonal into the interpersonal.

The cultivation of here and now awareness in Gestalt therapy goes hand in hand with another issue underlined by traditional psychologies, Buddhism in particular. Let us call it openness: to be aware of what is given here and now in our experiential fields involves a basic gesture of allowing—an indiscriminate acceptance of experience, which may be said to involve in turn a relinquishment of standards and expectations. Inasmuch as this openness cuts across mental content, it lies, again, in the transpersonal realm. It is expressed in Gestalt therapy in a number of ways, other than the injunction of being aware without self-manipulation. One of these is what Fritz Perls called (after S. Friedlander) "creative indifference." By this he meant the ability to remain in a neutral point, disengaged from the conceptual or emotional polar opposites at play in every moment of awareness. Perls displayed a striking measure of creative indifference as a psychotherapist by his being able to stay in the zero point without being caught up in his patient's games. I think of the zero point as a refuge of the Gestalt therapist in the midst of intense participation: not only a source of strength, but his ultimate self-support.

Another aspect of openness in Gestalt therapy, beyond the acceptance of experience and the relinquishment of attempts to control its content, is the acceptance of non-experience: the acceptance of nothingness. To this Perls gave so much importance that he described the successful therapeutic process as one leading "from the sterile void to the fertile void." By nothingness he meant no-thingness—i.e. non-articulate undifferentiated awareness, and in speaking of a fertile void he implied that being at home in this undifferentiated awareness is the foundation or ground for a healthy figure formation of articulate awareness in the here and now. Not infrequently the Gestalt therapist can observe the sequence of nothingness—psychological explosion, much as a partial death-rebirth, and even though Perls knew well that "to die and to be reborn is not easy," it is this eminently transpersonal process that he saw as the gist of therapy, and even life. His wholehearted involvement in it is reflected in one of the oil paintings which he left behind: a self portrait in which he is seen embracing his own skeleton.

Not only does Gestalt therapy share with Buddhism (and other spiritual paths) its prescription of virtuous relationship and awareness cultivation, the awareness of pain and death included in particular; it also shares with ancient prototypes its embodiment of the fierce guru, who pierces and tramples on the human ego. Hesse has remarked that there are teachers who are outwardly compassionate and teachers whose compassion speaks through the blows of a stick. Fritz, like the archetypal Zen master, was a wielder of the stick: he was a master of ego-reduction before Oscar Ichazo introduced the term, and his tribe has cultivated this ability, taking it so much for granted that we do not think of regarding it as a technique.

More than a Zen master, however, Fritz resembled the earliest transpersonal individual and therapist: the shaman. Shamanistic, too, is the precedent of the Gestalt therapist's role—that of an experience-guide, a consciousness conductor. This is also the role of those who work with body awareness, with fantasy, or with guided meditation; it may be said that contemporary therapy is becoming increasingly shamanistic in style, in this as in other regards. What makes the role of the Gestalt therapist particularly shamanistic, however, is its versatility, being characterized by an organic movement between the sensory, affective, cognitive, interactive and imaginal domains, and, potentially at least, that of consciousness as such.

Beyond this role as an experience-guide, however, the Gestalt therapist is likely to carry, to a greater or lesser extent, the imprint of Fritz Perls in his being, and Fritz was shaman in more than his role: in his reliance on intuition, in his scientific-artistic orientation, his combination of power and ordinariness, his unconventional ways and defiance of tradition, his familiarity with heavens and hells, and perhaps most importantly, his Dionysian-mindedness and appreciation of surrender. I think, too, that he was not unlike a true shaman when he described himself as "50% son of God and 50% son of a bitch." The transpersonal in the interpersonal.

Chapter Two

Gestalt and Meditation— and Other Topics[1]

When Joe some days ago asked me what I would be talking about today, I asked him, "Could I talk not about one thing, but about a number of things?" He agreed, and I am now grateful for the freedom to make of this talk a series of mini-lectures.

One idea that I had upon being invited to talk to you was to read fragments of the first chapter of a book completed in 1970 and subsequently lost, which included the recently published "Techniques of Gestalt Therapy." Of this opening chapter I happened to have a carbon copy at the time when the typescript was lost in a xeroxing place even though part of it was published by Ornstein in his anthology, *Nature of Human Consciousness*, I felt inclined to share parts of it today, as a complement to my statement on techniques. Its very title will tell you why: "On the Primacy of Attitude and the Transmission of Experience." I don't want to begin my presentation proper with reading, however—much less with the reading of old stuff—and so I turn, for now, to my second idea.

Another thought I had, on occasion of this invitation, was to complete the now independent book on

[1] This chapter is an edited version of my opening address given at *The Gestalt Journal's* Second Annual Conference on the Theory and Practice of Gestalt Therapy, Baltimore, 1981. It was edited for publication by *Journal* editor Joe Wysong, and was published in the Spring, 1982, issue (5-1) of *The Gestalt Journal*. Reprinted with permission.

techniques. As you may know, this ends with a chapter on "Techniques of Integration," where I speak of such things as the undoing of projections, intrapersonal encounters, and the dramatization of sub-personalities. I always felt unfinished about that chapter and thought I would finish it with the stimulus of this invitation. I was too lazy or busy, I must say.

Anyhow—let me say a few things more on the subject. As you know, intra-personal encounters frequently take the form of topdog vs. underdog or superego vs. id. I like Fritz' set of terms; it offers a descriptive terminology independent from the assumptions of instinct theory, and implies the recognition of the reactive ("anti-topdog") aspect of the underdog. We need not get stuck on terminology, however. Obviously, the polarity in question is the same observed by transactional analysts when they speak of parent and child.

When you carry out these encounters, sometimes the outcome is that one sub-self gets rid of the other. Underdog says, "Go to hell," and the problem is apparently solved. I think that is a valid temporary solution, the expression of a re-balancing of the psyche. But I can't believe that it is a definitive solution. I believe in the integration of personality more than in that: that is, in the achievement of a functioning in which somehow the energies that have been crystallized in these conflicting entities come together.

Inviting the split personalities within the individual to talk to each other is certainly a step toward integration, and it may even prove enough on occasion. Still, one of the most important questions in psychotherapy is that of how we may expedite this integration. Rather than tackle the issue at the technical level, however, let me propose that—in this, as in many other cases—our understanding and attitude count more than a "how to" approach.

Already to *aim* at integration makes a difference, and once we are as therapists conscious of this aim, techniques proceed from our intent. I have frequently used the analogy: "How about imagining that both of you will live forever in the same boat; you will always inhabit the same body. Can't you start moving towards contracts? Can't you think of a way of living better with each other?" If—once the aggression and pain have been ventilated—you make the suggestion that topdog and underdog are chained for life or have to live in the same room forever this may bring an integrative orientation to their dialogue.

In addition, certain things may be said about the nature of the superego that can be helpful. As you know the superego was interpreted by Freud as introjective. The first conception of the superego was this: we "should" ourselves as the world once did to us. Then Fritz Perls' most trusted mentor, Karen Horney, formulated an alternative interpretation of the superego: that it results from the idealization of our early strategies in coping with the environment. We idealize meekness, we idealize toughness, we idealize coolness, and so on. In general we make virtues of our strategic needs.

I want to propose to you still another view of the superego: one perfectly compatible and even implicit in both the introjective and strategic views. And I think most important to make explicit: we may say that topdog is, originally, a way of protecting ourselves, and in this regard a self-created parent. So our superego really wants to help. Topdog is destructive only in that it doesn't take into account the reality of the situation of the total person. Topdog commands underdog that it immediately, right now, be different, which is an impossibility. And yet at heart it wants to help.

Much of what happens in the course of effective Gestalt therapy can be viewed as a transmutation of energies. Usually the process is akin to an exorcism in which the act of expression serves to bring awareness of a deeper motivation underlying the apparent one—a motivation that is organismic and of which the surface expression is a vicissitude. The same can be held to be the case in regard to the fate of the superego in successful therapy. To put it briefly: its "topdoggish," destructive aspect, can be exorcised when it can become conscious of its deeper intent as self-created parent—i.e. helpful collaborator.

I have been made most aware of this issue through a booklet by the Argentinian psychotherapist, Norberto Levy—entitled "From Self-Rejection to Self-Assistance." He develops precisely this idea of a transmutation of energy: of the transmutation of self-rejection until it becomes "intelligent" enough of its original intention. He describes this in the form of a cartoon—or, more precisely, a set of two cartoons—reprinted here. The first shows a man going out to work in the morning with his briefcase, drops of sweat already flying from his pores as he rushes—with a clock in the background showing his struggle with time. Then he's shown in a bus surrounded by other unhappy people—all half dead. Next he's shown at work with his boss—who points his finger down over the head of our little man. There are several episodes like these, until he's shown coming to bed at night—lying down and starting to dream. And then he dreams that he is at the beach with a beautiful girl. And he dreams that he, at his desk, is pointing his finger at somebody else. And then there is a moment in the dream where his dream-self looks down and sees his body sleeping... and he looks further... and sees the content of all the previous cartoons. He sees himself leaving for work, the bus ride, at the office with a huge pile of papers on his desk. And he's so disgusted at all this life that he *shoots* at the fellow down there. In the final

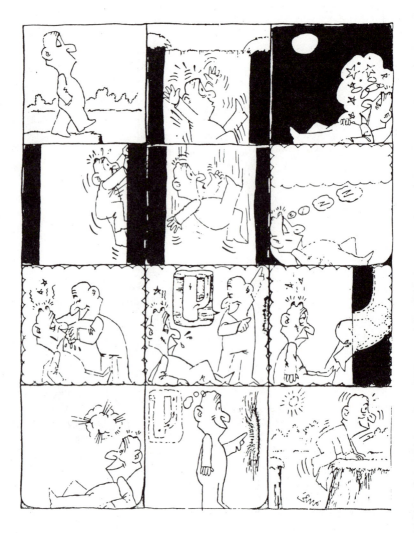

drawing the man on the bed is shown with blood dripping from his temple.

Here we have the gist of the topdog "torture game," as Fritz called it. There is pain and we want to avoid it. We create a wonderful image of ourselves that doesn't suffer and has a different identity—a wonderful false identity. Then this grandiose, proud identification—a substitute self—looks down at the individual's reality, doesn't like it, and becomes either suicidal or a chronic killer.

The second cartoon shows somebody falling into something like a well, knocking himself out, trying to climb out. Impossible. He falls down and knocks himself further. Loses consciousness. Starts dreaming. And in the dream this healthier person dreams with himself coming to his rescue. Somebody with his features comes to his rescue as he's lying there on the bottom of the well and shows him something which in the cartoon is not expressed in words but in a drawing of the empty well with a communicating shaft on the side. He wakes up. "Ahah!" He goes and—just as his dream anticipated—finds a hole in the wall. Through this narrow tube he can creep to the surface.

A self-same psychological entity—the "ego-ideal," if you like—is the protagonist's alter-ego in both instances (though in the service of repression in the first case) then, in the context of an acceptance of experience, in that of "self-assistance."

As another part of this Gestalt collage that I am bringing to you, I described to Joe over the phone as "Gestalt, Meditation, and Lust." I don't know how much that conveys. There is plenty to say about meditation and Gestalt therapy. And there is plenty to say about Gestalt and lust. It is an interesting polarity, this one of meditation and lust. Meditation has to do with being beyond desires; with a centeredness that is not needy, that doesn't require the support of things going one way or the other. Lust, on the contrary, involves an intensification of desires, a glorification of desires, even. There are two ways of thinking of this polarity. You can assign positive value to one of its sides: "Meditation is good: nonattachment, a great philosophy. Lust, however, is a passion to overcome; lust is oral aggression, neediness, the essence of neurosis." This is easy to defend: nonattachment is precisely one of the factors of growing up. Maturing is becoming less dependent than a child was, less needy, less oral—more self-supporting.

Yet in another sense of the word—present when Irving Stone calls his biography of Van Gogh *Lust for Life* —the word stands for something positive. And one of the most interesting things that can be said of Gestalt as a way of growth among others, new and old, is that it contains this polarity of mental inwardness and expressiveness; or, if you like, of nonattachment and desiring. Not as an aim, and that is a distinction worth holding in mind, but as a therapeutic process.

Let me first go into detail in regard to the first part of this subject and discuss "Gestalt and Meditation."

There are many points of contact between Gestalt therapy and meditation. In some sense you could say that Gestalt therapy is meditation in an interpersonal context. The first commonality between the two domains is that Gestalt is an awareness training and a major component of meditation is the cultivation of awareness. The practice of attending to ongoing experience, deepening this awareness of the here and now, is common to both. However, meditation is usually practiced in isolation whereas Gestalt therapy occurs in relationship, and meditation traditions know a stage of awareness beyond the awareness of the here and now: an awareness retroflected unto itself, which devours itself and dissolves into a condition of consciousness without an object—

consciousness without a subject, "nondual aware-ness," *sunyata*, cognition of the "ground of Being."

There are many techniques of meditation, each with a different focus. Within the classical repertoire there is none more related to Gestalt therapy than the form called Vipassana—the royal road to enlighten-ment in early Buddhism (and present Theravada). Vipassana consists essentially in sustained practice of here and now awareness while sitting with eyes closed. Much emphasis is placed during this practice on the awareness of body sensations. I don't think Fritz Perls knew much about Hinayana Buddhism, but he rediscovered the importance of "coming to one's senses" and unwittingly created an interper-sonal extension of the old technique.

Another common factor between meditation and Gestalt therapy is the suspension of concep-tualization. This brings Gestalt closest to Zen—as Emil Weiss pointed out in the fifties, an observation of which Fritz was subsequently very aware.

There is, even further, the related concept of function-without-thought or moving without think-ing. Engaging in action without "computing" what you are doing. This can be viewed as another exten-sion of sitting meditation, embodied in traditional forms like Tai Chi.

Beyond these rather formal parallels between meditation and Gestalt, however, there are more im-plicit ones. For instance, I remember coming away from a workshop with Fritz many years ago and commenting that to me the gift of those days had been Fritz's "so-whatness." In the face of great drama, these magic words would come out of his mouth: "So What." The thought that you could just drop it—that the drama was unnecessary—the awareness that much of suffering is creating problems for ourselves, could not be more succinctly expressed.

Meditation is the most direct way the mind can work on the mind, right now, beyond content. It involves a change of attitude. And Gestalt is full of that in the most creative way. My experience of Fritz working was, to a great extent, this. By being in front of another, and by being a little freer, by realizing the unnecessary problems of the other or, let's say, by realizing where the dysfunctional attitude of the other came in, by virtue of the "creative indifference" of which he spoke and of which he was such an exemplar, he was a silent therapeutic presence, conveying another attitude toward experience, another way to be. Something like: "In the face of this awareness, in the face of whatever is here and now, in the face of painful sensations, in the face of pain in your life, in the face of painful emotions even, why not make the best of it?" Not with self-deceiving optimism, but with the more functional position of enjoying the most in the midst of discomfort. I don't know if I am coming across in what I am saying. It's like rolfing. A good thing about rolfing is that you learn to relax while you are in pain. It's not the same thing to relax in a comfortable arm chair as it is to relax when somebody—especially Ida Rolf, rolfs you. She would use her elbow in a terrible way, and was at the same time, obviously, the good earth mother incarnate. She inspired trust and gave you the feeling that she knew what she was doing. That was part of the therapy, as I see it. Gestalt has much to do with that. Of going through the pain, not in a contorted way, but in a "so what" way. Behind all the dropping of "games" there is this element of nonattachment which is the gist of meditation.

Beyond that, meditation aims at self-support, like Gestalt, though meditation stresses it further, for it talks of a degree of self-support where you can relinquish *anything*. It invites you to a state of mind that is fully unsupported and does not *need* to be supported. It is a paradoxical fact that if you give up support, you don't fall, but on the contrary, start flying. Buddhism and Taoism speak of this letting go of all supports, outer and inner, as a being supported in emptiness. In something which, looked at from the outside, can be only described as nothing at all—even though a most fertile nothingness.

We could say that this center is our true being. The outer layers constitute our character. Our outer being is the system of the fixed (and thus partially obsolete) responses that we call "our personality." Insofar as we identify with our personality, we are the "little self" or "little mind" of mystical writers, the "ego" that—as Fritz makes explicit in *Ego Hunger and Aggression*—interferes with organismic self-regulation.

Let me insert here some further remarks on the issue of "being oneself" that I have tangentially brought into this discussion. As some of you may know, Paul Goodman did not care for the notion; I don't share his view in this regard, and I think many Gestaltists don't. If the theoreticians have not emphasized authenticity, it is "in the air" so to say. Here is an illustration: Joe Wysong was just telling me on the way from the airport how Fritz helped others by being himself — and how it also happens that some, instead of following his example and being *themselves*, became Fritz. Another: some years ago I interviewed Jim Simkin on videotape for the "Gestalt Therapy Record," and this was one of the questions I posed to him: "Do you regard being oneself an important tenet in Gestalt therapy?" "The most important one," was his answer.

The theory of psychotherapy in general is something that lags behind the fact, and this is much the case in Gestalt. Life, like art, contains more than theory spells out. In this case, the theory has emphasized Gestalt formation and allowed the notion of genuineness to recede into the background—even though everybody in the Gestalt subculture was implicitly acquainted with the issue. Yet I think that "being oneself" is a more fundamental theoretical proposition for Gestalt than "Gestalt formation"—which after all, is one of a number of metaphors that we may use for the shifting of the stream of consciousness. Fritz was something of a shaman, and in that a trickster. Obviously, Gestalt psychology was a strong ally to have on the road to academic accreditation, and it sounded impressive to draw the equation: "What associationist psychology is to Freudian psychoanalysis, Gestalt psychology is to mine." People didn't seem to realize that, in regard to theory, the emperor had no clothes—and they are still looking for the mysterious connection between Gestalt psychology and Gestalt therapy with questionable success.

Meditation may be described as a moving towards one's center and toward the suspension of one's character. When we use the expression "being oneself," however, we don't think so much of being-in-stillness as of being in action; and in Gestalt therapy there is an element that is most coherent with the spirit of meditation but which the meditation schools of the past may be said to have neglected: the *expression* of freedom. Meditation of course seeks to develop an inner freedom, a psychological permeability, we might say—an openness to process and experience. Yet there is also an outer freedom to be considered: a communicative freedom which might be regarded as the proof of openness. (We can communicate what we can accept.) And beyond the freedom of mere verbal communication, expressive freedom proper, the freedom of affective communication.

In this Gestalt and meditation are wonderfully complementary to each other—meditation emphasizing attention, Gestalt expression. Yet the two rest on the same pillars—as the good life itself: awareness and spontaneity. What is spontaneity? We may be closer to it if we clarify what it is not: it is *not* impulsiveness, it is not the mere expression of urges and emotions. The topic of spontaneity brings us back to that of being oneself. The idea of being true to oneself implies, of course, the existence of a "self." If this term is to have any meaning, that must be the counterpart to character structure, the uncondi-tioned—and, implicitly, the organismic.

Yet the usual situation in practice is that one runs into the question of what "self" to be true to. Thus, I want to point out that the issue of spontaneity cannot be separate from the issue of integration. While there are sub-selves, sub-personalities with boundaries be-tween them, there cannot be a self one might be true to. And while there is "character," there is a defensive structure and sub-selves. The only thing that can be called a self is an integrated totality, and that is the way Fritz used the term in his later years, when he wrote of the topdog/underdog and the mute self witnessing. The mute self hardly exists ordinarily because it has been swallowed up into the fragments. The process of healing can be seen as the melting of the parts into organismic function.

Let us now turn to Gestalt and lust. Generally we understand lust as related to the indulging of desires and in that sense we might say that Gestalt therapy is "lusty"—for there is in most Gestaltists an implicit belief in the therapeutic value of asserting, express-ing and gratifying one's desires. Also, lust is con-nected with a thirst for excitement that is typical in the Gestalt atmosphere. One thing is excitement, another the *thirst* for excitement—which is the other side of a propensity to boredom. And still another is pseudo-excitement. I remember that when I first worked with a Gestalt group in Germany and went around the room with the question, "How are you feeling now?" I found that everybody was "excited." It was very clear to me that "excitement" in their language was idealized anxiety. (By the way I don't buy Fritz's slogan that anxiety is excitement minus

oxygen. It can also be excitement minus a cigarette.
Anything can take away your anxiety and turn it into
action or rather distraction.)

I was made aware of lust as a personality bias
when I was exposed to the characterology that was
part of the Arica system. Or, if you like, of the "Fourth
Way" psychology tradition which was introduced to
the west first by Gurdjieff and in greater detail by
Oscar Ichazo. This involves a typology akin to that of
the seven deadly sins of Christianity (only that it
includes fear and vanity as sins—enlarging the
seven-fold into a nine-fold). One of the deadly sins,
as you know, is lust, which I had always interpreted
very literally, just as I had interpreted gluttony
literally too, not giving a second thought to subtler
meanings. On being acquainted with the characterology of the "Fourth Way" (as this tradition within
Sufism sometimes calls itself), I knew that gluttony
stood for a certain kind of orality. In the case of lust
what is meant is a kind of character that has been
often delineated in the psychological literature. Reich
talked about it as phallic narcissistic character;
Fromm called it the exploitative personality, noting
its connection with the psychoanalytic notion of oral
aggression. Lowen speaks of the "psychopathic
type," Horney spoke of a "vindictive character" and
most of us simply use the expression "sadistic." It
was unavoidable, after being exposed to this characterology, to start typing all of my acquaintances and
people I had met in my life—and Fritz could not
escape from the diagnosis. Ah, he was a lusty one!
Having a clearer focus on Fritz's characterological
bias than I had before made me immediately aware
of the projection of his personality on what became
the Gestalt therapy movement. There is a fraction of
Gestalt therapy that is independent of personality
and another fraction that is an imitation of Fritz, and
we need to discriminate in this, to take what is valid
and leave what is arbitrary. I think by now almost

everyone is doing Gestalt in his or her individual style. But still it is useful to keep the distinction. Not long ago I heard a definition of Gestalt as "the work of a psychopath teaching obsessive compulsives to become hysterics." The joke reflects the observation of how lust puts value on excitement in itself, how expression, at best a tool, comes to be regarded as an end. Intensity replaces depth, and conversely, entertainment is idealized as therapeutic achievement.

A subject related to the lust bias in Gestalt therapy is the assumption in Gestalt of an ethics of self-expression and self-indulgence. Obviously surrendering to impulse is a useful Gestalt technique. The same can be said of the invitation to members of a group to be as transparent in the group situation, as open with each other as possible and willing to experiment with new behaviors. The great thing about Gestalt is that it involves at the individual and group levels the opportunity of experimenting with self regulation. You can go beyond your boundaries, there. You are in a situation that is for that. Yet it is generally assumed either implicitly or explicitly that this is the way to live and you go out into the world bitching or you go out grabbing for your part of the pie, making room for yourself as you are urged to do in the context of assertiveness training. The outcome in the two situations is different, however. In therapy groups what happens is what I have called a "psychological judo." You take a dysfunctional impulse—it may be destructive, it may be greedy, whatever—and in expressing it, you get to the core of that experience (the intelligence of its intent)—by which awareness it is transmuted. Gestalt therapy is like an exorcism, in that regard, but in real life the exorcism doesn't go deep enough. The situation doesn't lend itself to going deep enough, and my impression is that it neither works very well for the individual nor does it work well at all for society. Behind the bias toward cathartic therapy over the attempt to extinguish dysfunctional behavior through inhibition is of course the tendency to believe in intensity and the bias against frustration, a bias toward permissiveness over control and excitement over inhibition that should be questioned. And we gain a better perspective over it, I am proposing, in the light of this idea of a "cultural disease" of Gestalt, a characterological contamination.

Lust has generated jewels—*and* let us be on the alert for a possibly limiting bias. I think people like Moses, Buddha and others were highly inspired in their conception of "virtue." The ways they proposed in regard to being among others may be seen as valuable works of psycho-social engineering. In them, the individual is urged to exercise ego continence in daily life, to inhibit his greed and destructiveness, and to practice contentedness. Essentially the yogic precepts and religious ethics constitute on the one hand a therapy through the inhibition of "character"—and on the other a means of making society a better place to live in. I think that there is plenty of room for an ego, inhibition practice and that this is more conducive to good relations than the behavior appropriate in a therapeutic group.

I mentioned Oscar Ichazo as one who introduced me to the "Fourth Way" typology. Oscar Ichazo had a saying that I remember on many occasions and in connection with many things in life ever since. It is one of the best sayings I have heard: "The devil doesn't know for whom he works." In regard to Fritz's intensity bias and his hedonistic propensities, I think this is very true. He hated neurotics; so he set out to exterminate neurosis. He hated dependency—so he helped people stand on their own. He also hated phoniness. He was hostile to it. In his presence you were encouraged in your genuineness and discouraged in your phoniness. Because of his lusty search for excitement, his active nature, his liking for friction, he was bored by verbalization. He didn't like words—he liked the expression of emotion, engagement. He was a contact freak. Yet from his appreciation of contact derived the valuable Gestalt approach of watching for the interruption of contact as a psychotherapeutic clue. Not even contact was enough for him. The actor in him enjoyed dramatization best, and this proved an inestimable therapeutic asset. If the individual undergoing therapy engages in a discipline of awareness and spontaneity—or awareness and authenticity if you like, or awareness and surrender to organismic regulation—what the therapist does is urging him or her, like a stage director, to "be this," to "be that."

I don't know whether anybody has pointed out that such invitation to dramatize is intimately connected to a form of traditional meditation: meditation with an object—which leads to "absorption." Every spiritual tradition knows absorptive meditation in one form or another. You visualize something and then you become it. You contemplate some archetypal representation—give life to it—and then absorb it into your being—you become Dionysus, Shiva, a bodhisattva, whatever. This act of becoming one with archetypal material Fritz turned into that of becoming one with your body, to become one with your hand, with your tears, with your voice, your dream-self, *yourself*. This amounts to a democratization of absorptive meditation—much like that which Freud brought about with his interpretation of dreams. David Bakan, who wrote a book on Freud and the Jewish mystical tradition, claims that a significant inspiration for Freud was the cabalistic tradition of interpretation of symbols. (Interestingly, his colleagues called him "the new Joseph.") He may be said to have made the process "democratic" in that he did not interpret traditional symbolic material, but assisted his patients in interpreting their *own* symbols, their personal unconscious creations.

Where Freud put interpretation, Fritz put dramatization—expecting insight to flow spontaneously from it. I think that Fritz's democratic tendency too had something to do with his lust-style. The "lust character" tends to be a little more popular in his inclinations: it stands for the underdog, is sensate, doesn't like religion, doesn't like abstractions. It is frequently the type of the revolutionary.

What I have been saying illustrates how a personality bias, in the presence of genius, *can* produce wonderful fruits. The mechanism is something like the formation of a pearl. As you know, the pearl is a disease of the oyster; it grows around a grain of sand that has fallen into the oyster's delicate body, and we harvest the outcome of the irritation.

Let me point out something important about Fritz's bias as a vindictive, phallic-narcissistic type. His tendency as a bully, as one who wanted to top everybody, was to deny everything else. To put down psychoanalysis, put down character analysis, put down all human wisdom before him if possible. As a consequence, of course, some things were left out of the formation of Gestalt. The first thing I want to try to bring in, especially since it ties in so much with what I have been saying in the context of meditation, is the notion of nonattachment. I think this is a very forgotten aspect of the process of human maturation and transformation. I already mentioned that we go from the oral attachment of the suckling to a certain measure of ego strength in the good sense of the term in classical psychology. And that means a certain forbearance, and qualities such as patience that come from adult growth and don't go along with greedy lust. There is a background of nonattachment in Gestalt that is not ordinarily seen, I think, because of its characteristically Dionysian and orgiastic foreground. Actually you need nonattachment even for that orgiastic foreground, because there is no letting go without nonattachment. You need nonattachment to stop whatever you are doing, to stand still, to just sit as Zen people do, to drop whatever games, to just be there, to soberly stay with the awareness of your perceptions of the moment rather than go into fantasies or play games; all that needs nonattachment. And you *also* need nonattachment to flow, to surrender to expression. So this is a valuable theoretical proposition, nonattachment. And one that because of a certain anti-theoretical bias or a lack of interest in formulations stemming from the spiritual traditions, especially the far eastern ones, was left out.

The same can be said of love. It is a bias of the lusty-sadistic propensity to be a champion of aggression and to put love in the background. It is hard not to agree that love, like nonaggression, is part of health. Freud put it very simply when a journalist asked him, "Dr. Freud, what is the aim of psychoanalysis?" That's always a challenge to get very simple and come to basics. He said, "The ability to work and love." That was spelled out much further by Fromm. I am very fond of his elaboration on the subject in *Man for Himself*. His statement is that ethics rests on a way of being rather than on behavior, and that the virtuous way of being, "if we are going to call anything that, rests on one's ability to love oneself," out of which in turn flows the ability to love others. If it is a characteristic of health, if it is a part of the therapeutic process to transcend childish ambivalence, as psychoanalytic parlance puts it, maybe it is useful to have that in mind. Not as a trap for dutifulness: to "try to love" of course never worked. As centuries of Christianity have proven, trying to love leads to the puritanical impasse. But that does not mean giving up as a therapist an orientation toward the ideal of love, an orientation to love as a therapeutic goal. In connection with love enhancing therapy as an alternative to "trying to love," I want to bring in some words on the therapeutic process known, mostly on the west coast and in South America, as the Fischer-Hoffman process. Before doing this, however, let me interpolate a general remark:

I regard the Gestalt therapeutic attitude and "way" truly a "teaching"—and a high one at that. No rules: only awareness. Awareness and spontaneity. Or, better: awareness and naturalness. Naturalness is not impulsiveness, but something that Fritz had the intuition to articulate—a synthesis of spontaneity and deliberateness. (You have much of that in Zen, especially in Zen art.) Spontaneity, but controlled spontaneity. *And* controlled spontaneity. A high synthesis, and the utmost of psychotherapy as art. Creative psychotherapy by implicit definition. Against psychotherapy as art are the underlying systems of psychotherapy with their rules and techniques and rituals. Gestalt is rich in its repertoire of ready-made psychotherapeutic tools—and yet it is also more than that, particularly in view of its implicit emphasis on healing through authentic encounter.

The Fischer-Hoffman process is remarkably effective I think, in spite of constituting a canned system, a systematization. A precious can. You have the art of psychotherapy and you have technologies, and you can become so slick in the refinement of technology that the average therapist may be able to do better with good technology than a bad artist working with a great form.

Among the new systematized therapeutic processes—including such as primal scream therapy, scientology, est, and NLP, I think the Fischer-Hoffman or Quadrinity Process is of particular interest to Gestalt therapists, for it does the following important things: Firstly, it takes the individual through a guided catharsis of the pain and anger experienced in the course of growing up with father and mother or surrogates. Also, it involves a guided analytic process of insight into one's early life and present personality. However, the process does not stop at catharsis and insight, but proceeds to a guided "crossing" to a further change in attitude toward one's past and parents.

In the great Gestalt form you work *organically*, and invite the catharsis of the past as it surfaces in the flow of experience, the continuum of awareness. There is something great about doing it organically in the moment when it emerges, and there is something to be said for having the whole ground covered. There is a "time track" as the scientologists say. We have "memory tapes," and each specific memory its pain component, and there is something to be said for completeness in going through this time track both chronologically and in terms of the issues reflected in it. Sometimes in a Gestalt session you will express a lot of anger toward your mother for this or that, for instance, and in that particular session you don't express or even think of anger toward your mother for such and such other. Eventually, however, it is important that all our experience be transmuted and that we may come to have an embracing and integrated grasp of our life, character and situation. This particular approach, the Fischer-Hoffman process, does that. It stresses the complete catharsis of the pain involved in relations with the parents for it rests on the assumption that our relationships are screwed up because our relationships with our parents got screwed up first. In this it echoes the psychoanalytic view: our contact with the world has gone wrong because our contact with our first world, our original world, went wrong. We are bound to the repetition compulsion because we were never finished with our parents.

But what is finishing with our parents? I propose: what is unfinished is what we have not forgiven. At one point we betrayed our love relationship with the first human beings in our life. Those most important human beings were just not sane enough to truly love us and we ended up inhibiting our original, spontaneous love and consciously or unconsciously resenting them. We were not ripe enough for compassion. We were too scared to trust and went into an emergency response, a stress mechanism. To end with the projection of our experience of our parents onto the present world as the repetition compulsion we must *finish* with them, and this involves forgiving them for whatever pain we suffered. Perhaps the most original contribution of the Fischer-Hoffman process I think is its sub-process of reaching forgiveness through understanding of our parents' conditioning as a response to their conditions. And then guiding the individual to the point of burying the hatchet, dropping the past, and beginning to love again.

I am curious. How many of you have heard about the Fischer-Hoffman process before? I see that only a minority of you. Let me tell you a bit of the story then. It was called psychic therapy at first when Bob Hoffman saw people individually. He was a tailor become a psychic. A man who discovered his gift in the aftermath of the death of his mother, as he wanted to believe that there was an entity beyond the grave, that his mother could still be communicated with. Even though he had no strong religious beliefs, he was persuaded to go to a church where a psychic answered questions from those present. This led to an impressive experience on his part, which motivated him to join a psychic development training group convening in the same church. Eventually he developed as a psychic and was contacted by a spirit who identified himself as Dr. Fischer, a Viennese psychoanalyst whom he had previously known. In time, Dr. Fischer therapized him and he went through considerable personality change. This sufficiently motivated him to carry out Dr. Fischer's wish to introduce the process to the world at large. I was one of his early patients and in spite of having been psychoanalyzed and self-analyzed, Gestalted, dianected, LSDed and so forth, I found the experience important in my personal and professional life. In the early days of SAT (a psycho-spiritual school that I formed in the early seventies, closed, and am now opening again) I applied for the first time the Fischer-Hoffman concepts as a group process, and Bob Hoffman soon did the same much better, proceeding thereafter to train trainers.

When I bring the Quadrinity Process to the attention of Gestaltists, I do not expect Gestalt therapists to begin leading Fischer-Hoffman groups—though that could be a good complement to specifically here-and-now work, work on late traumatic material and present conflicts and on dreams. Rather I expect that what this therapeutic system embodies may be "disembodied" by chewing up and assimilation, so that its virtues may enrich the organic process of Gestalt. To enrich it with an invitation to completeness and a contribution to "closure" in relationships and to enrich Gestalt-synthesis by a measure of synthesis between the organic and the systematic, the Dionysian and the Apollonian, spontaneity and deliberateness. After all, the integration of spontaneity and deliberateness was one of Fritz' late interests, and its conception one of his more original and important contributions. Spontaneity plus deliberateness equals intelligent naturalness— the Gestalt way.

I have talked to you about integration as the resolution of the topdog/underdog impasse, about Gestalt and meditation, Gestalt and lust, the place of "being oneself" in Gestalt therapy, about filling Gestalt theory holes with the concepts of nonattachment and love, and about what Gestalt can learn from a pop psychology, and I see that I won't get to reading my chapter on the primacy of attitude and the transmission of experience. I really had it with me for my security, to be sure that I wouldn't run dry before the due time. That is one of the hangups that I have never transcended: fearing that I will say everything that I have to say in five minutes.

I will say something else, however: I have drawn your attention to the Gestalt attitude of putting down everything else. A corollary to that observation is that it has left out things that it would do well to reinvite. In establishing itself, Gestalt (or rather the early Gestalt clan) needed to say "Here I am, I am the best." Now that it is established, it could well drop that game. I think, for instance, that there is an important place for character analysis in the therapeutic process, for the assistance of self-insight, self-understanding, understanding of one's life and the structure of one's character—not only implicitly through illuminating experiments in relationship and Gestalt expressive techniques. Also, I think that there is a place for more sophisticated bodywork than what may develop organically in the course of a session. I think that there is a place for lots of home work too, for making the best of the individual's opportunity to work all the time on his or her self in daily life.

Which brings me to what will be my closing statement—on the place of Gestalt in the process of psycho-spiritual guidance. I like that label— "psycho-spiritual guidance," because I don't think that the psychological process can be separated from the spiritual.

In my own practice, I have come to use Gestalt as part of a mosaic. A "holistic" mosaic. A mosaic of bodywork, feelingwork (with Gestalt as the basic tool), spiritual work proper (largely through meditation) and intellectual nourishment. Issues like understanding the meaning of life, or the connection of life to the cosmos are important to consider and don't have to be called "bullshit." I like to read Sufi stories to people I work with because, just as Buddhists are masters of silence, Sufis are masters of the word.

I think I have said enough.

Chapter Three

Dick Price:
A Memorial Baptism[1]

My immediate reaction to Joe Wysong's invitation to contribute to this anniversary issue of *The Gestalt Journal* was to transcribe a recent session. Then I received the transcript of a not-so-recent session, and, in honor of the synchronicity, I added some comments. Yet, after that, as I searched my files for materials to include in a forthcoming book, I happened on some pages that seemed much more fitting for this occasion: an even earlier session, yet that of one who is very present in the mental horizon of the Gestalt community.

I suppose most readers of this journal know who Dick Price was. If Michael Murphy was the brain and pocket of Esalen, and Fritz—the genius in residence—its heart, Dick, program director of Esalen from its beginning till not long ago, was its gut.

It is to Dick Price's nose that we owe the full flowering of Fritz and his work and its coming into the wide world, for his appreciation was in the background of Fritz's decision to make of Esalen his home after migrating to the West Coast.

I think that those who knew Dick—a champion for openness—will share my feeling that he would have enjoyed this post-mortem visit and sharing of himself with them through the pages of *The Gestalt Journal* on its tenth anniversary.

[1] *The Gestalt Journal*, Spring, 1987. Reprinted with permission.

The session I describe took place in May or June 1971, soon after my return from Arica, Chile, where I underwent experiences that influenced my Gestalt activity as well as everything else in my life in ways which I will not stop here to spell out. I would not characterize my work here as anything innovative, however: only empathic and creative enough to have had the intuition of asking Dick—immersed in the experiences of wateriness and childlikeness—to crystallize his experience further by "bringing his child to the fountain." It seems that in doing so I was alluding to a dream image earlier in the session. I will not comment further on the transcript—unfortunately a fragment—which begins like this:

DICK PRICE: ...I'm thinking of a particular passage... says Lao Tzu... who running dirty, runs clean like still water... (weeping) It's like I do this very well for others... (weeping)

CLAUDIO NARANJO: Just go over it once more.

DP: (weeping) Who, being dirty, running dirty... (pause)... I can't recall exactly... Who running dirty comes clean like clear water. Who being still brings others to fullness of life. I am kind of running like a stream, like I am turbid here, like I have a flow here, and my flow is just very slight...

CN: Just go over it once more.

DP: (weeping) Who, being dirty, running dirty... (pause)... I can't recall exactly... Who running dirty comes clean like clear water. Who being still brings others to fullness of life. I am kind of running like a stream, like I am turbid here, like I have a flow there, and my flow is just very slight...

CN: Please, can you still get in touch with that flowing of tears?

DP: Let me read in Lao Tzu a little bit. "I running dirty, come clean like clear water. I being still... like I kind of hold back my flow, and am afraid to show my weakness... "

CN: Yes, let go more. That's it—the child...

DP: The child, yes, that's it. I'm afraid to show my weakness: I can never cry. But I being still bring others to fullness of life. (weeping) Like I never... you know, myself how well I really do that...

CN: Yes.

DP: But I being still bring others to fullness, and I still do not fully allow my own life.

CN: My impression is that you have to allow yourself to be weak, and put all your toughness in the service of your weakness. I suggest you explore right now how you can allow your weakness.

DP: Yeah, like I need to be that child. I need to be that child unattacked... yeah, by letting be—you know. I can get done. Just let me be, just let me be. Let me be a child; let me be a butterfly. You don't have to drown me... It's almost the opposite. You won't allow my child, my fears, you won't allow my own moisture. And as Dick you want to drown me. The opposite: you want to dry me up. (chuckles) Dick, you want to dry me up; you won't allow me my own posture... I was looking for another word... you won't allow me my own posture... with the action, something of that sort. My own tears, my own process. It's been I've been trying to show you something, to plead with you, and I'd like to draw you into my life which allows tears (pause) and allows weakness. As Dick, well you know, never allow, I'm too stubborn... I won't allow you, I'll never show weakness or tears, you know. Maybe I'll love you... you know, occasionally, one tear, one tear. Just enough for life...

CN: Yes. You have that voice saying that, in you, but perhaps you could take some action in service of what you know are your best interests. I have a suggestion that you go through a little ritual. Sometimes rituals have the effect of bringing into life something. What I would suggest is taking that child to the fountain to which your dream mind wants to take him, and see if the dream develops differently.

DP: All right. See, I'm wondering if it is safe to let Dick change back from a butterfly to a child and kind of let Dick cradle me, and just let Dick take me to the fountain.

CN: Be Dick now. Be Dick taking the child.

DP: O.K. You are back as a child. Let's see. I feel the coldness of my hands. I both want to stroke and give you life and yet something in me, uhm, at least in goals, you know... my goal is to give warmth (chuckles)... my hands right now are really cold... yeah, so, what I have to do is cradle you with capability of means. So I can cradle you like that and I have to hold my hands out... there is another solution... rather than giving warmth in some way I am going to take warmth from the child...

CN: It can be together.

DP: Yeah, yeah. Perhaps it is possible for me to take warmth from you. I feel the pillow, I feel you as quite a bit warmer than my hands. I then give you warmth with my forearms and arms, but with my hands I have to take warmth from you. And, yeah, I can take you out by the fountain. (weeping) Where I am is like under a night sky and open pavilion, which is really very safe, uh—it is like a garden. There is a kinda, maybe a fountain that is almost as big as the room in diameter, fairly shallow, and it is just in the middle bubbling. A bubbling fountain. And, yeah, as Dick I feel no need to drown you. (pause) Yeah, like you are accompanying me in just watching the fountain... I can stroke you and give you strength, and give more warmth, and I can take your warmth. And we can just watch the play of the fountain together, there is no...

CN: Um-hum.

DP: We can wash and drink. There is need to... you know, there is no need to kill you. I have no need to kill you. I need your life.

CN: You are satisfied with contemplating this fountain together. I am curious as to whether the child has any other idea. Maybe since you are there you might do something else with the fountain.

DP: As a child, immediately I want to jump in and swim around and play under the water... you know... tsu, tsu, su... water comes down on me, kind of splash around, float. My legs are not too strong yet, but I can kind of, you know, move in the water... splashing, splashing a little water on Dick. It's not too cold. Try not to get my clothes wet. Yeah, now I feel that I can really both give strength and take strength from you. And that, uh, yeah, I really need you. I need your vitality in me. It's like a child. I need your unspoiled perceptions. I can't just operate on pseudo-strength and knowledge.

CN: And the child says, "Yeah, you need me..." (group laughter) Well, that sounded like a pact. That sounded like more or less the kind of pact that sometimes is held on the side of fountains and rivers, deaths, first baths...

DP: Yeah, bubbling—you know, just bubbled, and water and uh, plenty of room for, you know, the whole group could get into my fountain. You are welcome to play with my child... (pause) Now, you know, as the fountain, I am strong and I am steady; I just have endless vitality, you know. I keep circulating, and have room for warmth and moisture. Endless recirculation, you know... Perpetually giving life, strength. Room for both vitality and quietness. A lot of room, a lot of room... Like right in my center, like whesssh, just like bubbling, like you can also be quiet in me, in my reaches, yeah, you can have passion bubbling or you can have a quiet and peace in me, and you get to choose. I'm here, just steadiness and strength in this continual life, night and day...

CN: I feel very happy having been present at your baptism. I trust that when it happens once, it keeps happening.

SOMEONE IN THE GROUP: Can't operate without Kleenex.

ANOTHER: Not with big fountains. (group laughter)

DP: I have the feeling my tears are a lot more acceptable to me now, not equated with "I cry therefore I am weak." I cry with strength.

CN: Sure. Tremendously wise dream, your child having to be brought to the fountain, and against this archetypal process, ego getting in between, with revenge... (laughter)

DP: There is a statement attributed to Buddha: "I alone and the world... " I was never comfortable with that. You know, I am going to take some steps...

CN: Would you go through the moves; I think it would be a very good completion for the ceremony, giving the child his total rights. (group laughter)

DP: I'd rather change the (word missing) not alone and the world honorable...

[The transcript is all I have, and this sentence doesn't make sense to me. However, there is an allusion to the story of Buddha's birth, where, as is usual in the Sutras, he is addressed as the World Honored One. Dick here enacts the legend of the new-born Buddha taking seven steps after his birth and proclaiming his divinity.]

(laughter)

DP: O.K.... five, six, seven... (group laughter)

CN: I once heard Allen Ginsberg say that there was a time when he would go around the Berkeley campus saying "I am God" in a tone of voice that made others feel that they were not. It takes time to discover that we can all be.

Chapter Four

Gestalt Exercises

Psychotherapeutic exercises have been a particular interest of mine since early in my career. I started introducing these systematically in certain workshops at a time when I worked at Esalen in the late 60s. After Fritz left for Canada, I conducted two kinds of workshop there: Some (in collaboration with Bob Hall and Jack Downing) were regular Gestalt workshops (Jim Simkin conducted the training workshops at the time); in others I took advantage of the opportunity given to me by my sponsors to be innovative and devoted the mornings to meditation, the evenings to Gestalt hot seat work, and the afternoons to something in between: exercises in small groups where I explored the interface between meditation and encounter.

I think that much of what happens in psychotherapy is truly the doing of the patient, inasmuch as it is an internal process out of which converge the will to see and the will to heal. Psychotherapy, from one point of view, might be seen as a context in which this inner event can happen: as support for a self-therapeutic process. Whatever the measure of help that can be offered by the being and skill of the therapist anyhow, there is such a thing as working on one's self psychologically, and many people do so gropingly even without exposure to formal psychotherapy or spiritual guidance.

This view of mine on the possibility and importance of work on self therapy—supported by Fritz's own invitation to self therapy in the Gestalt exercises in the beginning of the 1951 classic, *Gestalt Therapy*—always interested me in devising interpersonal structures that would embody general therapeutic principles and might thus be helpful ways for people to carry out mutually assisted work on themselves. In the course of the years I have even refined the mini-lab situation to the point of obtaining substantial therapeutic results through the supervision of such a process of people working with each other.

I had occasion to use therapeutic exercises for small groups intensively in the early 70s, in connection with the teaching experiment that became "SAT Institute"—an aspect of which was the engineering of a group into a self-healing system. Small group exercises in this venture served both a therapeutic and a training aim, and among them there was a series of "Gestalt drills" in which I sought to provide an opportunity for participants to concentrate on the development of specific skills such as listening, monitoring their awareness continuum, observing body language, reflecting, and so on.

The Gestalt exercises that I have collected in this chapter have in common a dual relevance to therapy and training. The first three—emphasizing the sense of presence and the sense of *I/You* as distinct from *I/It* in place of the other—I have come to regard a desirable background to all psychotherapy training, along with all aspects of the awareness continuum. The particular description of the latter, given next, is taken (except for the introductory comments) from a workshop transcript, and illustrates one particular variation of that genre which I am calling "the awareness continuum in a meditation context." "Meditation context" here stands not only for the "meditation field" provided by the meditative attitude of the listener, but for the confinement of the meditation awareness itself in view of an understanding of meditation through selective emphases on such issues as letting go, body awareness, feeling awareness, panoramic awareness, and so on.

Also the last series of exercises, concerning topdog/underdog conflict, constitute an excellent opportunity for training as well as a therapeutic opportunity, in that the coaching of a person through its four stages involves, besides the exercise of intuition, the skill to stimulate emotional expression, and anger in particular.

When I did and shared my spiritual recipe, I could not fail to appreciate Fritz in retrospect for the I/You exercise that he prescribed that I had failed either to practice or pass along with the rest of the Gestalt heritage. Fritz's exercise was one in which two people were actually saying strings of I's and You's in different combinations and rhythms in alternation.

Just as I then felt that the experience did not go much further than a word game, there may be others who have failed to appreciate the important issues involved: I-am-ness in balance with the sense of other-ness. Some of the exercises I discovered myself and described for others may be of help for others who have never focused before on the I/You issue. I have applied them to many groups of people who have found them both personally meaningful and a substantial aspect of their professional training.

Though I have presented here the three "I/You" exercises in such little space that they may be read in virtually no time, I think that the experience of each deserves the opportunity of deepening through practice—particularly in group situations through rotation among group members over many meetings. Also, in the course of time, I have come to know well the training value of many of these exercises, particularly since the time I first devised a therapeutic training program, during the 70s in the SAT Institute. Since then I have liked best a situation that is neither one of pure therapy nor one of professional training: a hybrid one of developing the potential therapists among laymen, while shaping groups into self-therapizing psychological self-maintaining systems.

Though in this activity of combining sophisticated microlab work and therapeutic training I have drawn on inspiration beyond Gestalt therapy alone, my practice has naturally been strongly influenced by Gestalt; for the purpose of this chapter I am selecting some exercises that can be regarded as direct embodiments of Gestalt ideas.

I.   I/You exercises

The first exercise, below, may be seen both as a development of something implicit in Gestalt therapy and as a borrowing from Sufism: the exercise of focusing on the sense of presence or selfhood. The second, likewise, may be regarded both as an elaboration of something already present in the Gestalt approach and a borrowing: the cultivation of the sense of personhood of the other, the sense of "You" in contradistinction to the experience of "it." Working separately both with myself and with others on these two techniques, I naturally discovered the power of their combination: the exercise of being at the same time mindful of self and of others' presence and being.

1. Presence

Sit face to face with one another—and close your eyes.

Pay attention to your body sensations, posture and facial expression, and make any corrections in posture or attitude as such awareness may invite.

Be as you want to be—moment after moment.

Now open your eyes, yet remaining still in body and thought.

Relax your eyes, yet remaining still in body and thought.

Relax your body and let yourself be at ease, not trying to do anything and as you allow your mind to become silent, concentrate on the sense of existing—

Feel "I am here."

After some time concentrating on the I-sense while relaxing with a silent mind, bring your breathing into awareness and shift your attention from "I" to "here" and mentally repeat I—am—here in synchrony with in-breath, pause, and out-breath (don't attempt to do anything in particular during the out-breath pause).

Go on with as much continuity of attention as possible.

2. You-ness

As before, begin by sitting face to face, closing your eyes, optimizing your posture, attitude, and state.

Then, after a time of letting yourself be in peace as much as you can, open your eyes, while you sit, physically relaxed and centered engaging in neither verbal nor nonverbal dialogue—forget yourself as much as possible while you focus on the sense that the person before you *truly exists*, is a person and not a thing, a conscious being seeing you.

3. I/You

After preparatory centering as before, here the two continuing to sustain mental silence with open eyes and with the support of physical relaxation, concentration on both "I" and "you," while at the same time evoking a sense of infinity around them.

Try it—seeking to intensify at the same time the sense of presence in self and other and a sense of cosmic depth.

Let the sense of infinity support your relaxation and dissolve your mind.

Perhaps you may find it useful to say at times subvocally

I—You—Infinity.

II. *The awareness continuum in a meditation context*

The awareness continuum is to Gestalt therapy what free association is to psychoanalysis: both the beginning and the end of therapy. The beginning, in that it provides the mirror in which a person's psychological difficulties are reflected and from which the therapist takes his cues; the end, in that, just as the ability to free associate without resistance may be regarded as a sign of completeness of analysis, the ability to experience fulfillment and depth in every here-and-now is the goal of Gestalt.

I believe that, despite much talk about the awareness continuum, its practice is not given all the attention it deserves—for it tends not to be viewed enough as a *practice*—the practice of a healthy present-centered attitude—but, rather, merely a point of departure for other therapeutic interventions and directions.

Since I regard it as a valuable psychological exercise in its own right, and one which will be best carried out with the stimulus of interpersonal communication, I usually schedule it as a complement to therapy proper, and—in variations such as the one below—as a part of training.

Those who have experience with the awareness continuum exercise cannot have failed to notice that, as is the case with psychological exercises in general, it is sometimes fulfilling and productive, sometimes superficial: a string of seemingly meaningless self-reports, most typically an inventory of perceptions: now I look at the rug, now I hear a car passing by, etc. Where is the mystery? What is it that makes the act of becoming-aware-of-the-moment something deep; that which causes on occasion the act of awareness to be profound?

I think that the answer can be approached in several ways, one of which is the experience of *presence*, the experience of "I am Here." There are times when we experience ourselves as *things* and times when we experience ourselves as *humans*. This might seem to be a matter of grace—as the perception of the world in general: sometimes the tree before our house is of little interest to us, whereas at other times we see its beauty shine; the world is sometimes opaque, whereas at other times it has meaning—(not an intellectual but an affective deepening of mind that is the object of meditation practices); yet a listener may be able to help in a way completely different from what is usually cultivated in the practice of psychotherapy: not through anticipating, not through the effort to understand, but through a concern about *being there* in a more substantial way, by increasing so-to-say the density of his being, so that a deeper silence may attract to it a deeper communication. This is the exercise I want to propose to you now: a "here and now" exercise in which one person performs the classical Gestalt exercise (about which I will add certain details), while the listener listens in a particular manner.

Let me now describe a bit further the role of both as well as the role of a third party, who will be in the position of a supervisor. We will be working in groups of three, rotating so that each person will have ten minutes to work.

I have just used the word "work," a word prominent in Fritz Perls' vocabulary. Though working with him (or with other therapists) involved a willingness to follow directions and not to become defensive in the face of painful truths, this awareness continuum exercise (the basic Gestalt situation) is already "work" enough by itself. It is, in the first place, work of attention. Attention can be superficial or deep, gross or subtle, sustained or intermittent. And it is also work to dare, and there is work in relinquishing the habitual manipulation of our own mind. Just as in the life of meditation it may require much work to come to the state of peace, so that non-doing is effortful before it can become effortless, there is work in going with the mind where *it* wants to go. I think that this organismic aspect of the flow of experience is sometimes not given enough attention in Gestalt practice. I think that even Fritz Perls' word "continuum" in the expression "continuum of awareness" may have implied a quasi-poetic allusion to the multidimensionality of awareness and the fact that at every moment we can attend to innumerable possible experiences: sounds, visuals, emotions, what we are doing, our voice, and so on. Not only do different fields of awareness intersect in every moment so that any one of them can beckon to us and lead us in a particular direction; if we resist the temptation of becoming an active manipulator of our experience, but are truly sensitive to where our attention *wants* to go, there will be a particular psychic flow—whether we interpret this in terms of figure/ground formation, self-regulation, or simple spontaneity or inspiration. This very simple act may take much daring, to surrender to what comes. It requires much courage and also humility; it requires many things, this "being open to experience."

If you are willing to say what you have not rehearsed, if you are willing to be surprised by what you say, you might have to let go of your self image. You either express or impress. Much of what gets done in the awareness continuum is still within the bounds of a role, within the boundary of not creating a bad impression. And I say all this because I think what happens in an exercise of such simplicity depends on your degree of freedom; depends on how much you allow to occur and how much you appreciate the indefinite potential of your exploration. It is up to you to make it into a trivial exercise or a great occasion; it all depends on how open you are and sincere in your desire to work.

I want to recommend to those who are speaking—in a monologue—to take into consideration the three basic realms of awareness: perceptions, feelings and actions. At any time you are aware of what comes to you through the outer senses as well as through your body sense. You are aware of what you are doing, not only with your body and voice, but intrapsychically (such as waiting to have something to report, or choosing between attending to one thing or another), and you are aware of your emotions. I want to suggest that you don't remain stuck in any particular realm. Be sure that your exercise does not result only in an enumeration of perceptions or in the observation of what you are doing. Keep moving, keep rotating, yet emphasizing the observation and expression of *feelings*. It is feelings that interest us more. It is the feeling life that needs to be unveiled; yet it is useful, in order to become aware of your emotions, that you are grounded in your perceptions, so that you can inquire into what you feel *on the occasion* of each one of your perceptions like this. Do not simply report the movements, postures, inflections of voice that you observe, but use observations of your actions to inquire as to how you feel *while* you act: use your actions as a mirror for your feelings.

Now I turn to instructions for the listener. The listener sits face to face with the speaker and inhibits not only verbal language (as is appropriate to a monologue) but body language as well. Offer your partner the experience of having a *mere* witness, one who is simply there without giving cues, without approving or disapproving. Inhibit smiles, shoulder shrugs, and so on, and adopt a meditative stance: do nothing but being present. Relax your face, relax your eyes, relax your tongue (which is active even during internalized, nonvocal talk). And I want to invite you also to not try to understand what your partner says. You will probably notice that by not trying you will understand better, not less. Instead of trying to understand, put your effort *in attending;* putting your attention both inside and outside: what you see, the voice and words you hear and also how you feel moment after moment. In ordinary conversations there is a certain amount of implicit preparation for responding. Here, let yourself be at rest without another task than that of attending to the moment—to your partner. Let your only exercise be that of continuous non-judgmental attention. What you are offering your partner is pure presence. Nothing more—and yet something the effect of which, I think you will observe, is not just trivial. And not so easy—since there is so much compulsion to help, compulsion to respond, and the speaker may sometimes feel abandoned.

The third person is a supervisor. He sits next to the couple. Two people are facing each other and the supervisor sits between them on the side. The supervisor will do one of the things the therapist does: point out the infringement of the Gestalt rule—i.e., point out when what is said is not an expression of experience: when he is going on a tangent, into explaining, into abstraction, telling a story, anticipating, and so on. The supervisor also attends to the compulsive gestures of the listener who is supposed to stay relaxed: nods, automatic gestures, etc., and brings them to his or her attention.

III. *Topdog/underdog exercises*

I think we all know how a topdog/underdog encounter often constitutes the peak of a Gestalt session—the point of an explosive transition to a healthier state.

Since anybody who has internal problems has a topdog or superego, and since to every topdog there is an underdog, I think that the issue of self-control, self-hate and self-manipulation is ever present in the neuroses. Thus one may choose at any moment to focus upon this essential split that sustains the conflict. This being so, it lends itself ideally to systematization, and the series of exercises I describe below constitute a stepwise progression that I have devised for a mutually assisted therapy setting.

First Stage:
Self-accusation as a catharsis of superego rage

Catharsis, Aristotle tells us, is the very point of drama; this being so, it seems most appropriate to use dramatization as a means for making explicit (and thus bringing into awareness) the hateful self-control that is normally implicit in neurotic function and psychosomatic disorders. (The Argentinian psycho-analyst Angel Garman used to speak of "the biting of the superego on the gastric mucosa.")

On beginning this exercise I usually explain that when the behavioral channels for the expression of anger are blocked through an internalized prohibition, it will be difficult to experience the emotion of rage, and that conversely, the dramatization may facilitate access to the feeling. (I here may use the metaphor of "priming the pump": "hamming it up," as Fritz used to say, until the water of emotion begins to flow into the words, voice, and gestures.)

Second Stage:
Underdog reversal

Rather than replaying the usual topdog/underdog game, I skip to underdog reversal — the most dramatic application of reversal technique I know in the implicit Gestalt heritage: I here ask group members to impersonate their underdog (that is, the personality that was the target of topdog's accusation in the earlier exercise), but not a pleading, guilty and suffering underdog; rather, one who is aware of the deformity and destructiveness of topdog's injunctions; to take the side of the oppressed not to stay oppressed; to rebel, to throw off topdog's yoke and tell topdog off with a full display of anger in words and gesture.

Third and Fourth Stages:
Topdog reversal and working towards a contract

When the above described exercise is wholeheartedly engaged in, it may—as in some successful hot seat sessions—bring about a major psychological breakthrough: a measure of liberation from topdog and consequently increased internal freedom. It is my impression that this is not a definitive freedom, however, nor is the state of seeming freedom from topdog enduring. Another layer of psychological obstruction is likely to become apparent in time, and in the end topdog is not amputated but assimilated. The end of the topdog/underdog situation, with slashes in each polarity, in other words, is a process of synthesis, integration, dialectic purification.

For this to happen, I believe, topdog needs to abdicate—from within as it were—out of a full understanding of what he is doing and wish to come out of an impossible situation (which implies a wish to serve the healing process).

The reversal of underdog is only half of healing the basic split of the psyche. The other half is the reversal of topdog: the willingness on the part of our controlling, angry self to give up its tyranny of the psyche and to become vulnerable and feeling.

I think that this reversal involves nothing short of diving into the part of topdog, for the superego is like a parent we have created to protect and assist us, originally, and our superego only wants to help.

The trouble is that our superego is impatiently angry, wanting us to be different *now*—and that is not in the nature of things. Couldn't we perhaps educate topdog into a perception of the impossible situation that it is creating, an understanding that through its tyrannical assertion in the psyche it can never find the satisfaction it so greedily demands? Couldn't we perhaps persuade it into a willingness to help toward the realization of its ideal without imposing it? Therein might lie some possibility.

Topdog reversal (through which the person is invited to switch from angry accusation to getting in touch, as topdog, with his frustrated wishes and to express them in an attitude of vulnerability), seems like such an appropriate gateway to further dialogue between the dominant and dominated subselves, that only conceptually I distinguish between these stages. In practice I propose them as steps in an uninterrupted process. As I introduce group members to this stage of the process, I suggest that they begin by giving topdog (the inner parent) a voice, while in an attitude of willingness to listen to underdog in a child and its needs. I compare the situation to that of two subpersonalities condensed, sharing the same body, and underscore the importance of learning to live together in the best possible way. I also invite the working out of agreements, the moving toward a new contract.

As may be imagined, in a training situation—where individuals are receiving the stimulus and support of one or more peers in small groups—the power of this series of exercises may compare with that of a nonstructured Gestalt session, and I have even witnessed, at least once, the occurrence of a psychological death experience—an "ego death," the gist of which was a heartfelt abdication of superego from its tyrannical rule.

Chapter Five

Gestalt and Protoanalysis[1]

I

I want to begin with a question: what is it that psychotherapy cures, or what is it that it seeks to cure?

We may answer "neurosis," but sometimes a distinction is made between healing the symptoms and healing the root of the trouble—curing what is *essential* to neurosis. Perls frequently used the expression "impasse," and used to say that most of psychotherapy stops before reaching "that which the Russians have called the 'sick point'." He never did more than mention this concept of Soviet psychology — to the effect that there is a structure that no psychotherapy can modify, so that all our attempts at psychological healing only reach a certain level. As is well known, this was a notion that Fritz endorsed inasmuch as *conventional* psychotherapy was concerned, while he claimed that with his approach (surpassing others) it was indeed possible to go beyond the impasse.

Now what is this central structure, this root of an individual's psychopathology?

[1]This is an edited transcript of a presentation given at the Second International Gestalt Conference in Madrid in 1987, to which I have added a brief description of the nine character types according to protoanalysis, and some references to pertinent illustrative material in other chapters of this book. "Protoanalysis" is a registered service mark of the Arica Institute, Inc.

Transpersonal psychotherapy would answer with a word that it employs in a way different from psychoanalysis: the "ego". (Unlike psychoanalysis, which equates ego and self, transpersonalists designate "ego" as internal obstruction, a false personality that stands in the way of the deeper self.) The best translation for "ego," in the sense that both the transpersonalists and the spiritual traditions use it, is not the "ego" of psychoanalysis but "character"—that is to say, the sum total of conditionings, the sum total of adaptation responses learned in childhood that are not truly ourselves and are not appropriate to life in the present.

The conception of sanity in Gestalt therapy is inseparable from the notion of organismic self-regulation; or we might say that character is that subsystem within the psyche that is not open to organismic control—but (to use Perls' expression again) has become "control-mad," compulsive. We know well enough how this compulsive or "non-organismic" personality within us arises from the experience of childhood pain and, once an emergency response, has become ingrained through phantom danger and anxiety.

The notion of character as the essence of psychopathology is, I would say, somewhat implicit in Gestalt therapy. Reich, who was Perls' analyst, formulated the idea that character is in itself defensive; Fritz went beyond, however, in claiming that the ideal person is a person without character. This, in the English speaking-environment in which he dwelt during his more significant years of work, constituted a defiance in face of the common use of the word. This meaning is also present in Spanish when we say "a man of character," but particularly in a culture of puritanical descent "character" stands for will, self-control, and idealized rigidity. Perls rebelled against this ideal in his view of the healthy person as one who responds creatively to the situation at hand, rather than out of ingrained obsolete responses.

This, of course, is something difficult to reach, yet I think that the symptomatic neuroses are only secondary complications of the implicit character neurosis that practically everybody develops (as the consequence of growing up in the atmosphere of the culture's "emotional plague.") And since it is the pathological style of relations implicit in the character neurosis that underlies all our inner conflicts, interpersonal problems and the consequent suffering, I think that character—bedrock of the repetition compulsion—is the most fundamental issue in any psychotherapy that seeks to be deep and complete.

If this is true, the perception of character on the part of the therapist is highly relevant to the therapeutic process. Indeed, I believe that much of the success of therapists has to do with a good clinical eye with regard to character—the capacity to see in the way of walking and the gesture and manner of speech of an individual the reflection of a life style. This is something that is not always made explicit, however, nor does the perception of character derive from experience alone, but also from the therapist's mental health: one who lives "organismically"—i.e. with the creative flexibility that is part of health, perceives the deadness in the other. Character is that which is dead, it is the non-self of the other, a *rigor vitae*—as Perls called it, in analogy to *rigor mortis*.

Also, just as a Zen master may respond with the stick to any utterance that comes from unenlightened consciousness, a good Gestaltist confronts the repetition compulsion—the automatic games people play—with severity or irony. Perls gave a precedent, since he exhibited this capacity in great measure—particularly since the satori experience (described in his autobiography) which was the prelude to his most rewarding personal and professional life. He had an exceedingly good eye and also a long experience at the time of his California years, when I knew him. (I once congratulated him on a certain piece of work after a group session at Esalen, and he answered with a German saying to the effect that "the devil knows more because he is old than because he is a devil.")

Aside from the factors that help the therapist see the deformities of the other—self-understanding and personal health on the one hand, and clinical experience on the other—the perception of another person's character is something that can to some extent be trained. Much of clinical education consists precisely in this: in learning to discriminate what an obsessive character is, to recognize a histrionic character, a narcissistic personality, etc. However, there is much chaos in the psychopathology of character, and considerable confusion in regard to its discrimination—with a consequent low reliability of diagnostic judgments. Yet precisely because of this (in addition to the fact that character is a basic issue to healing, and its perception particularly significant to the healing process), I think the information that I am here calling "protoanalysis" is of great meaningfulness to psychotherapy in general and to Gestalt therapy in particular.

II

We have been living through times when the fashion of diagnosis has become slightly *passé*, perhaps through the abuses of the post-Kraepelinian era, where the diagnostic and taxonomic passion seemed to take the place of living understanding and the ability to listen to patients. As a reaction, there has been a wave of opinion to the effect that it is better to work improvisationally in view of the ongoing personal and interpersonal process with as few preconceptions as possible—diagnostic preconceptions included. I think that this "romantic" attitude in psychotherapy may have provided a healthy antidote to an exaggerated "classicism" and yet should not be made into a cult or dogma. We can be phenomenological and intuitive in our approach and still use (and benefit from) a theoretical perspective; in other words, we can profit from generalized experience without being blinded by preconceptions. I am bringing this subject matter to you today because, after more than 15 years of experience with protoanalysis, I can say that it has been the single greatest influence on my practice after the inheritances of Perls and Simkin, and because I have seen my appraisal of its value confirmed in the testimony of many who learned protoanalysis with me: both therapists who felt that their work improved and non-therapists who, without intending to, became good amateurs. In 1971 I began a group in Berkeley in which I explicitly indicated to the participants that this should *not* be regarded as a training group, but an activity offered for personal development. The fact that, after a year and a half of meeting, almost every nonprofessional in this group became an amateur with helping ability and several professionals became charismatic figures in California was due, among other factors, I think, to this particular tool toward self-insight and toward insight into the experience and behavior of others.

III

The word *protoanalysis* came into use through Oscar Ichazo, a spiritual teacher in the "Fourth Way" tradition (a Sufi lineage of which the best known exponent in the West has been Gurdjieff). The particle "proto" alludes to what is basic, and the word as a whole to a self-insight process geared to the basic structure of an individual's personality. Since such a process is supported in a particular view of the psyche—a body of traditional psychospiritual theory—the expression "protoanalysis" has by extension also been used in regard to this body of ideas—just as "psychoanalysis" has designated not only the therapeutic method but its theoretical perspective. In sum, then, we may say that protoanalysis is the experiential and theoretical understanding of one's personality or ego in the light of Fourth Way psychological ideas.

A distinction is drawn by Gurdjieff and Ichazo between "essence" and "personality"—much as Fairbairn and the objects-relation theorists today draw a distinction between a "deep self" and a "false self." The "personality" or "ego" that is the object of protoanalysis and other stages in the Fourth Way approach may be viewed as a subsystem in the psyche, constituted of cognitive, emotional, and behavioral conditionings that interfere with attunement to what may be called either "Tao" or "divine will"—or, in the language of Western psychology, organismic self-regulation.

The ego or personality—our apparent identity— may be likened to an island within the psyche and within our neural network, a part that controls the whole and stands in place of the whole: it admits within its boundaries only that which is coherent with its directives; it is no different from what we have been calling character: a structure predicated on an active unconsciousness, the fixity of which was born as an emergency response to childhood suffering and which in turn perpetuates suffering and unconsciousness.

This sphere of personality is mapped in protoanalysis in reference to the three categories of mental phenomena acknowledged by western psychology since Brentano: the cognitive, the emotional and the conative. In Ichazo's language these are referred to as the intellectual, feeling and instinctive or moving "centers." A peculiar feature of the psychological theory summarized in this personality map is that it is not a single-instinct theory like Freud's (before his conception of death instinct), but one that recognizes the interplay of three instincts or innate goals in the psyche: self-preservation, the sexual drive, and the social (relationship) need that Maslow called instinctoid, and that Object Relations Theory now emphasizes against the sexual emphasis of classic libido theory.

In view of the three-centeredness of the psyche and the threefoldness of the instinctual realm, the "anatomy of the ego" is presented as a structure with five domains as in the graph below.

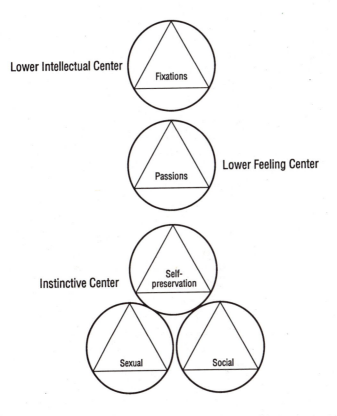

Though simplified here into a triangle, the figure mapping the structure of each of these five centers or realms is called an enneagram, (familiar to those who have read Ouspensky or other accounts of Gurdjieff's teaching). They will also be familiar with the notion that two more centers lie dormant in the ordinary individual: the "higher emotional"—in contrast to the "lower emotional" center of the ego—and the "higher intellectual". (Both are aspects of the essence, and the object of disciplines beyond protoanalysis.)

A feature that distinguishes the Fourth Way view from the usual religious formulations (and approximates it to contemporary psychotherapy) is its view of instinct as essential rather than egoic. The process of ego transcendence that is the goal of this school is understood as a detachment from the passions and the "fixations" (wrong assumptions about reality that constitute the ego's cognitive aspect) and is seen not as a liberation *from* instinct but *of* instinct— so that in the process of maturation the "bound" or egoic state of the instincts (contaminated by the passions) is replaced by a free and unconditioned state.

Those acquainted with Gurdjieff's work will know that, next to the practice of self-observation moment after moment, the main focus of the self-insight process is the discrimination (among such "snapshots of oneself") of a pattern usually called a person's "chief feature"—a key structure in the personality upon which it is recommended to concentrate one's further efforts in the work.

According to the psychological system presented by Ichazo, the chief feature is no other than the person's "fixation"—the cognitive structure that goes hand in hand with the person's ruling passion— while any of the nine egoic emotions in the psychic system of the individual may be, according to his or her personality, in the foreground. (I usually explain this by saying that, even though we all embody the nine passions mapped in the enneagram, our psyche is like a nine-faceted solid that lies on one or another of its particular facets, which thus presents itself as a fundamental one for the individual.)

More than a mere collection of types, the characterology of protoanalysis involves a view as to how these types are related to each other—for they are mapped on a circle in such a way that each may be seen as a hybrid of the adjoining ones, and the enneagram lines connecting its numbered points represent psychodynamic processes within the individual psyche. Without elaborating on this, however, I now present below the enneagram of the passions and a series of brief descriptions of the nine character syndromes.

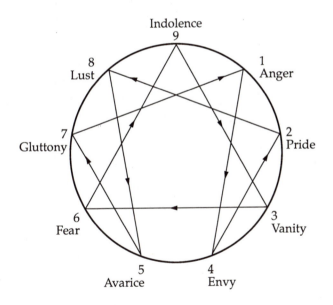

Type I, in which the ruling passion is anger, is not characterized by obvious aggression but by perfectionism, where anger is expressed intellectually through criticism of self and others. This is typically the personality of a do-gooder, the "fighter for a good cause," the puritan, who controls (self and other) through an excessive concern with moral goodness. The perfectionistic character corresponds to DSM[2]-III's "compulsive" and is illustrated in this book by Gerald's session, in which he displays a surface good-boyishness and intellectual dryness, and in which emotional exploration leads him to the phantasy of warding off blows and the desire to "smash." Unlike many encounter group leaders, I have rarely suggested a physical fight in the course of a session, and I think that its usefulness here (as a means for the patient to be less fearful of causing harm and to relinquish the overcontrol of aggression) was an outcome both of the motivation (arising from insight into the situation) and appropriateness to character-structure.

Type II is the pride type. We must also distinguish the pride of type II from the arrogance of type VIII, the vanity of type III, and the pride of still other personalities. The specific situation here is one of an inflated self-image more than obvious bragging or an achievement orientation. The enhanced self-concept—i.e., the sense of being a very special person—is supported partly through imagination, partly through the appreciation of people who are both seduced and given value as authorities. Type II people are those who indulge most in what Idries Shah has called "MCO" for Mutual Comfort Operation. It is characteristic of this personality to adopt a position of pseudo-abundance out of an avoidance of the humiliation to acknowledge needfulness. Because of this, needs are expressed in a manipulative way, and also become a source of impulsiveness. This is what today is called

---

[2]*Diagnostic and Statistical Manual of Mental Disorders,* Third Edition, Revised (Washington, D.C.: American Psychiatric Association, 1987).

a histrionic character, a predominantly emotional ("touchy-feely") type.

Type III, at the corner of the inner triangle in the enneagram, involves *identification with* the self image, rather than its *amplification* and it corresponds to an achieving character, since here the idealized self needs to be implemented in the world rather than validated through personal convictions as in pride. Since validation is sought through the matching of objective (and usually quantitative) standards, form becomes a substitute for being. The syndrome corresponds to that described by Fromm under the rubric of the "marketing orientation" so prominent in American culture.

Type IV, which follows vanity in the circle, corresponds to the passion of envy, and we may say that envy is a frustrated vanity: a combination of vanity with a chronic thirsting, a sense of *want* that makes envy the most passionate of passions. It is most frequent in women and corresponds to what Fritz used to call the "tragedy queen," a person full of demands and complaints who tends to resist the therapeutic process through competition with the therapist. (I more than once heard Fritz say to a person like this, "How many therapists have you defeated?")

Type V corresponds to avarice, among the traditional "deadly sins." It stands for a more generalized retentiveness than the hoarding of money. As in envy, there is a sense of hollowness and depletion. Instead of manifesting as the "wet depression" of the envy type (which stands on the hysteroid region of the enneagram), the sense of lack here is part of a schizoid "dry depression" that manifests as apathy and lack of zest. Not only do Kretschmer's and Fairbairn's "schizoid" coincide with type V but also with the personality disturbance that Kohut and Kernberg (but not DSM-III) discuss under the label "narcissistic," which is characterized by little access to feelings and a cold aloofness.

Type VI is one in which the dominant passion is fear; the person lacks trust in his or her own responses. The fear of doing the wrong thing or making the wrong choice that is part of compulsive doubting makes the person dependent on the support and guidance of authority figures or ideologies. Richard's case and Len's illustrate two subtypes of the fear structure. Richard, predominantly counter-phobic, is in protoanalytic language a social coward (who will dutifully risk his life at war rather than face his father). Len, predominantly ingratiating, illustrates the preservation type VI: weak, warm and in need of protection.

In type VII the dominant passion is gluttony — not necessarily a gluttony for food (just as avarice does not necessarily involve a greed for money) — but a gluttony for love, appreciation, approval, and, generally speaking, *more* of whatever the case may be. The characterological syndrome is that of a non-aggressive, soft, sweet, helpful yet inwardly afraid and covertly greedy individual. It has not been much discussed in psychological literature except by Abraham and others in the description of the optimistic "oral receptive" character.

Type VIII, in which lust predominates, not only lusts for sexual satisfaction but for intensity in all forms. It corresponds to Reich's phallic narcissistic character and might also be called (as Karen Horney proposed) "vindictive"—or sadistic. It is characterized by the denial of fear and the suppression of soft or compassionate feelings—in the struggle for power and dominance. Fritz—a bully in his childhood whose chief adult game (as I once heard him say) came to be to "outfritz" everybody, embodied a type VIII character and I have elaborated already[3] on how the practice of Gestalt therapy with its characteristic confrontativeness and its penchant

[3]In the Second East Coast Gestalt Conference Keynote address reproduced in Book Two, Chapter Two.

for excitement has carried the imprint of his personality.

The passion corresponding to type IX is one for which there is no appropriate name in today's language, though the monks of the middle ages had it in their vocabulary: *accidia*—which in time was translated as "sloth." The laziness implied, however, is not that of the body but a spiritual laziness: a resistance to self-insight or interiority, and a resistance to change. This inner deadening (for which Gurdjieff had the fitting name of "the self-calming devil") may involve outer laziness but is most often associated, on the contrary, with intense activity (for activity can help distract attention from one's experience of self and world). In regard to adaptation, the problem here is the opposite of the more usual one: a pathological *overadaptation*, an excessive passivity toward the demands of the world—which is the other side of a negligence of the deeper self or (to speak in religious language) a "forgetfulness of God."

IV

As I set out to describe in retrospect how an acquaintance with protoanalysis has contributed to my experience as a Gestaltist, I must begin by saying that I never sought to deliberately apply protoanalysis to Gestalt therapy. I just conducted workshops and saw clients, and found myself drawing on an enhanced perception of the workings of people's personalities as well as on a sharpened intuition in regard to intervention alternatives. In some cases the most substantial part of a session became a guided inquiry into a person's dominant passion or main characterological strategy—something that might be the content of a Gestalt session anyhow, yet in these instances was facilitated by a trained capability to type. In many cases this perception of

character structure was reflected in different suggestions with regard to work in the awareness continuum: either paying attention selectively to a
particular mental state, exaggerating it, or inhibiting
it.

A more specific way in which I have noticed that
perception of character has helped my work has been
that it has given me a better sense of what to support
in a person. Being clear as to what a person's
psychopathology consists in, involves, of course, a
sense of the way out. This was brought home recently
in a session with a young man who tortured himself
with a feeling that he should either define himself
before the world as a homosexual or quit being one.
For many years he had struggled to change his sexual
orientation, and he had become a happier person
when he gave this up. Now he demanded of himself
the heroism of defining himself to be one thing or the
other rather than to continue exploring the issue.
Knowing him to be a "fear type," where duty and
intolerance of ambiguity are central issues in the
neurosis, I could see that his pressure to define himself implied the yielding to an obedient son's superego, and I was able to steer his exploration—through
inner dialogues—to the point where he applied his
courage, instead, to a position of *not* having to decide,
not having to take a position, but living, in this
regard, according to his uncharted decisions at the
moment.

Still another way in which protoanalysis has
been useful to me has been through the notion that
to each character type there exists a dominant passion—or, more exactly, an emotional state that is at
the same time pathologically intensified *and* rejected
(since our dominant passion is also something
toward which we harbor an especially intense taboo).
In my experience, work on self-accusation and
catharsis is specially productive when it focusses on
this dominant passion. Self-accusation in this case

makes the person aware of an implicit self-accusation that is part of her chronic mental atmosphere; the dramatization of the dominant passion, in breaking the chronic taboo, helps bring a repressed emotion into consciousness. Through this, it makes possible that transformation of energies—so well known to Gestaltists—that sometimes may be compared to an exorcism. I remember, as I say this, the session of a perfectionist (anger type) who, as usual, suffered from an exaggerated criticism towards himself and others while being at the same time an overly polite individual who had trouble in getting angry. Seen from outside, his dramatization of wrath was like the eruption of an extinguished volcano; subjectively his experience of anger beyond judgments of good/bad brought him to an experience of inner fire that he associated to the Scandinavian god Loki. We may say that this transpersonal and archetypal experience was nourished from his anger, though it didn't belong any more to the sphere of passions, since it constituted an impersonal *disinterested* anger without a specific issue. Loki constituted for him an antidote to the rigid personality in which he felt locked. Much of his therapeutic process afterwards derived from a purpose to permit himself to be more "Loki-like" in his daily life; to permit himself to be what his rigid super-ego reproved, instead of being so concerned with form.

Only artificially can the three issues that I have just discussed be separated, however: in many a session the dramatization of the ruling passion will flow naturally from the exploration of character, and both will occur in the context of either subtle or explicit support/confrontation. Thus, in a session with a type II (pride) woman, I (as I rarely do) broke the initial silence inquiring as to whether she saw herself in an attitude of asking. When she clarified that, indeed, she had been asking for guidance during her silence, I pointed out how this was missing in her communication, for in this I could already see reflected the psychology of the proud character type: too proud to ask and not explicit in the communication of needs. This led me to suggest some experimentation with the expression of wants to other group members, which in turn brought to her attention the need to be important to others. At this point the words "I want to be important to you," repeated at my suggestion, served as an expression of her proud self. After her dwelling for some time on this wish, however, I invited her to make a round telling each of those present, "I want you to love me without my having to be important."

Again my familiarity with the pride dynamics (in which the person seeks to be important and loving in order to deserve and attract love, while at the same time repressing the awareness of the childish love need) not only incited me to explore in this manner the reversal of pride (and a *de*reversal of neediness) but stimulated me to facilitate the group exchanges that followed in such a way that she could come to believe the feedback that she was getting—to the effect of *not* being expected to be important to be loved. Later in the session she said, in tears, "It is so important to me—that I *not* have to do anything, and have what support I need. I want to be loved that way." Toward the end of our meeting, she was able to let herself be nurtured without occultation of the childish love thirst and without having to step into the adult role of doing or pretending something in exchange. The session as a whole was a lesson in that it indicated to her how to work further in herself.

At other moments this perception of a patient's character helped me not to be "sucked into" games or manipulations that I might not have seen in early years. I can recall an instance in a group in Italy where the patient began expressing a concern about her aloofness and after some work on that came to focus on her judgmentalness. Being an American in a group of Italians, she at some point requested for my interventions not to be translated into Italian, since she could understand my English. Of course this meant leaving the group out for her convenience, and met not only protest on their part but that of the translator, who was unwilling to proceed that way. After allowing for some time the battle between the translator (supported by the group) and the patient, my interventions aimed at making her aware how she was turning her desire into a demand, and finding support for her demand in an invalidation of the refusal of her wish through the judgment "childish." Behind her self-righteousness, thus, there was a childish disregard for the needs and views of others; behind her protest, a not taking others into account. I do not remember in detail how I did it, but I do remember that she did understand that her condemnation of the translator had been biased by self-interest. The whole event illustrated the usual way in which the self-assertion of perfectionists is like an "egoism in the name of the law," a need to have things go their way rationalized as morality, maturity or "common decency." My showing this and pointing out how closed she had been to the preferences and perceptions of those she accused turned out to be the most important thing she took back from that workshop. I think that, except for acuity in recognizing her way of manipulating, it would have been easy for me to fall for it, to automatically yield to her apparently reasonable imperiousness rather than to confront her.

Another way in which protoanalysis can be applied in a Gestalt session—and I see that I have done so now and then—derives from the notion that for each type there are "antidotes": one may work toward internal states contrary to the dominant passion and the corresponding fixation.

Even though traditionally the "psychocatalysts" or "holy ideas" constitute meditative exercises at a later stage than protoanalysis (because they presuppose substantial meditation training), I think that they may be glimpsed through Gestalt enactment in an "as if" attitude, and that they lend themselves to applications in connection with the awareness continuum.

An example is the following excerpt from a session with a type I man who had before this followed my instruction to exaggerate a sense of social awkwardness, and who in so doing had presented a caricature of his ordinary self. Impersonating his audience, as I suggested, he accused himself of "farting around, with all this reflective stuff." "He says something and then he goes up another level and comments on that, and then goes up another level and comments on *that*... Why do that all the time?"

To make his stance for of this part of himself even more explicit, I had asked him how he felt about his "performance" (his word), and he acknowledged: "This performance thing is a huge thing in my life— Yeah, I mean I am performing very often before people and being concerned with what they think. Even meditation is performance."

Up to this last statement, all has been ego clarification, and the ideal stage had been set for an exercise, well known among Gestaltists, that—I think— originated with Jim Simkin and was here particularly appropriate. I proposed to him: "I'll tell you what I see, as the dominant characteristic of what you have been doing: hitting yourself over the head. 'I am not performing, I am not producing, I am not doing what I should be doing, not knowing what I should be doing,' etc. And so the direction in which I would be interested in seeing you work is that of getting to be less of a judge to yourself, to give up the prosecuting attorney. So try the continuum awareness again and watch for this, the judgmentalness; inhibit it for a while."

Though necessary to his psyche, dumping judgmentalness was not something he could easily do, so that in the process of carrying out my instruction he had occasion to observe how he was not only evaluating but even keeping score. Later, however, I proposed the prescribed antidote to perfectionism: the idea of perfection (i.e., the intuition that all is perfect). Such an "idea" which only the "higher mind" with its contemplative faculty can comprehend, cannot, of course, be faked. Still, "pretending" that all is perfect can serve to suspend criticality and open the way to genuine appreciation, as in the brief experiment that followed. I introduced it by saying:

"Let's drop the whole thing for a while, and pretend everything is perfect. Let's see whether this works as an antidote to your compulsion to judge. Let's take for granted for now that everything is perfect, that the whole universe is perfect—including what are supposedly its most imperfect features— that everything is in process and it is doing the best it can, given its past and present conditions. Also you are doing your best. So go back to the continuum of awareness but now with this underlying attitude."

I quote his response: "All right, it's all right. We'll just sit here then. It's pleasant. There is no need to really do anything, to get our money's worth or to make sure that this is an entertaining session, or that I'll go away with something I can harvest... you know, *harvest*. And I think about that a little bit, and then immediately this other thought comes, 'Well, oh yeah, but if you just sit here it will get boring, and you can get something out of it if you keep talking, and hear Claudio talking, and doing something.' But what is wrong with that? I mean, that is perfect too. That is just the way the machinery works. Claudio nods and that is very nice; it is all perfect, yeah. This is pretty good. And then I think, 'Well, why can't I keep this up?' But then that is perfect too, it is just a particular program. All right, it is kind of nice, yeah, but I say I could sit here and not talk. But it is fun to talk too, so I'll talk."

Though not dramatic, the exercise did put an end to his self-consciousness, and while not the intuitive apprehension of the "Holy Idea" (Ichazo's terminology) potentially accessible in a contemplative state, it was, as the process in the session reported earlier, a lesson: a glimpse of a way out: an inspiration for working on himself in daily life. Yet there can be instances where bringing in the "antidote" to the person's "chief feature" may be as dramatic in a Gestalt session as in the life of contemplation. I have already presented such an instance in this book without a comment — in the transcript of Dick Price's session. Even though in the brief introductory note (written upon its publication in the *Gestalt Journal*) my only commentary was that, after my return from Arica, my work was different in a way that I did not feel like stopping to analyze at the moment, I have in the course of this discussion stopped long enough to observe that at least one source of this difference was my awareness of protoanalysis. Dick, I was well aware, was "a lust type." I was particularly aware of this since he had visited Ichazo and some days before the session had shared this visit with me. If his characterological bias was, accordingly, one of toughness—the way out, it could be assumed, would be that of tenderness. Yet in protoanalysis the word employed to designate the psychocatalyst of the vindictive type is not "tenderness" but "innocence"—a word that evokes childlike spontaneity. At no moment during the session did I mention "innocence," yet I was well aware of the polarity of punitiveness versus innocence as I worked with him and supported his identification with the child in his dream.

Still another situation worth mentioning in which I have appreciated the sharpening of perception contributed by protoanalysis is that of working with dreams. Most of the people who work with dreams interpret them in a way that does not reflect the relevance of personality structure to the symbolic material at hand. (Jung, for instance, spent a lifetime working with dreams, but his discussion of them focuses mostly on the transpersonal archetypal aspect, with relatively scant reference to the interpersonal dimension.)

Here is an example of working on a dream from the perspective of character awareness: a woman has dreamt that she goes in her car following another car. Probably she goes to a party, a reunion (this is a little vague in the dream). She stops before a traffic light; looking to her left, she sees her husband passing by the side on a bicycle. It is clear he is going to play tennis since he is dressed appropriately; he conveys a sense that he knows where he is going. She delights in how he knows. This pleasure causes her to laugh. But when the light changes from red to green, she realizes that she has distracted herself, and now she cannot find the other car. She has become lost and does not know which way to follow.

I think that my ear would not have been as open to the message of this dream if I had not recognized in the person of the dreamer the syndrome corresponding to the type IX of protoanalysis. The psychology of indolence is that of a person who is moved by habits and does what others do; an over-adjusted personality that goes hand-in-hand with a heedlessness with regard to attending to her inner voices, taking care of her needs. The indolent have a great need to belong; they may be patriotic and like to be part of a team, anything from a football team to a political party. Also in their love life they tend to be symbiotic, filling their sensed lack of being with the being of another.

From this perspective the dream becomes very clear: she *follows* and she does not even know well whom; she then *entertains herself in a vicarious manner* instead of concentrating on her following—with the consequence that her participation urge, thus perverted, leaves her lost and alone.

V

Before the relative loss of interest in character that went along with the loss of interest in diagnosis around the 50s, the subject was far from fully explored. I have been personally surprised while rereading Freud's cases (looking for pertinent illustrative material) to find how little the father of psychoanalysis dwelt in this domain of discourse. (In spite of having opened discussion on the subject with his classic paper on anal character, I find that he moves between symptom and childhood memories, bypassing his patient's relationship patterns almost completely.) It was, of course, Adler, Horney, and Reich who brought the subject matter to the foreground; certainly Reich has to be credited for the generalized awareness of character in later psychoanalysis. It has been mostly the typology of Reich's disciple Lowen that has survived throughout the years of humanistic psychology, and I am sure that many Gestaltists with a background in bioenergetics will agree in that awareness of the Lowenian type helps the Gestaltist by sensitizing him to attend to and anticipate aspects of the person's behavior.[4]

Yet protoanalysis is not merely a descriptive system and an education in the recognition of

[4]Even if such support for attention and extrapolation were the full extent of the service of protoanalysis, its comprehensiveness and accuracy recommends it over the Lowenian system. From the experience of matching my diagnosis of some eighty people with those of two bioenergetic specialists (Dr. Antonio Asin in Spain and Blanca Rosa Añorve in Mexico) I come to the following conclusions in regard to equivalences: type IX corresponds to Lowen's "Masochistic" and type V to his "Schizoid"; while type IV is perceived in bioenergetics as "oral," and type II is frequently seen as oral; types III and I are lumped together as "rigid"; types VIII and VI as psychopathic; type VII is usually described as mixed.

character types. The idea of a ruling passion is one that offers a psychodynamic interpretation particularly appropriate to each type according to the emotional background underlying behavior, and the notion of particular strategies and views of self and reality involved in each character type are full of suggestions and inspiration for the therapeutic process.

If I am not mistaken in the premise that character is the central issue in neurosis and a substantial issue in psychotherapy, I will not be mistaken in recommending protoanalysis to Gestaltists.

Chapter Six

Gestalt in the Context of the Ways of Growth[1]

It is an honor for me to be here before you, all the more since the invitation to open this conference fell originally on Laura Perls, and only because of her present unavailability has it fallen upon me. Since the presence of Laura was wished by the organizers, I think it is appropriate to make her present, at least in the form of a brief homage—and say that even though Laura was not with Fritz during his years in California and Canada (which I deem those of the ripeness of his work) not all know the measure in which she was an inspiration and a powerful influence to the gestation of Gestalt therapy. Fewer still are those who know that she was the author of a good part of Fritz's first book, *Ego Hunger and Aggression.* Being a disciple of Dalcroze since an early age, Laura (along with Reich) was an influence on Fritz's attention to the body in the therapeutic process, and his insistence on the "awakening of the senses."

It is not only an honor for me to be before you today, but a very happy occasion as well. I think there is much truth in that Spanish saying *"la tercera es la vencida"* (there is triumph at the third time); at least, in my life this has often seemed true. This is the third

[1]Keynote address at the 2nd International Gestalt Conference (Madrid, 1987).

time I have been called to open a Gestalt conference (since the first of all of them, in Berkeley), and it seems to me that the recognition I am implicitly receiving with this invitation to open the 2nd International Gestalt Conference in Madrid constitutes something like a punctuation mark in an important transition in my life—a transition that is both internal (in that I feel that my years of pilgrimage are coming to an end and that, somewhat late, I am coming to maturity), and, external—in that the focus of my activity is shifting from the U.S. to Spain.

Like Pancho Huneeus, who sits by my side at this table, I started my life in Chile—though with not very patriotic sentiments, since I never felt much at home when I grew up and lived there, but rather a stranger. I arrived in Berkeley as to an oasis, and began there my years of apprenticeship, years of pilgrimage. I now have a feeling that in Spain I will spend a good part of the best of my life. At the moment I feel drawn to it through the invitation of colleagues and friends who have asked me not only to teach here (I begin a three-year summer course beginning this year) but through the generosity of Ignacio Martin Poyo, who has offered me a place to live and work: in the "Kingdom of Babia"—near Almería.

But to end with personal digressions (Gestalt-like as it may be to be personal)—I turn to the first of two topics that I want to discuss as aspects of Gestalt in a context: the place of Gestalt among the old and classical "ways of growth."

I will begin by speaking of some affinities between Gestalt and certain spiritual traditions, then about what I think Gestalt unnecessarily excludes from its credo and practice and by which it might be enriched.

We live in a time in which we are experiencing the simultaneous presence of a great multiplicity of therapeutic and spiritual methods. Just as in the history of music there was a time when one lived in the present, yet since music recordings became available and we have lived more and more before the simultaneous presence of all musical history, so are we now, in our increasingly global planetary times, and in the domain of personal growth—before a *simultaneous* presence of the contributions of all cultures.

When I ask myself, before this varied repertory of methods, which is the closest to Gestalt among them, the first answer that I give myself is one that I have already commented upon in my book *On the Psychology of Meditation* (with Robert E. Ornstein, New York, 1971) of nearly 20 years ago: it is, naturally, *vipassana*, the meditation which constitutes the first and most characteristic technique of Buddhism—and which is nothing other than attention to the "here and now." The main difference between them is that in classical Buddhist meditation the practice of attending to the "immediate data of consciousness" (to use Bergson's expression) is not an interpersonal activity, but, rather one typically carried out in a retreat situation, and more generally, in silence and stillness. Because of this it may be said (as Jim Simkin did) that Gestalt theory is the practice of the "here and now" in the context of the "I and Thou."

Yet the parallelism of Gestalt with Buddhism does not stop in Hinayana tradition, of which *vipassana* is the main practice. Even though Gestalt may be seen as a rediscovery (if not application) of *vipassana* in the interpersonal situation, Fritz was much closer to Zen than to the Hinayana tradition. This was an influence that came to his life especially through his friend and disciple Emil Weiss in New York, and later through his own journey to Japan. When he moved to California, this influence and affinity was of particular interest to the local culture, which (more strongly than any other in the west) was in those years open to the orient—especially through the brilliant interpretation of Zen by Alan Watts.

The theme of Gestalt and Zen has been dealt with in many papers. I think that the most important resemblances are the invitation to suspend conceptual thinking, the appreciation of spontaneity, and a characteristically cutting, severe style on the part of teacher/therapist.

Still greater than in Hinayana and Zen, however, is the parallelism to Gestalt in Tantric Buddhism—also called the *vajrayana* or diamond path. In spite of the resemblance between *vipassana* and the continuum of awareness exercise, this early Hinayanic form of Buddhism differs from Gestalt in that its general style is one of austerity, which stands in contrast with the hedonistic therapies in general. Whereas in Hinayan there is a great insistence on the cultivation of discipline, it is spontaneity and the expression of impulses that are emphasized in Gestalt. Although the appreciation for spontaneity is present in Zen, it is emphasized even more in Tantric Buddhism where, in addition, one finds much stress given to the "transformation of energies": the transmutation of the passional and pathological motivations that are characteristic of unenlightened consciousness into different qualities of enlightenment (symbolized by the Dhyani Buddhas and their corresponding colors). In this process of transformation, use is made of visualization exercises in which the most important aspect is not visual imagination proper but the evocation of mental qualities and the act of imaginatively becoming them. Even though in Gestalt it is not an identification with gods or archetypes that is invited, but, usually, identification with dream images, sub-personalities, ways of being reflected in body language—the relationship of Gestalt to Tantric Buddhism in this regard resembles that between the interpretation of religious symbols in the kabbalistic tradition and the interpretation of dream symbols undertaken by Freud.

Even though it is possible (as David Bakan proposes, in view, among other things, of certain books in Freud's library) that Freud may have been under the influence of Hassidic ideas, in the case of Fritz the technique of identification with symbolic materials certainly did not come from the orient but, as we know, from theater, and particularly from his apprenticeship with Max Reinhard.

Yet it is in the least known and more advanced teaching of Buddhism that we find the closest parallel with Gestalt—in the *Dzogs-chen* or Ati-yoga, which only lately has come to be taught and written about in the West, the two pillars of which are precisely the cultivation of attention and naturalness. Though the practitioner may come to Ati-yoga after experience in the preceeding "vehicles" or *yanas* and though it comprises *guruyoga* and introductory practices, it may be said that on the whole it rests basically on the intrinsic cultivation of attention and the recognition of perfection. That parallels the gestalt situation in which the sense of lack is viewed as a residue ("unfinished business") from the past, and the patient is invited to turn from an unfulfillment that is linked to the operation of thought (memories and anticipations) to the ever available possibility of finding fulfillment even in painful situations when these are lived with sufficient awareness and with a healthy attitude.

Important as the Buddhist parallels may be, resonances between Gestalt and other traditional ways of growth do not end here. Just as it may be said that Gestalt is a crypto-Buddhism, Gestalt is also a crypto-Taoism. Fritz was an exemplar and practitioner of living Taoism, and this was perhaps the main element in his affinity with Esalen (perhaps the most significant neo-Taoistic mini-culture in America). Coincidentally, there also lived in Esalen during the first years (while Fritz and I were there) Gia-Fu-Feng, who had recently arrived from China and whose presence seemed to condense and also make more felt the Taoism in the atmosphere of community there living by the meadows, the red-woods, and the sea. Frequently his calligraphies adorned some wall, or one could see his silhouette on the edge of the property while he practiced Tai Chi in the company of some students. Also the brightest spark of this early Esalen—without which it surely would not have prospered—was Alan Watts, who contributed so much to the diffusion of Zen but who, more characteristically, vibrated with the spirit of Taoism, so eloquently conveyed through his books and talks.

The spirit of Taoism in Gestalt is very strong. Taoism speaks of a "Tao of heaven" and a "Tao of man"—the "Tao of things" and the "Tao of the individual." This "Tao of the individual," a deep and intrinsically wise spontaneity beyond the pro-grammed willfulness of the conscious ego, is no different from the Gestalt ideal. Gestalt is also Taoistic in its being naturalistic (nature is a frequent translation for Tao): it is a spirituality that embraces not only the actual and concrete but the body in particular, and the instinctual sphere.

Yet if we speak of the consonance of Gestalt with Buddhism and with Taoism we cannot fail to mention, also, its affinities with Sufism—especially that form of Sufism that has been called the Fourth Way.

The influence of Gurdjieff and his school was important in my life, and there was a time when I was hoping to meet a second Gurdjieff. In the years when I came to California I lived in the hope that I might come to meet a person of such training and mastery. I would say that the person most resembling Gurdjieff I have ever met was Perls. I do not know how much you may know of this Russian Socrates, who became known shortly before the Russian revolution and emigrated to Turkey—and then to France. He worked with attention and what he called "conscious suffering," which is nothing but the non-evasion of suffering or the acceptance of the suffering entailed by growth. Perls was not only a proponent of the "secret of awareness" but, psychologically speaking, a surgeon. His therapeutic success rested, to a considerable degree, on the invitation to not escape the pain occasioned by his own powerful confrontation. Interestingly, a key word in Gurdjieff's language was "work." There are people who have been schooled in this tradition and refer to this by simply saying "I am 'in the work'." This was also a key word in Perls' vocabulary, so that the typical invitation to therapeutic involvement in the groups that he conducted was "Who wants to work?" It was through him that this word has become a commonplace with group leaders.

In the same way in which Perls was a crypto-Buddhist, a crypto-Taoist, and a crypto-Sufi, we could not fail to notice that there was much of the Hassidic rabbi in him. He was certainly somebody who—like the Hassidim—reminded one of the *joie de vivre*, the joy of mental health: not only Freudian "maturity," the serious maturity of the person who is not a child any more, but the overflowing health that has integrated the child and its spontaneity. One link between Hassidism and Perls was, of course, Buber, with whom he had so much in common implicitly—if not explicitly. Though Buber was deeply steeped in the Hassidic tradition and expressed himself through the medium of writing while Perls expressed himself through his activity rather than his reflection, both have in common their rising above their specific professions—of philosopher and therapist respectively—to what might be called prophetic significance.

It is particularly in the Buber of *I and Thou* and later in whom we find a special kinship to Perls, for this was the time when Buber, known as an exponent of Hassidism, disidentified with the Hassidic form of expression and allowed himself even to doubt the existence of God. At this time Buber became, without ceasing to be deeply religious, anti-mystical—in that he ceased to be interested in any experience of the divine through inwardness, and any religiosity divorced from human contact. Perls, like Buber, was a prophet of contact, and I think it is proper to say "prophet" (even though we do not find in his work Buber's rhetoric of salvation) because he in effect was one of the most powerful change agents in the days of the emergence of humanistic psychology and the "consciousness revolution." We may also call him a prophet of the here-and-now, a personal influence in people's approach to life, first in California, then in the expanding "Human Potential Movement."

I think that the most striking similarity between Perls' approach to that of Buber can be summarized in the word *presence*, and Buber's reflections on presence should be an inspiration to any Gestaltist, for Gestalt assumes that therapeutic action rests on presence more than on technique. While the word presence in Buber has an implicit connotation of *loving* presence—i.e., caring—the presence cultivated in Gestalt is more a matter of attention in the present: attention to self, attention to the other, and genuineness in the I/You encounter. We might say that Buber's formula for the ideal attitude vis-a-vis the other is one of presence and caring whereas in Perls' implicit credo it is presence and authenticity (even if this authenticity involves the acknowledgement of one's limitations to care and the expression of anger).

In regard to the expression of anger, however, we find again a similarity between Perls' spirit and that of Buber—perhaps obscured by the very different rhetoric of each. In the recent conference "Envisioning the Future and Healing the Earth" held in Zurich in 1987 I had the pleasure of hearing Maurice Friedman (Buber's translator into English and biographer) pronounce a generalized criticism of the "new age" spirit in psychology that indulges in an enjoyment of togetherness without a proper acknowledgement of differences. He did this from the perspective of Buber's attitude of generously wrestling with our fellow beings about such differences and our duty to offer them our disagreements. Although Fritz was disliked shouldistic language, he was certainly a master in healing through confrontation, and one who knew deeply that "contact is awareness of differences."

Yet an important difference between the spirit of Gestalt and all the old traditions discussed is, I think, that of being a spirituality that does not seem to be one. It is certainly a very embodied spirituality, and one steeped in the awareness of the dangers of seeking spiritual experience (in this Buber agreed) as an evasion of earthly problems. In addition to this, Fritz's attitude was anything but pious, if "pious" means petitionary prayer and conventional virtue—which he saw as consequences of being a "good boy" or a "good girl." In its down-to-earth and seemingly low spirituality Gestalt resembles, more than anything, that of shamanism. Surrender is common to the prophetic western stream of spirituality and to shamanism as well, yet comparably speaking, civilized religion has also a strong Apollonian ingredient, while shamanism entails a more unconditional surrender—and, consequently, a greater familiarity with madness.

I have pointed out that the new psychology (which has inspired the labels "humanistic" and "transpersonal") is, more than an academic event, a vast cultural phenomenon that may be interpreted as a new shamanism, and that the shaman may be called the archetype of our Zeitgeist. It was an aspect of Esalen's pioneering activity to have brought together in the 60s many of us, sympathetic to this spirit, when it sponsored events on the issue of "the positive value of psychotic experience" in the Sixties, the event that was followed by the creation of an alternative "handling" of psychosis along the lines intuited by Laing, Perry, Silverman and others.

Psychotherapy is rather Dionysian on the whole, yet the only psychotherapists that I could call more Dionysian than Fritz in the way he practiced Gestalt during his California period are some psychedelic therapists. I think that it may be of interest to point out that the transition between Fritz's early "east coast" Gestalt and the therapy done by him in the 60s was his significant psychedelic treatment in Jerusalem. (Though the east coast has tended to point at him as one that became a hippie, I see him as one of the few that have dared to defy the world and become a "fool"—he learned to dance around the age of 70.) He lived at Esalen, not only the California capital of the Taoistic spirit but the prototype of today's growth centers and a major force in the development of today's Dionysian spirituality (so well observed by Sam Keen in *To a Dancing God*).

It seems significant to me that the occasion on which I met Fritz was when I first visited Esalen, in the company of Carlos Castaneda. A now well-known American anthropologist—Michael Harner—had invited us to join him in the presentation of a workshop on Shamanism. Esalen had just opened its doors and Fritz had come to reside there; he still did not work, and he was just beginning to show who he was at Esalen. We had the honor of having him in the audience during that workshop, during which we had brought along Elsie Parish—a Pomo Indian healer. I remember Fritz commenting during a break something to the effect that if what Elsie did was indeed shamanism, he was a shaman too. Truly so, since shamanism is characteristically an intuitionism, one of the typical

forms of expression of which is the moment-by-mo-
ment direction of another's stream of experience—so
characteristic of the Gestalt situation. Also characteristic of a shaman is that "energy contagion" which
was so much a part of Fritz's success, as in the work
of other great therapists. Yet most importantly,
shamanism is the most Dionysian among the
spiritualities, just as Gestalt therapy (together with
psychedelic therapy) is the most Dionysian among
the new "ways of growth."

I now want to turn to my second topic, and say
something about the holes in Gestalt and the potential role of Gestalt in a holistic growth program.

You are familiar with this concept of "holes" that
Fritz put forth. An individual may not have eyes but
instead feel seen; another may alienate his heart but
need somebody else's warmth. Others are not in
touch with the experience of their bodies, and are in
contact with abstractions instead. Each one of us
scotomizes some aspect of his experience, part of his
experience-field. I think something similar occurs to
Gestalt as a cultural-social phenomenon. Fritz often
used the word "disowning." As you know, he
defined the ego as an identification phenomenon: an
act by which we assert "this is my limit," by which
we set a barrier and say: "what is beyond it is not me,
it is not I." Similarly, Gestalt therapy has been saying
"*that* is not Gestalt." It has erected its barriers, and
said of this or that, "it is not Gestalt therapy."

I would say that Gestalt therapy came into the
world affirming itself competitively—and very effectively at that—at the beginning of what we now call
the humanistic movement. Fritz was very competitive. He did a very good job when it was necessary
to compete with the monopoly of psychoanalysis: a
dogmatic monopoly that had exiled some of its best
talent (such as Horney) and continued to oppose
much of the ongoing creativity. Fritz was the first
who managed effectively and single-handedly to

compete with psychoanalysis in the U.S., in such a way that it was of Gestalt that it was first said, "Here is something with greater therapeutic power." I am convinced that this is what opened the path for the humanistic movement in general, for ideas follow upon practice and not the other way around. Though many of the other approaches—TA, encounter groups, etc., by themselves had not achieved such success, these suddenly flooded the scene after the supreme authority of psychoanalysis was challenged.

It was in this competitive attitude and context that Fritz had to say, "This is not that, and this is much better." For instance, he emphasized how many years he had lost on the couch, and never ceased wreaking vengeance on Freud for the little attention he had paid to him on his visit in Vienna. Yet I would say that it is not only unnecessary but impoverishing to throw overboard the insight process in psychotherapy, or to minimize insight—as is common in the implicit Gestalt movement. It seems to me that all deep therapy operates through insight, even when it is not interpretation but behavioral experiment such as risking, group interaction, dramatization, fine attention, or personal sharing on the part of the therapist that leads to this insight. I believe that it is not necessary to give up the simple process of sharing perceptions and understandings on the part of the therapist. Intellectualization is not good during a Gestalt therapy *session*, yet there are many today (Abe Levitsky being perhaps the most representative among them) who have discovered that they don't need to practice Gestalt in every single session, or who alternate in a single session the Gestalt modality with the interpretive modality. There are even analysts today who declare that Gestalt techniques are a contribution to psychoanalysis (which I think is reasonable if by this is meant not an analysis in which the original adherence to a specific theory blots out the phenomenological aspect of therapeutic activity and the free play of therapeutic intuition).

Not only are the theoretical recognition of insight and the practical use of interpretation holes that arose in Gestalt from the repudiation of psychoanalysis, but also the use of free association—which Fritz denigrated and called free dissociation. I think that it is useful sometimes to explore the flow of thinking (rather than feeling—doing—perceiving of a patient), just as it is useful to interpret—not dogmatically, but in the spirit of saying "This is what I see."

Let me say something on the so-called "bullshit." This is a very useful term for a certain kind of defensive intellectualization, and the distinction between regular *bullshit* and *"elephantshit"* is no less appropriate. Yet we must have in mind that Fritz was very ambivalent in regard to his own theorization. One may see in his autobiography how on one page he makes brilliant observations on time, space and awareness and on the following laughs at himself for philosophizing. On the one hand he injected into Gestalt a view according to which there is no place for theory and, on the other, he tells us, also in his autobiography, that if he came to be a holy cow one day *he* would like to use his prestige to promote an integration between psychology, medicine and philosophy.

It is clear, I think, that Fritz's personality involved a strong anti-intellectual prejudice, and we should not be blinded through that to the recognition that intellect, just as emotion and action can be part of the path of growth. It is precisely out of this recognition that have arisen what traditionally are called "teachings." The Oriental ways, for instance, comprise—each one of them — a *view* of the world—partly a cosmology, partly an anthropology; a view that supports or stimulates the transformative process.

Such perspectives (*drishti* in Sanskrit) are ways of seeing things that make the path easier. I think that Gestalt could also operate in the context of a vision of things (and I say this in spite of scant enthusiasm in "traditional"—i.e., Paul Goodman's—theorizations). This has been another hole in Gestalt, and that has arisen from its competitive claim to be able to do everything without its support. Fritz's Gestalt in the later years was a good historical demonstration, to the effect that it is possible to do therapy without theory, but it is not necessary to rigidly uphold this position, and to continue training therapists to regard an understanding of the psyche, psychopathology, and human maturation as bullshit.

Something similar can be said concerning meditation. Fritz personally meditated—at least at the time of his life when I knew him, but as a consequence of his scant willingness to give praise to any way other than his own, he gave the impression of looking down upon everything related to spirituality. In consequence, some of today's Gestaltists are not cognizant of the fact that meditative consciousness constitutes the deepest self-support. Most Gestaltists are familiar with the concept of growth as a movement from environmental support to self-support. While much has been said about the support that comes from being grounded in sensory awareness and more generally in awareness of experience, we may have to learn from the spiritual traditions about the support that comes from giving up support in anything and through that openness—developing the sense of existence beyond the awareness of content—an *awareness of awareness,* a pure presence or pure wakefulness (*bodhi* in Buddhism) that confers both a sense of invulnerability and an ability to be empty handed.

There is a hole in traditional Gestalt (if early Gestalt can be called that when it was so much a thus far untried traditional thing), a hole that arose early from its assumption and presumption to the effect that the attention it gives to the body in the course of a session is enough. Gestalt needs to be praised for its awareness of the body, the attention to posture and gesture in the course of the therapeutic process as well as its attention to the body sensation as both a part of waking up and as mirror of feelings—yet I think both Fritz and Laura have been somewhat arrogant in their contention that this was enough; and I praise Gestaltists of our generation such as Bob Hall, Richard Bloomberg, Ilana Rubenfeld and those who have integrated Reichian and other elements of "bodywork" into Gestalt. Essentially the situation of the individual is one of being able to receive from therapy, but being able to help himself better through attention to undoing the physical end of the body armor. To be effective, bodywork in any of the major schools needs a certain amount of attention and time. Whether it be Feldenkrais, Alexander, or older methods such as yoga and Tai Chi, the techniques will require time for instruction and some sustained dedication.

Another hole in the therapeutic repertory that might come about by a therapist adhering too closely to the established boundaries of Gestalt could be the systematic abstention from the advantages of advice and behavior prescriptions. These all important aspects of behavior therapy and modern family therapy are undoubted resources in the hands of psychotherapist and spiritual guide alike, and I would like to challenge the rather prevalent view of Gestaltists (taken over from earlier psychoanalysis and from Rogerian therapy) to the effect that in-fluencing patients by advice is something to be avoided. However non-directive a Gestalt therapist may be in his support of spontaneity, he can be very directive in his way of prompting behavioral ex-perimentation in the course of a session—and there is no reason why this should not extend (as Jim Simkin frequently did) to the prescription of tasks beyond the therapeutic time proper—that is, in advice for self-work in ordinary life.

Thus far I have been talking of holes in terms of the non-incorporation of a value resource, the omission of an activity that could contribute to the therapeutic process, in the name of Gestalt purity. I would now like to deal with holes the nature of which is more psychological. One of these I can describe as a bias of Gestalt toward "toughness" over "tenderness." However valuable the contribution of Gestalt may have been in its systematic support of the expression of anger, I think that its championship of rudeness has sometimes implied a certain forgetfulness of the ideal of love; an ideal which I believe as Freud did, cannot be separated from our understanding of healing. It is true that the exposing of conflicts and pain is by itself enough in many cases to remove the barrier to spontaneous integration. It is helpful, however, to have the integration process explicitly in view; to know that we are working for the restoration of the ability to love without which there cannot be deep satisfaction or an end to suffering. In this regard Gestaltists may have much to learn (as I have already claimed) from the Fischer-Hoffman process—not that they must turn into Fischer-Hoffman style therapists, but because the emphasis there given to the all important factors of love and forgiveness in psychotherapy may be inspiring to their Gestalt practice.

Another bias in Gestalt that has as a consequence the perpetuation of a hole is the greater appreciation for pleasure above pain in the transformative process. As I characterized it in its early years, Gestalt is a "humanistic hedonism." True, the expression of impulse has helped the undoing of repression; the injunction to not hold back has helped the process of becoming conscious of impulses, yet this should not lead us to think that the reverse process of inhibiting impulses is not without fruit as an approach in itself. Spirituality has traditionally been not hedonistic but ascetic, austere, out of a recognition that restriction too can *sharpen* our attention to our wishes and emotions. If we look in a subtle way at Gestalt practice we can see that both these aspects are reflected in it. Part of Gestalt is a daring to be without a topdog (to a greater extent than in real life), yet part of it consists in an ability to "stay with" one's experience without acting out, as when a group member (for instance) says, "I feel uncomfortable with what you said," instead of making a critical remark. The chief expression of this hole in Gestalt practice lies in the injunction for daily life that most people carry after Gestalt sessions. The usual attitude is that one should live the "Gestalt way" at all moments, and therefore express one's negative feelings in the family and at work. I disagree with that advice, for I have all too often observed how it leads to an endless circle of irritation in groups that are not psychotherapeutically oriented or assisted, and in which this becomes destructive rather than constructive. I think the rule of transparency is very valuable for Gestalt therapy within its boundaries, yet the traditional formulas for inhibiting one's destructiveness in daily life can be the best background for complementary work on oneself.

I think that Gestalt therapy, such a revolutionary method 15 years ago as it flowered and emerged into the culture, today runs the risk of turning into one more orthodoxy, a monopoly not unlike that of psychoanalysis in the past. And I think it will be appropriate today—when Gestalt is widely recognized—that it make its boundaries more flexible so that it facilitates the development of a wider Gestalt: a wholistic approach in which the capacities of the individual to work on him- or herself are employed in meditation and awareness practice in daily life and in which bodywork as well as a mental perspective on human development contributes to the individual's growth process—in addition to the therapy sessions proper. Gestalt therapy will then serve its function even better, as a precious element in a mosaic that would at the same time complement and support it.

Chapter Seven

GESTALT AFTER FRITZ[1]

I must confess that I was never interested in the history of Gestalt Therapy nor did I feel I had anything to contribute to it before Riccardo Zerbetto asked me to prepare a statement for the twenty-year retrospective that was anticipated for last year. That retrospective didn't come to pass, however, and Dr. Zerbetto, who became one of the organizers of this Conference, told me that he wished I would still contribute with some reflections on the subject. Later, still, he had in mind a session devoted to the history of Gestalt in which my report on "Gestalt after Fritz" would be part of a trio performance, along with speakers addressing themselves to the New York and California years of Perls' lifetime. The task that I undertook of reviewing the Gestalt literature and the *Gestalt Journal* in chronological sequence led me to see some things more clearly and to feel now truly interested in sharing my reflections on Gestalt history.

Since nobody from New York has shown up and Abe has preferred to speak most personally of his process of becoming a Gestaltist, I have felt inclined to speak not only of "Gestalt after Fritz" but also of what Gestalt I was exposed to during Fritz's Esalen years. More recently, I have felt inclined to emphasize what I see as the experiential root of Fritz's late (West Coast) work: the "new beginning" that he

[1]An edited transcript of a talk given at the Fourth International Gestalt Conference, in Siena, Italy, 1991.

experienced at the time of his crisis as a sexagenarian in Israel. It is because of this that when Riccardo, weeks ago, asked me over the telephone how I would *call* this talk, I said (not wanting to make an already extended long distance call any longer) "Gestalt Therapy after Jerusalem." He sounded startled, as if taken aback at such apocalyptic language. I suppose that he assumed that this is how it would sound to people not aware that Fritz's visit to Israel was the turning point of his life—an inner event that made him, more than the talent he had been, a master. Also, although the title I suggested in haste was appropriate to my meaning in view of its double reference—both to Fritz's months in Israel and to something of "apocalyptic" proportions. It was certainly not exact in a technical sense, since Fritz did not spend much time in Jerusalem, and the exact site of his life changing pilgrimage was Einhod[2].

Let me then begin my account with a consideration of Fritz's coming to Einhod. Einhod is a colony of artists south of Haifa where Fritz stopped in the middle of his wandering when he (as he tells us in his autobiography) felt "imprisoned in life," condemned to life and not even depressed, though in despair. In response to Dr. Simkin's invitation he had come to California and then decided to return from California to New York not Eastward, but Westward, around the world.

He first stopped in Japan and he fell in love with Kyoto. When, after this journey around the world, he ended up by establishing himself in Esalen (to a point, for he was always a "gypsy") two places competed in his mind with Big Sur—Kyoto and Israel—

---

[2] Though I have decided to speak of Fritz's activity in his late years as well as of Gestalt Therapy after Fritz, as I go into print I have decided to keep the original "Gestalt after Fritz" title because of its double meaning—according to alternative senses of the word "after." For Fritz's Gestalt Therapy after his "Jerusalem" was "after" him in the same sense of the word intended when we speak of a painting after Rembrandt.

the stay at which was for Fritz like a pilgrimage within his pilgrimage. He had made contact with the hippie spirit in Einhod and this had a great impact on him because he had been running after glory and fame and achievement, and surely did not have a conception of what it was like to do nothing.

He has told us in his autobiography what a profound impact it was on him to find people who were only seeking, and seeking something of a different order than the agitation that had moved him thus far. He devoted himself to painting and seriously considered dropping out of the therapeutic profession. The person who became closest to him in those days, Hillel (one of the founders of the village actually and a very remarkable person of a long lineage of saints in Israel) reported to Jack Gaines on occasion of his book of the seventies:

"He told me directly he didn't want to be a psychiatrist any more, he didn't want to do any more psychotherapy, he wanted to devote his whole life from now onwards to painting and art, to painting and music, actually he said. He dropped his past; however, he came back to psychotherapy, and he came back to that which he had dropped after an experience which was like a new birth."

This perception coincides with that of Dr. Kulcar, a psychiatrist to whose facility Fritz came every week to work on himself under the effects of LSD. Dr. Kulcar had developed great admiration for Fritz, claiming no merit for these sessions—which he did not even regard as psychotherapy, since Fritz was able to work effectively on himself: "He treated himself and it was not depression; it was pain of growth, it was pain of a new birth."

When I knew Fritz at Esalen—and when the whole world came to know Fritz through Esalen, for by now he had become a highly charismatic person— he was not exactly the same Fritz we had known previously. I think we can say he had always manifested a great talent, but now had come the time of flowering of his genius. There is a great difference between talent and genius. Genius is not just a potentiality, nor is it just instrumental abilities, but it involves a deep contact of a person with the core of his or her being. The greatness that those of us who knew him in this second stage of life sensed in him, was, I think, the expression of his ripeness, and not something that had been evident in the first stage of his life, great as his talent may have been.

Yet it was not just the flowering of Fritz's genius that underlay the striking "Gestalt explosion" of the mid-sixties; another factor in it was Esalen, or, more generally, the beginnings of the "California Phenomenon." There was a providential synergy between his coming to California with something important to offer and the remarkable community there. For not only in Israel, but also very especially in California, people who were essentially seekers in a more than intellectual way were finding an oasis and forming a movement that launched a counter-culture into being.

Not only did Fritz have something substantial to offer: he had come to a different level of self-realization and authoritativeness—as he states very clearly in his autobiography, when he says that he has found "the Tao and the truth." Though he sometimes qualified this statement (as when he says, "I have not made it to the final enlightenment grade, if it exists") he was in a position of abundance and fulfillment, and this was expressed through a natural sense of authority. I felt that those of us who came into contact with him treated him very much like Zen masters are treated, not in virtue of any traditional investiture, but because there was an implicit sense that "he knew." And surely the intuition was not wrong, for his perceptions were confirmed again and again. The extent to which this was true was surely a factor in his psychotherapeutic effectiveness. I give you an example: Hillel, his host and teacher of painting in Israel, says: "We didn't have to talk much, we read each other's thought" and he tells that he (Hillel) was not only a painter but that he had attempted to be a writer, and that he had stopped writing because it was very difficult for him, hardly compatible with his family life. He was in a conflict between having a space to write and having the sense of isolation required by him to write, and had felt very interrupted by his wife. In spite of his not having communicated to Fritz, Fritz once approached him and said, "Hillel you should write, not paint. But when you get back to writing, you should have your own room and don't give your wife a copy of the key." This may be regarded as quite an elaborate clairvoyant feat. He never talked about this, but I think this extreme intuition was more an explanation of what he could do than any theoretical framework.

What was Fritz like during this time I call the "flowering of his genius"? What were the qualities of his mind? What were the aspects of his being that accounted for this extraordinary effectiveness? I speak of the time when people started coming to Esalen from the East Coast—people from all walks of psychotherapy—including psychoanalysis—almost as if to see a miracle worker in action.

Things happened in one hour of therapy for which there was no precedent. Sometimes it is said that Milton Erickson was a genius like that. If there is anybody that could be compared, it would be Erickson, for I doubt that Freud had a comparable therapeutic genius notwithstanding his momentous contribution to psychology and culture. We felt (and by "we" I mean people like Virginia Satir, Jerry Greenwald, William Golding, Abe Levitsky, and others from my first training group), that we were before something unique, something totally new. And it was, though we may now feel that this became commonplace.

One element of that was what today is beginning to be called "dialogical." I should remark that even though Fritz was quite aware of Buber, only very slowly is Buberian language coming into the Gestalt discourse. It is the Old (New York) word "contact" that is mostly used. I am a little unhappy with it because of its ambiguity. Of course, it points in the right direction; but it may refer to being in touch with the inner world or with the outer; sometimes it makes a reference to sensory contact, sometimes to motor contact, for instance, and these are quite different things. I think it is more useful to reserve the word *awareness* for contact with one's experience, for instance. Also when we refer to the interpersonal situation and borrow the word "contact" from the mechanical world, there is something missing, for it fails to evoke something bigger than sensory-motor contact, which happens to be the most essential part of human contact: that contact "from heart to heart," from essence to essence or center to center—that Buber calls "encounter" or "relationship." Though there is some differentiation in Buber's use of "encounter" and "relationship," both have to do with the *sense of the other as subject,* a sense of the other as something beyond an object of thought, manipulation or desire. There is a gratuitousness in the approach involved in the ability to perceive the "other" as "you," and the "I" that sees "You" is not the same as the "I" that sees "It" (as Buber points out at the beginning of his *I and Thou*).

I think this was something that Fritz had to an extraordinary degree: the ability to be present, to be there. To be present as living and lived existence, and to make you feel that you were there. Sometimes he might make a psychotherapeutic intervention out of that. "*Who* is telling me this?" When I once answered him, "I am saying this," he retorted, "*Are* you?" "I don't hear *you*." It's not just the external behavior that is the target of such statements—such as somebody looking at the floor or looking at somebody else instead of making face to face contact. Sometimes all the external signs of contact may be there, and *still* something deeper is missing. "Are you talking to *me*?" Fritz could then say, "I don't feel that you are addressing me." That is very subtle. It is in another realm—a realm of personhood and presence beyond biological input and output.

I think this subtlest realm of contact was *one* element of his "dialogical" activity. If we take "dialogical therapy" to be synonymous (as M. Friedman does) with "therapy through meeting," he was *extremely* dialogical, and I think that Friedman has been most unfair to him in his book on the subject[3]. When I met Friedman some time ago in Switzerland at the Conference on "Healing the Earth and Visioning the Future," I had a very good feeling for him, and I felt his way of talking about Buber was particularly coherent with what could be said of Fritz, principally in regard to Buber's conception of a "holy struggle" with the other and the responsibility of challenging. Also "Fritzian" was the distinction Friedman drew between confluence and contact: he was challenging the "New Age" spirit inasmuch as it involves an indulgence in dwelling on feelings of brotherhood and sameness without proper acknowledgement of differences and boundaries.

When after this meeting with Friedman I got his book, I was amazed to find that he gives more credit to Jungians, to object relations therapists and to practically every school of psychotherapy than to Gestaltists! Amazed, because it seems to me that Gestalt has contributed more than any other approach to the liberation of present day psychotherapy from fixed roles and techniques, and especially the Gestalt example has been an inspiration to psychotherapy in general for the greater freedom that it has given the

[3] Maurice Friedman, *The Healing Dialogue in Psychotherapy* (New Jersey: Jason Aronson, 1985).

therapist for using oneself as a person rather than as a mirror and a technician.

Fritz was a great person manipulator too; indeed, in one of my first conversations with him, he defined his activity as precisely that. But beyond that, he was one who used *himself;* if we can say "use" for what derives from believing in the primacy of encounter over everything else. Only in the case of R.D. Laing can we say, I think, that therapy and life were so close; that the distinction between therapy and the situation outside therapy was so slight.

Another element in that very extraordinary presence of Fritz was an element that already in the sixties (after one of his workshops) I called his "so-whatness." It took me some time to realize that what I was calling his "so-whatness" was of the same nature as that which he called "creative indifference." An expression of it was his extraordinary ability to withstand manipulation. He would not be sucked into any games, and was able to stand in his neutrality. Of course, it is part of the golden rule in psychoanalysis to cultivate neutrality, but that is a more "gimmicky" or at least procedural neutrality, embodied to a large extent in what words are said or not said and in whether you sit behind the couch or not, whereas his was a more profound neutrality, which had more to do with what in the Buddhist language is called detachment or non-attachment. Fritz had attained spontaneously a remarkable degree of non-attachment, and this was very visible in the presence of "drama"—i.e. in the presence of a person dramatizing pain; it was in these cases where he might say, "So what? Are you going to weep over the past forever?"

This was an invitation for a more salutary attitude in the here and now, a more healthy attitude of accepting the pain of life for what it is, as well as from a familiarity with the "poor me" game and the notion that consciousness is restricted to the extent that we avoid pain. It was part of his implicit theory of psychotherapy that because we don't want to suffer, we cannot see, and it was part of his practice to invite and even push toward the direct confrontation of pain. This was quite explicit, and Fritz often compared himself to a surgeon.

Another trait that I find very characteristic of this stage of Fritz's life is something that might be called a perfection-in-imperfection. There was a kind of greatness to him, but a very paradoxical greatness, as I was pointing out yesterday in some of the anecdotes that came to my mind as a result of the invitation to share memories of him at the end of our pre-conference dinner. It seems to me that when one talks about Fritz, one naturally gravitates to these controversial (apparently very "shitty") doings of his. And yet we sense (and perhaps this is our interest in such anecdotes) that it was not just that he was being a son-of-a-bitch. It's more what he once said of himself—that he was "50% son-of-a-bitch and 50% son-of-God." It was in that integration that lay his uniqueness, the integration of holiness and ordinariness; a deep authenticity and a freedom to be not an animal (i.e., a biological being), and even a freedom to be selfish. I am reminded of Freud's answer to Binswanger when, later in his life, Binswanger reproached Freud for having insisted so much on the animal aspect of human life. Freud's reply was, "I have endeavored to remind man that he is *also* an animal."

There was something of this sort, but also something more—I cannot avoid using the word—mysterious. Something that has been scarcely talked about or written about, except in the worlds of Buddhism and Sufism, in both of which there is a recognition of a high wisdom that seems to wear the garb of behavior or speech that comes across as outrageous or even idiotic. In addition to the matter of an upside-downness of wisdom in an upside-down world alluded to by Idries Shah's *The Wisdom of the Idiots*, I think "crazy wisdom" involves a phenomenon that seems not to have been spelled out. There are people who have evolved very much in whom even their idiotic part becomes a wisdom for others and even their mistakes become beneficient. I tried to express this in an interview quoted by Jack Gaines in his book[4] by saying that in Fritz hatefulness became a gift to his patients and an asset in the destruction of their neurosis. Dr. Schnacke—a Chilean psychotherapist who wrote the introduction to the Spanish translation of Gaines' book and who never met Perls—thought that I had not understood him properly, and that I did not give him enough credit for being a loving person. She voiced the opinion that I should have said that Fritz wanted to destroy their ego, not destroy *them*. I think this falls short of the mystery, and Fritz himself would have objected to such depersonalizing language. It is something of a mystery, in people who evolved enough along the path of transformation, that their shortcomings spontaneously become aligned with their fundamental orientation without any intention on their part, and so—as Faust's Mephistopheles, they do good without intending to be good. I think this rare phenomenon was aptly grasped by the person who wrote the jacket blurb for the same book, which says that the phenomenon of Fritz Perls was that he "had horns and a halo at the same time." His kind of halo was one that arose from the acknowledgement of horns, perhaps.

When, at the age of 75, Fritz needed to be hospitalized in Chicago (on his way back from Germany to Vancouver) and died there after a surgical intervention, the fact that hundreds of hippies congregated outside the hospital in which he lay was a

[4] Jack Gaines, *Fritz Perls: Here and Now* (Integrated Press: Tiburon, CA, 1979).

testimony to the fact that his activity has impinged
not only on the individual lives of many patients and
on his contemporary colleagues, but on the culture at
large. His presence (as I have said on other occasions)
had acquired prophetic stature. Though the healing
potential of awareness and the "here and now" had
been known to Buddhists and had been richly spelled
out by Heidegger in *Being and Time* and though Ram
Dass (through his book *Be Here Now*) and Alan Watts
through his lectures contributed much to the
popularization of the theme after Fritz, it is Fritz Perls
who, more than anybody, deserves to be called a
"prophet of the here and now" in our modern times.
His living rather than intellectual influence was the
most substantive in this regard, both on
psychotherapy in general (beyond Gestalt) and in the
"new consciousness" that was to spread from
California to the whole Western world.

Gestalt Therapy has continued to expand both
geographically and within our own society. It has
come to be taught in India and Japan, and personal
acquaintance with Gestalt Therapy in the U.S. has
become very widespread. Most striking in this stage
has been the expansion of Gestalt Therapy into the
culture, as distinct from the counter-culture (in
which it originated) as it has come to be taught in
universities, applied to business and so forth. Related
to this diffusion of Gestalt Therapy into mainstream
society has been what we may call its institutionaliza-
tion: 1) in that it has penetrated the established in-
stitutions, and 2) in that Gestalt practice has
crystallized into a large number of Gestalt training
centers throughout the world that are practically (if
not academically) accredited and offer, in turn, accreditation. While we may assume that in this
process there have developed refinements in Gestalt
education and supervision, we should also be aware
of how the adoption of psycho-spiritual values by the
establishment and society at large also entails a

process of compromise. Thus it is legitimate to ask whether—along with the great international and intercultural diffusion of Gestalt Therapy in the last 20 years and with the existence of excellent representatives of the approach in many countries—there has not also taken place a dilution, as in Nasruddin's famous "duck soup" joke.

The story goes that a kinsman came to see Nasruddin from the country, and brought a duck. Nasruddin was grateful, had the bird cooked, and shared it with his guest. Presently another visitor arrived. He was a friend, as he said, "of the man who gave you the duck." Nasruddin fed him well. This happened several times. Nasruddin's home became like a restaurant for out-of-town visitors. Everyone was a friend at some remove of the original donor of the duck. Finally Nasruddin became exasperated. One day there was a knock at the door and a stranger appeared. "I am a friend of the friend of the friend of the man who brought you the duck from the country," he said. "Come in," said Nasruddin. They seated themselves at the table, and Nasruddin asked his wife to bring the soup. When the guest tasted it, it seemed to be nothing more than warm water. "What sort of a soup is this?" he asked the Mulla. "That," said Nasruddin, "is the soup of the soup of the soup of the duck."

Jim Simkin, whose best wisdom was usually expressed in the form of humor, once addressed the same phenomenon through the story of a lady who goes to a rabbi requesting a "broche" for a Christmas tree. Very orthodox, he excused himself from involvement with something so idolatrous as the blessing of a tree, and suggested asking the rabbi of a reform congregation. He, in turn, declined and recommended another, a rabbi of a new age congregation. When the lady formulated to him her request for a "broche" on the Christmas tree, however, his response was, "A Christmas tree? I have no objection—but what is a 'broche'?"

If something similar has happened with Gestalt Therapy, then it has not escaped what seems to be a historical law, observable in the unfolding of all social movements and even civilizations which, as Spengler, Toynbee, Sorokin and others have pointed out decades ago, have their springtime, their summer, their fall, and their winter seasons.

There is still another topic I want to mention, for without it, this retrospective on the history of "Gestalt after Fritz" would be incomplete. In addition to being a story of remarkable geographic and intracultural diffusion with rather unremarkable creativity, this has been a story of *division*—a division that originally reflected the distinctiveness of an East Coast and a West Coast network, but now permeates the world as the presence of two contrasting orientations.

This division of East and West was not truly a division of a whole into two, however, but the long-term consequence of an increasing opposition that Fritz Perls and his activity met on the part of his older associates, so that it may be said to have existed in seed-form in the split between Fritz and his collaborators, even while he was alive and while, after his sexagenarian crisis, he became established on the West Coast.

It is not surprising that those associates of Fritz who during the New York years competed intensely with him (as Simkin used to recall) became only increasingly competitive once Fritz embraced his late and anti-theoretical and intuitionist creed, when the words "bullshit" and "mindfucking" became prominent in his vocabulary and when he considered the Gestalt Therapy book of the fifties obsolete and sought new associates and relationships. It is easy to understand how they did not only respond to rejection with rejection but also, taking Fritz's West Coast triumph as a defeat, sought its (and his) invalidation.

Subtle and restrained in the expression of their disapproval in the course of Fritz's lifetime, after Fritz's
death they have supported an increasing denigration
of Fritz, as if wanting to bury him and to minimize
his imprint in the annals of history—at least in the
sense of taking away his preeminence vis-a-vis Laura
Perls and Paul Goodman.

Public expression of this criticism has brought
about a sort of counter-reform or "restoration"
period in the history of Gestalt, already ushered in
when Paul Goodman had the bad taste of criticizing
Fritz at the memorial celebration that the New York
group took the initiative of "celebrating" a little after
the one that took place at the Masonic Auditorium in
San Francisco in the days following Fritz's passing.
The chief landmark in the expression of such
criticism has been Isadore From's *Requiem for Gestalt*[5]
and an interview on his training with Fritz where he
claims that Fritz had not been able to provide Gestalt
Therapy with a theory, while Paul Goodman did
accomplish it[6]. It is my impression that Dr. From has
not only sided with his brother Paul against his
oedipal rival, but implicitly claimed authority as Paul
Goodman's representative among the living.

Since then one can see that a subtle rewriting of
the Gestalt Therapy history has gradually unfolded
through the pages of the *Gestalt Journal*. Fritz has been
made to look as if in becoming somewhat of a hippie
he had lost seriousness; and as if his dedication to
group workshops had been mostly an expression of
his narcissistic need and lack of caring. He has certainly been criticized for not continuing to be interested in theory, and very unjustly accused of relying
excessively on techniques. People even started

[5] "Reflections on Gestalt Therapy after Thirty-Two Years of Practice: A
Requiem for Gestalt." *The Gestalt Journal*, Spring, 1984, Issue #74.

[6] Joe Wysong, *An Oral History of Gestalt Therapy: Interviews with
Laura Perls, Isadore From, Irving Polster, Miriam Polster and Elliott Shapiro*
(Highland, NY: The Gestalt Journal Press, 1988).

saying here and there—in books and in articles—that Fritz didn't practice therapy in California. If you read about it you find that he only *demonstrated* Gestalt Therapy, he didn't *do* therapy. In sum, the coming to fruition of Fritz's genius has been presented to the "official world" as an intellectual and moral decadence.

As I have mentioned, when I was first asked by Riccardo to speak of "Gestalt after Fritz" I was not excited about it. Since then I have read everything that has been written on Gestalt in preparing for this; I have re-read every line of Paul Goodman (whose formulation I never appreciated very much, and which I find full of mystification), and as a result I have developed a real motivation to talk about it. It has become clearer than ever to me that Gestalt— which once originated as a revolutionary movement—has developed an orthodoxy. Max Weber observed that in the history of every religion there is a transition from a "charismatic stage" to a "bureaucratic stage." When the established church condemns those who don't abide by the "holy book," the bureaucratic stage has already arrived. Isadore From's contention is that the (charismatic) Gestalt of the West Coast is endangering the movement—yet we know that the real danger to every movement lies not in its flexibility but in its fossilization.

Unfortunately, I am told that my time is up, which doesn't allow me to document what I have said as much as I would have liked. I hope, however, that the older gestaltists in my audience will feel that my words are particularly supported by the obvious yet increasingly obscured fact that the personal story of Fritz Perls was one of ongoing evolution, and that his work, after migrating to the West Coast, far from being degenerate, was his ripest. Perhaps the fact that West Coast gestaltists have not felt the need to create an institution constitutes a tribute to Fritz's taoistic spirit and his faith in spontaneous unfolding.

INDEX

INDEX

Centeredness, in meditation, 211
Centering, in Gestalt exercise, 239
Character, 78, analysis, 21, 228, and characterological bias of Gestalt, 215-222, basis of psychopathology (in Gestalt and protoanalysis, also character types), 249-271 definition of, 33, 201, 250, neurotic, 138-139
"Chief feature," 256, 268
Childhood, in therapeutic techniques, 20, 76, 88, 146-147, 150-151, 250, 254, 270
Chile, for Naranjo, 230, 273
Christ, 34
Christian(ity), 36, 41, 223, seven deadly sins, 218
Chuang-tzu, 24
Classicism, in psychotherapy, 253
Cohen, Ben, xxiii
Communication, of awareness, 25-32, 83, 216, 240-241
Compassion, 203, 226
Comus (Milton), 38
Conative (category of mental phenomena), 254
Concentration, 102, 200, 239
Conceptualization(s), 54, 200, 213
Conditioning(s), 26, 76, 226, 250, 254
Confrontation, 57, 109, 137, 141, 263, 278, 280, 298
Consciousness, in Gestalt, 22-33, 38, 78, 174, 196, 197, 204, 212-213, stream of, 216, 251, 263, 274-279, 285, 297
Contamination, characterological, 220
Control-mad (compulsive), 250
Counter-aggression, 106
Counter-culture, 300
Creativity, in therapy, xxxi, 119, 283, 302

Crypto-Buddhism (Taoism, Sufism), of Gestalt, 277-78

Dalcroze, 272
Dante, 38
Death, 19, 37, 59, psychological, 73, 248, 98, instinct, 255
Death-rebirth, 203
Defense(s), 3, 30, 65, 108, 112
Defensiveness, 144
Demands, 76, 265
Depression, 105, 259, 292
Desensitization, 26
Desoille, 137
Detachment, 256, 297
Devil, 21, 220, 252, 261
Dhyani Buddhas, 275
Diagnosis, 57, 80, 218, 252, 270
Dialogical (therapy), 295-296
Dianetics, 22, 146
Dionysian, 227, 281, 282, -mindedness, 204
Dionysus, 221
Do-gooder, 258
Downing, Jack, 235
Dramatization, in therapy, 98, 142, 146, 206, 245, 263, 283, for Perls, 221-222,
Dream(s), 50, 146, 208-211, for character awareness, 269, in therapy, 79, 93, 97, 108, 109, 112, 142, 147-150, 155, 169-175, 230-234, 268, 276, re-enactment session, 176-193
Drishti, 285
Drug(s), 51, 146
Drunkenness, spiritual, 197
Dryden, John, 38
DSM-III, 258, 259
Dzogs-chen, 276

Eating, exercises for, xiii, 116-117
Ecclesiastes, 35
Education, clinical, 252

Dear *Gestalt Therapy* Reader,

If you have enjoyed this volume of Dr. Claudio Naranjo's work, you may wish to pursue your inquiries in this field. This volume was intended to be of use both to practicing professionals in psychotherapy and to novices or lay readers interested in the ideas and methods for their intrinsic value.

No matter what your motivation for using this book, you may be interested in other books by Dr. Naranjo or other related training materials. For information on available publications, audio and videotapes of Dr. Naranjo, and future training events sponsored by the SAT Institute in Europe or Latin America, you may contact the publisher at the address and phone number shown below.

If you have questions or comments that you wish to address to the author, we will be happy to forward your letters or memos directly to him.

The Editors
Gateways Books
P.O. Box 370-GT
Nevada City, CA 95959

Phone:(916) 432-1716
FAX: (916) 432-1810
In U.S. only: (800) 869-0658